Moving Hadoop to the Cloud

Harnessing Cloud Features and
Flexibility for Hadoop Clusters

Date: 1/8/18

Bill Havanki

Beijing · Boston · Farnham · Sebastopol · Tokyo   **O'REILLY**®

Moving Hadoop to the Cloud

by Bill Havanki

Printed in the United States of America.

Published by O'Reilly Media, Inc., 1005 Gravenstein Highway North, Sebastopol, CA 95472.

O'Reilly books may be purchased for educational, business, or sales promotional use. Online editions are also available for most titles (*http://oreilly.com/safari*). For more information, contact our corporate/institutional sales department: 800-998-9938 or *corporate@oreilly.com*.

Editor: Marie Beaugureau	**Production Editor:** Colleen Cole
Copyeditor: Kim Cofer	**Proofreader:** Christina Edwards
Indexer: WordCo Indexing Services, Inc.	**Interior Designer:** David Futato
Cover Designer: Karen Montgomery	**Illustrator:** Rebecca Demarest

July 2017:   First Edition

Revision History for the First Edition

2017-07-05:   First Release

See *http://oreilly.com/catalog/errata.csp?isbn=9781491959633* for release details.

978-1-491-95963-3

[LSI]

Table of Contents

Part III.   A Simple Cluster in the Cloud

Foreword

Apache Hadoop as software is a simple framework that allows for distributed processing of data across many machines. As a technology, Hadoop and the surrounding ecosystem have changed the way we think about data processing at scale. No longer does our data need to fit in the memory of a single machine, nor are we limited by the I/O of a single machine's disks. These are powerful tenets.

So too has cloud computing changed our way of thinking. While the notion of colocating machines in a faraway data center isn't new, allowing users to provision machines on-demand is, and it's changed everything. No longer are developers or architects limited by the processing power installed in on-premise data centers, nor do we need to host small web farms under our desks or in that old storage closet. The pay-as-you-go model has been a boon for ad hoc testing and proof-of-concept efforts, eliminating time spent in purchasing, installation, and setup.

Both Hadoop and cloud computing represent major paradigm shifts, not just in enterprise computing, but affecting many other industries. Much has been written about how these technologies have been used to make advances in retail, public sector, manufacturing, energy, and healthcare, just to name a few. Entire businesses have sprung up as a result, dedicated to the care, feeding, integration, and optimization of these new systems.

It was inevitable that Hadoop workloads would be run on cloud computing providers' infrastructure. The cloud offers incredible flexibility to users, often complementing on-premise solutions, enabling them to use Hadoop in ways simply not possible previously.

Ever the conscientious software engineer, author Bill Havanki has a strong penchant for documenting. He's able to break down complex concepts and explain them in simple terms, without making you feel foolish. Bill writes the kind of documentation that you actually enjoy, the kind you find yourself reading long after you've discovered the solution to your original problem.

Hadoop and cloud computing are powerful and valuable tools, but aren't simple technologies by any means. This stuff is hard. Both have a multitude of configuration options and it's very easy to become overwhelmed. All major cloud providers offer similar services like virtual machines, network attached storage, relational databases, and object storage—all of which can be utilized by Hadoop—but each provider uses different naming conventions and has different capabilities and limitations. For example, some providers require that resource provisioning occurs in a specific order. Some providers create isolated virtual networks for your machines automatically while others require manual creation and assignment. It can be confusing. Whether you're working with Hadoop for the first time or a veteran installing on a cloud provider you've never used before, knowing about the specifics of each environment will save you a lot of time and pain.

Cloud computing appeals to a dizzying array of users running a wide variety of workloads. Most cloud providers' official documentation isn't specific to any particular application (such as Hadoop). Using Hadoop on cloud infrastructure introduces additional architectural issues that need to be considered and addressed. It helps to have a guide to demystify the options specific to Hadoop deployments and to ease you through the setup process on a variety of cloud providers, step by step, providing tips and best practices along the way. This book does precisely that, in a way that I wish had been available when I started working in the cloud computing world.

Whether code or expository prose, Bill's creations are approachable, sensible, and easy to consume. With this book and its author, you're in capable hands for your first foray into moving Hadoop to the Cloud.

— *Alex Moundalexis,*
May 2017

Preface

It's late 2015, and I'm staring at a page of mine on my employer's wiki, trying to think of an OKR. An OKR (*https://en.wikipedia.org/wiki/OKR*) is something like a performance objective, a goal to accomplish paired with a way to measure if it's been accomplished. While my management chain defines OKRs for the company as a whole and major organizations in it, individuals define their own. We grade ourselves on them, but they do not determine how well we performed because they are meant to be aspirational, not necessary. If you meet all your OKRs, they weren't ambitious enough.

My coworkers had already been impressed with writing that I'd done as part of my job, both in product documentation and in internal presentations, so focusing on a writing task made sense. How aspirational could I get? So I set this down.

"Begin writing a technical book! On something! That is, begin working on one myself, or assist someone else in writing one."

Outright ridiculous, I thought, but why not? How's *that* for aspirational.

Well, I have an excellent manager who is willing to entertain the ridiculous, and so she encouraged me to float the idea to someone else in our company who dealt with things like employees writing books, and he responded.

"Here's an idea: there is no book out there about Running Hadoop in the Cloud. Would you have enough material at this point?"

I work on a product that aims to make the use of Hadoop clusters in the cloud easier, so it was admittedly an extremely good fit. It didn't take long at all for this ember of an idea to catch, and the end result is the book you are reading right now.

Who This Book Is For

Between the twin subjects of Hadoop and the cloud, there is more than enough to write about. Since there are already plenty of good Hadoop books out there, this book doesn't try to duplicate them, and so you should already be familiar with running Hadoop. The details of configuring Hadoop clusters are only covered as needed to get clusters up and running. You can apply your prior Hadoop knowledge with great effectiveness to clusters in the cloud, and much of what other Hadoop books cover still applies.

It is not assumed, however, that you are familiar with the cloud. Perhaps you've dabbled in it, spun up an instance or two, read some documentation from a provider. Perhaps you haven't even tried it at all, or don't know where to begin. Readers with next to no knowledge of the cloud will find what they need to get rolling with their Hadoop clusters. Often, someone is tasked by their organization with "moving stuff to the cloud," and neither the tasker nor the tasked truly understands what that means. If this describes you, this book is for you.

DevOps engineers, system administrators, and system architects will get the most out of this book, since it focuses on constructing clusters in a cloud provider and interfacing with the provider's services. Software developers should also benefit from it; even if they do not build clusters themselves, they should understand how clusters work in the cloud so they know what to ask for and how to design their jobs.

What You Should Already Know

Besides having a good grasp of Hadoop concepts, you should have a working knowledge of the Java programming language and the Bash shell, or similar languages. At least being able to read them should suffice, although the Bash scripts do not shy away from advanced shell features. Code examples are constrained to only those languages.

Before working on your clusters, you will need credentials for a cloud provider. The first two parts of the book do not require a cloud account to follow along, but the later hands-on parts do. Your organization may already have an account with a provider, and if so, you can seek your own account within that to work with. If you are on your own, you can sign up for a free trial with any of the cloud providers this book covers in detail.

What This Book Leaves Out

As stated previously, this book does not delve into Hadoop details more than necessary. A seasoned Hadoop administrator may notice that configurations are not necessarily optimal, and that clusters are not tuned for maximum efficiency. This information is left out for brevity, so as not to duplicate content in books that focus only on Hadoop. Many of the principles for Hadoop maintenance apply to cloud clusters just as well as ordinary ones.

The core Hadoop components of HDFS and YARN are covered here, along with other important components such as ZooKeeper, Hive, and Spark. This doesn't imply at all that other components won't work in the cloud; there are simply so many components that, due to space considerations, not all could be included.

A limited set of popular cloud providers is covered in this book: Amazon Web Services, Google Cloud Platform, and Microsoft Azure. There are other cloud providers, both publicly available and deployed privately, but they are not included. The ones that were chosen are the most popular, and you should find that their concepts transfer over rather directly to those in other providers. Even so, each provider does things a little, or a lot, differently from its peers. When getting you up and running, all of them are covered equally, but beyond that, only Amazon Web Services is fully considered, since it is the dominant choice at this time. Brief summaries of equivalent procedures in the other providers are given to get you started with them.

Overall, between Hadoop and the cloud, there is just so much to write about. What's more, cloud providers introduce new services and revamp older services all the time, and it can be challenging to keep up even when you work in the cloud every day. This book attempts to stick with the most vital, core Hadoop components and cloud services to be as relevant as possible in this fast-changing world. Understanding them will serve you well when integrating new features into your clusters in the future.

How This Book Works

Part I starts off this book by asking why you would host Hadoop clusters in a cloud provider, and briefly introduces the providers this book looks at. Part II describes the common concepts of cloud providers, like instances and virtual networks. If you are already familiar with a cloud provider or two, you might skim or skip these parts.

Part III begins the hands-on portion of this book, where you build out a Hadoop cluster in one of the cloud providers. There is a chapter for the unique steps needed by each provider, and a common chapter for bringing up a cluster and seeing it in action. Later parts of the book use this first cluster as a launching point for more.

If you are interested in making an even more capable cluster, Part IV can help you. It covers adding high availability and installing Hive and Spark. You can try any combination of the enhancements, and learn even more about the ramifications of running in a cloud provider.

Finally, Part V looks at patterns and practices for running cloud clusters well, from designing for price and security to dealing with maintenance. Those first starting out in the cloud may not need the guidance in this part, but as usage ramps up, it becomes much more important.

Which Software Versions This Book Uses

Here are the versions of Hadoop components used in this book. All are distributed through Apache:

- Apache Hadoop 2.7.2
- Apache ZooKeeper 3.4.8
- Apache Hive 2.1.0
- Apache Spark 1.6.3 and 2.0.2

Code examples require:

- Java 8
- Bash 4

Cloud providers update their services continually, and so determining the exact "versions" used for them is not possible. Most of the work in the book was performed during 2016 with the services as they existed at that time. Since then, service web interfaces may have changed and workflows may have been altered.

Conventions Used in This Book

The following typographical conventions are used in this book:

Italic
> Indicates new terms, URLs, email addresses, filenames, and file extensions.

`Constant width`
> Used for program listings, as well as within paragraphs to refer to program elements such as variable or function names, databases, data types, environment variables, statements, and keywords.

`Constant width bold`
> Shows commands or other text that should be typed literally by the user.

`Constant width italic`
> Shows text that should be replaced with user-supplied values or by values determined by context.

 This element signifies a tip or suggestion.

This element signifies a general note.

This element indicates a warning or caution.

IP Addresses

Many of the examples throughout this book include IP addresses, usually for cluster nodes. The example IP addresses are drawn from reserved address ranges as specified in RFC 5737 (*https://tools.ietf.org/html/rfc5737*). They should never resolve to an actual IP address anywhere on the internet or within private networks. Change them as needed when using the examples in your work.

Using Code Examples

Supplemental material (code examples, exercises, etc.) is available for download at *https://github.com/bhavanki/moving-hadoop-to-the-cloud*.

This book is here to help you get your job done. In general, if example code is offered with this book, you may use it in your programs and documentation. You do not need to contact us for permission unless you're reproducing a significant portion of the code. For example, writing a program that uses several chunks of code from this book does not require permission. Selling or distributing a CD-ROM of examples from O'Reilly books does require permission. Answering a question by citing this book and quoting example code does not require permission. Incorporating a significant amount of example code from this book into your product's documentation does require permission.

We appreciate, but do not require, attribution. An attribution usually includes the title, author, publisher, and ISBN. For example: "*Moving Hadoop to the Cloud* by Bill Havanki (O'Reilly). Copyright 2017 Bill Havanki Jr., 978-1-491-95963-3."

If you feel your use of code examples falls outside fair use or the permission given above, feel free to contact us at *permissions@oreilly.com*.

O'Reilly Safari

 *Safari* (formerly Safari Books Online) is a membership-based training and reference platform for enterprise, government, educators, and individuals.

Members have access to thousands of books, training videos, Learning Paths, interactive tutorials, and curated playlists from over 250 publishers, including O'Reilly Media, Harvard Business Review, Prentice Hall Professional, Addison-Wesley Professional, Microsoft Press, Sams, Que, Peachpit Press, Adobe, Focal Press, Cisco Press, John Wiley & Sons, Syngress, Morgan Kaufmann, IBM Redbooks, Packt, Adobe Press, FT Press, Apress, Manning, New Riders, McGraw-Hill, Jones & Bartlett, and Course Technology, among others.

For more information, please visit *http://oreilly.com/safari*.

How to Contact Us

Please address comments and questions concerning this book to the publisher:

O'Reilly Media, Inc.
1005 Gravenstein Highway North
Sebastopol, CA 95472
800-998-9938 (in the United States or Canada)
707-829-0515 (international or local)
707-829-0104 (fax)

We have a web page for this book, where we list errata, examples, and any additional information. You can access this page at *http://www.oreilly.com/catalog/0636920051459*.

To comment or ask technical questions about this book, send email to *bookquestions@oreilly.com*.

For more information about our books, courses, conferences, and news, see our website at *http://www.oreilly.com*.

Find us on Facebook: *http://facebook.com/oreilly*

Follow us on Twitter: *http://twitter.com/oreillymedia*

Watch us on YouTube: *http://www.youtube.com/oreillymedia*

Acknowledgments

I'm well aware that barely anyone reads the acknowledgments in a book, especially a technical one like this. So, for those few of you who are reading this right now, well, first, I'd like to thank you for your diligence, not to mention your attention and support in the first place. Truly, thanks for spending time and/or money on what I've written here, and I hope it helps you.

Thank you to everyone who's helped to build up the amazing Apache Hadoop ecosystem, from its founders to its committers to its contributors to its users, for showing us a new way of computing. Thank you also to everyone who's built and maintained the amazing cloud provider services, for showing us another new way of computing and empowering the rest of us to use it.

This book would be worse off without its reviewers: Jesse Anderson, Jenny Kim, Don Miner, Alex Moundalexis, and those who went unnamed or whom I've forgotten. They each applied their expertise, experience, and attention to detail to their feedback, filling in where I left important information out and correcting what I got wrong. I also owe thanks to Misha Brukman and the Google Cloud Platform team for looking over Chapter 7. My editors, Marie Beaugureau and Colleen Toporek, did a wonderful job of shepherding the writing process and giving feedback on organization, formatting, writing flow, and lots of other details. Finally, extra thanks is due to Alex Moundalexis for writing the foreword.

One of my favorite aphorisms is by Laozi: "A good traveler has no fixed plans and is not intent on arriving." I've arrived at the destination of authoring a book, but no one observing my travel, including me, could have guessed that I'd have gotten here. The road has wound through a career with a few different employers and with a few more projects, and I was privileged to walk alongside a truly wonderful collection of coworkers and friends along the way. I owe them all my gratitude for their company, and their roles in my journey.

I owe special thanks, of course, to my current employer, Cloudera, for the opportunity to create this book and the endorsement of the effort. I specifically want to thank Vinithra Varadharajan, my manager for the past few years, for her unwavering faith in and promotion of my writing effort; and also Justin Kestelyn, who got the ball rolling between me, my employer, and O'Reilly. My teammates past and present on my current project have all played a part in helping me learn about the cloud and have contributed their thoughts and opinions, for which I'm grateful: John Adair, Asif Arman, Cagdas Bayram, Jayita Bhojwani, Michael Cudahy, Xiaohua Guo, David Han, Joe Heyming, Ying Li, Andrei Savu, Fahd Siddiqui, and Michael Wilson.

Finally, I must thank my family, including my parents and in-laws for their encouragement, my daughters Samantha and Lydia, and especially my wife Kathy.[1] They have been constantly supportive of me during the long effort it's taken to write this book, and excited for it to be one of my accomplishments. I love them all very much.

---

1 *Te amo et semper amabo.*

Introduction to the Cloud

The purpose of the first part of this book is to orient you. First, the exact meaning of "the cloud" when it comes to working with Hadoop clusters is explored, so that it is clear what the benefits and drawbacks are. Then, overviews of three major public cloud providers are provided, including a little of their history as well as their approaches to doing business.

## CHAPTER 1

Why Hadoop in the Cloud?

Before embarking on a new technical effort, it's important to understand what problems you're trying to solve with it. Hot new technologies come and go in the span of a few years, and it should take more than popularity to make one worth trying. The short span of computing history is littered with ideas and technologies that were once considered the future of their domains, but just didn't work out.

Apache Hadoop is a technology that has survived its initial rush of popularity by proving itself as an effective and powerful framework for tackling big data applications. It broke from many of its predecessors in the "computing at scale" space by being designed to run in a distributed fashion across large amounts of commodity hardware instead of a few, expensive computers. Many organizations have come to rely on Hadoop for dealing with the ever-increasing quantities of data that they gather. Today, it is clear what problems Hadoop can solve.

Cloud computing, on the other hand, is still a newcomer as of this writing. The term itself, "cloud," currently has a somewhat mystical connotation, often meaning different things to different people. What is the cloud made of? Where is it? What does it do? Most importantly, why would you use it?

What Is the Cloud?

A definition for what "the cloud" means for this book can be built up from a few underlying concepts and ideas.

First, a cloud is made up of computing resources, which encompasses everything from computers themselves (or *instances* in cloud terminology) to networks to storage and everything in between and around them. All that you would normally need to put together the equivalent of a server room, or even a full-blown data center, is in place and ready to be claimed, configured, and run.

The entity providing these computing resources is called a *cloud provider*. The most famous ones are companies like Amazon, Microsoft, and Google, and this book focuses on the clouds offered by these three. Their clouds can be called *public clouds* because they are available to the general public; you use computing resources that are shared, in secure ways, with many other people. In contrast, *private clouds* are run internally by (usually large) organizations.

 While private clouds can work much like public ones, they are not explicitly covered in this book. You will find, though, that the basic concepts are mostly the same across cloud providers, whether public or private.

The resources that are available to you in the cloud are not just for you to use, but also to control. This means that you can start and stop instances when you want, and connect the instances together and to the outside world how you want. You can use just a small amount of resources or a huge amount, or anywhere in between. Advanced features from the provider are at your command for managing storage, performance, availability, and more. The cloud provider gives you the building blocks, but it is up to you to know how to arrange them for your needs.

Finally, you are free to use cloud provider resources for whatever you wish, within some limitations. There are quotas applied to cloud provider accounts, although these can be negotiated over time. There are also large, hard limits based on the capacity of the provider itself that you can run into. Beyond these somewhat "physical" limitations, there are legal and data security requirements, which can come from your own organization as well as the cloud provider. In general, as long as you are not abusing the cloud provider's offerings, you can do what you want. In this book, that means installing and running Hadoop clusters.

Having covered some underlying concepts, here is a definition for "the cloud" that this book builds from:

"The cloud" is a large set of computing resources made available by a cloud provider for customers to use and control for general purposes.

What Does Hadoop in the Cloud Mean?

Now that the term "cloud" has been defined, it's easy to understand what the jargony phrase "Hadoop in the cloud" means: it is running Hadoop clusters on resources offered by a cloud provider. This practice is normally compared with running Hadoop clusters on your own hardware, called *on-premises* clusters or "on-prem."

If you are already familiar with running Hadoop clusters on-prem, you will find that a lot of your knowledge and practices carry over to the cloud. After all, a cloud instance is supposed to act almost exactly like an ordinary server you connect to remotely, with root access, and some number of CPU cores, and some amount of disk space, and so on. Once instances are networked together properly and made accessible, you can imagine that they are running in a regular data center, as opposed to a cloud provider's own data center. This illusion is intentional, so that working in a cloud provider feels familiar, and your skills still apply.

That doesn't mean there's nothing new to learn, or that the abstraction is complete. A cloud provider does not do everything for you; there are many choices and a variety of provider features to understand and consider, so that you can build not only a functioning system, but a functioning system of Hadoop clusters. Cloud providers also include features that go beyond what you can do on-prem, and Hadoop clusters can benefit from those as well.

Mature Hadoop clusters rarely run in isolation. Supporting resources around them manage data flow in and out and host specialized tools, applications backed by the clusters, and non-Hadoop servers, among other things. The supporting cast can also run in the cloud, or else dedicated networking features can help to bring them close.

Reasons to Run Hadoop in the Cloud

Many concepts have been defined so far, but the core question has not yet been answered: Why run Hadoop clusters in the cloud at all? Here are just a few reasons:

Lack of space
Your organization may need Hadoop clusters, but you don't have anywhere to keep racks of physical servers, along with the necessary power and cooling.

Flexibility
Without physical servers to rack up or cables to run, it is much easier to reorganize instances, or expand or contract your footprint, for changing business needs. Everything is controlled through cloud provider APIs and web consoles. Changes can be scripted and put into effect manually or even automatically and dynamically based on current conditions.

New usage patterns
The flexibility of making changes in the cloud leads to new usage patterns that are otherwise impractical. For example, individuals can have their own instances, clusters, and even networks, without much managerial overhead. The overall budget for CPU cores in your cloud provider account can be concentrated in a set of large instances, a larger set of smaller instances, or some mixture, and can even change over time.

Speed of change

It is much faster to launch new cloud instances or allocate new database servers than to purchase, unpack, rack, and configure physical computers. Similarly, unused resources in the cloud can be torn down swiftly, whereas unused hardware tends to linger wastefully.

Lower risk

How much on-prem hardware should you buy? If you don't have enough, the entire business slows down. If you buy too much, you've wasted money and have idle hardware that continues to waste money. In the cloud, you can quickly and easily change how many resources you use, so there is little risk of undercommitment or overcommitment. What's more, if some resource malfunctions, you don't need to fix it; you can discard it and allocate a new one.

Focus

An organization using a cloud provider to rent resources, instead of spending time and effort on the logistics of purchasing and maintaining its own physical hardware and networks, is free to focus on its core competencies, like using Hadoop clusters to carry out its business. This is a compelling advantage for a tech startup, for example.

Worldwide availability

The largest cloud providers have data centers around the world, ready for you from the start. You can use resources close to where you work, or close to where your customers are, for the best performance. You can set up redundant clusters, or even entire computing environments, in multiple data centers, so that if local problems occur in one data center, you can shift to working elsewhere.

Data storage requirements

If you have data that is required by law to be stored within specific geographic areas, you can keep it in clusters that are hosted in data centers in those areas.

Cloud provider features

Each major cloud provider offers an ecosystem of features to support the core functions of computing, networking, and storage. To use those features most effectively, your clusters should run in the cloud provider as well.

Capacity

Few customers tax the infrastructure of a major cloud provider. You can establish large systems in the cloud that are not nearly as easy to put together, not to mention maintain, on-prem.

Reasons to Not Run Hadoop in the Cloud

As long as you are considering why you would run Hadoop clusters in the cloud, you should also consider reasons not to. If you have any of the following reasons as goals, then running in the cloud may disappoint you:

Simplicity

Cloud providers start you off with reasonable defaults, but then it is up to you to figure out how all of their features work and when they are appropriate. It takes a lot of experience to become proficient at picking the right types of instances and arranging networks properly.

High levels of control

Beyond the general geographic locations of cloud provider data centers and the hardware specifications that providers reveal for their resources, it is not possible to have exacting, precise control over your cloud architecture. You cannot tell exactly where the physical devices sit, or what the devices near them are doing, or how data across them shares the same physical network.[1] When the cloud provider has internal problems that extend beyond backup and replication strategies already in place, there's not much you can do but wait.

Unique hardware needs

You cannot have cloud providers attach specialized peripherals or dongles to their hardware for you. If your application requires resources that exceed what a cloud provider offers, you will need to host that part on-prem away from your Hadoop clusters.

Saving money

For one thing, you are still paying for the resources you use. The hope is that the economy of scale that a cloud provider can achieve makes it more economical for you to pay to "rent" their hardware than to run your own. You will also still need a staff that understands system administration and networking to take care of your cloud infrastructure. Inefficient architectures, especially those that leave resources running idly, can cost a lot of money in storage and data transfer costs.

What About Security?

The idea of sharing resources with many other, unknown parties is sure to raise questions about whether using a public cloud provider can possibly be secure. Could other tenants somehow gain access to your instances, or snoop on the shared net-

---

[1] An exception: some cloud providers have infrastructure dedicated to US government use where stricter controls are in place.

work infrastructure? How safe is data stashed away in cloud services? Is security a reason to avoid using public cloud providers?

There are valid arguments on both sides of this question, and the answer for you varies depending on your needs and tolerance for risk. Public cloud providers are certainly cognizant of security requirements, and as you'll see throughout this book, they use many different mechanisms to keep your resources private to you and give you control over who can see and do what. When you use a cloud provider, you gain their expertise in building and maintaining secure systems, including backup management, replication, availability, encryption support, and network management. So, it is reasonable to expect that clusters running in the cloud can be secure.

Still, there may be overriding reasons why some data simply cannot be put up into the cloud, for any reason, or why it's too risky to move data to, from, and around the cloud. In these situations, limited use of the cloud may still be possible.

Hybrid Clouds

Running Hadoop clusters in the cloud has compelling advantages, but the disadvantages may restrict you from completely abandoning an on-prem infrastructure. In a situation like that, a *hybrid cloud* architecture may be helpful. Instead of running your clusters and associated applications completely in the cloud or completely on-prem, the overall system is split between the two. Data channels are established between the cloud and on-prem worlds to connect the components needed to perform work.

"Cloud-Only or Hybrid?" on page 220 explores the pattern of hybrid clouds, including some examples for when they are appropriate or even necessary. Creating a hybrid cloud architecture is more challenging than running only on-prem or only in the cloud, but you are still able to benefit from some advantages of the cloud that you otherwise couldn't.

Hadoop Solutions from Cloud Providers

There are ways to take advantage of Hadoop technologies without doing the work of creating your own Hadoop clusters. Cloud providers offer prepackaged compute services that use Hadoop under the hood, but manage most of the cluster management work themselves. You simply point the services to your data and provide them with the jobs to run, and they handle the rest, delivering results back to you. You still pay for the resources used, as well as the use of the service, but save on all of the administrative work.

So, why ever roll your own clusters when these services exist? There are some good reasons:[2]

- Prepackaged services aim to cover the most common uses of Hadoop, such as individual MapReduce or Spark jobs. Their features may not be sufficient for more complex requirements, and may not offer Hadoop components that you already rely on or wish to employ.
- The services obviously only work on the cloud provider offering them. Some organizations are worried about being "locked in" to a single provider, unable to take advantage of competition between the providers.
- Useful applications that run on top of Hadoop clusters may not be compatible with a prepackaged provider service.
- It may not be possible to satisfy data security or tracking requirements with a prepackaged service, since you lack direct control over the resources.

Despite the downsides, you should investigate Hadoop-based provider solutions before rushing into running your own clusters. They can be useful and powerful, save you a lot of work, and get you running in the cloud more quickly. You can use them for prototyping work, and you may decide to keep them around for support tasks even while using your own clusters for the rest.

Here are some of the provider solutions that exist as of this writing. Keep an eye out for new ones as well.

Elastic MapReduce

Elastic MapReduce, or EMR, is Amazon Web Services' solution for managing prepackaged Hadoop clusters and running jobs on them. You can work with regular MapReduce jobs or Apache Spark jobs, and can use Apache Hive, Apache Pig, Apache HBase, and some third-party applications. Scripting hooks enable the installation of additional services. Data is typically stored in Amazon S3 or Amazon DynamoDB.

The normal mode of operation for EMR is to define the parameters for a cluster, such as its size, location, Hadoop version, and variety of services, point to where data should be read from and written to, and define steps to execute such as MapReduce or Spark jobs. EMR launches a cluster, performs the steps to generate the output data, and then tears the cluster down. However, you can leave clusters running for further use, and even resize them for greater capacity or a smaller footprint.

---

2 If there weren't, this book would not be very useful!

EMR provides an API so that you can automate the launching and management of Hadoop clusters.

Google Cloud Dataproc

Google Cloud Dataproc is similar to EMR, but runs within Google Cloud Platform. It offers Hadoop, Spark, Hive, and Pig, working on data that is usually stored in Google Cloud Storage. Like EMR, it supports both transient and long-running clusters, cluster resizing, and scripts for installing additional services. It can also be controlled through an API.

HDInsight

Microsoft Azure's prepackaged solution, called HDInsight, is built on top of the Hortonworks Data Platform (HDP). The service defines cluster types for Hadoop, Spark, Apache Storm, and HBase; other components like Hive and Pig are included as well. Clusters can be integrated with other tools like Microsoft R Server and Apache Solr through scripted installation and configuration. HDInsight clusters work with Azure Blob Storage and Azure Data Lake Store for reading and writing data used in jobs. You control whether clusters are torn down after their work is done or left running, and clusters can be resized. Apache Ambari is included in clusters for management through its API.

Hadoop-Like Services

The solutions just listed are explicitly based on Hadoop. Cloud providers also offer other services, based on different technologies, for managing and analyzing large amounts of data. Some offer SQL-like query capabilities similar to Hive or Apache Impala, and others offer processing pipelines like Apache Oozie. It may be possible to use those services to augment Hadoop clusters, managed either directly or through the cloud provider's own prepackaged solution, depending on where and how data is stored.

Of course, these tools share the same disadvantages as the Hadoop-based solutions in terms of moving further away from the open source world and its interoperability benefits. Since they are not based on Hadoop, there is a separate learning curve for them, and the effort could be wasted if they are ever discarded in favor of something that works on Hadoop, or on a different cloud provider, or even on-prem. Their ready availability and ease of use, however, can be attractive.

A Spectrum of Choices

It's perhaps ironic that much of this chapter describes how you can avoid running Hadoop clusters in the cloud, either by sticking with on-prem clusters (either partially or completely), by using cloud provider services that take away the management work, or by using tools that do away with Hadoop completely. There is a spectrum of choices, where at one end you work with your data at a conceptual level using high-level tools, and at the other end you build workflows, analyses, and query systems from the ground up. The breadth of this spectrum may be daunting.

However, one fact remains true: *Hadoop works everywhere*. When you focus on the core components in the Hadoop ecosystem, you have the freedom and power to work however you like, wherever you like. When you stick to the common components of Hadoop, you can carry your expertise with them to wherever your code runs and your data lives.

Cloud providers are eager for you to use their resources. They offer services to take over Hadoop cluster administration for you, but they are just as happy to let you run things yourself. Running your own clusters does not require you to forgo all of the benefits of a cloud provider, and Hadoop components that you deploy and run can still make effective use of cloud services. This book, in fact, explores how.

Getting Started

Have you figured out why you want to run Hadoop in the cloud? Ready to get started?

If you already know which cloud provider you'll use, skip ahead to Part II for a primer on the major concepts of cloud instances, networking, and storage. Otherwise, continue to the next chapter for an overview of the major cloud providers so that you can understand the landscape.

## CHAPTER 2

Overview and Comparison of Cloud Providers

This short chapter provides a brief background and history of the three major public cloud providers that are covered in this book. If you aren't sure which one to use, this information may help you decide.

Amazon Web Services

Amazon Web Services (AWS) is, at the time of this writing, perhaps the dominant public cloud provider. It may be surprising to learn that its earliest services were launched in 2006, well before cloud computing grew popular:

- Elastic Compute Cloud (EC2), a service for provisioning computing resources on demand
- Simple Storage Service (S3), online storage for opaque data

The original primary intent of AWS was to resolve scalability issues within Amazon itself, but even in its initial proposal in 2003 it was recognized that the new infrastructure could also be offered to customers.

The next prominent services to be added to the AWS suite included:

- Elastic Block Store (EBS), persistent disk-like storage for EC2 instances, in 2008
- Elastic MapReduce (EMR), a service providing Hadoop-like clusters for running MapReduce (and later Apache Hive and Apache Pig) jobs, in 2009
- Relational Database Service (RDS), a service for managing relational database server instances running in AWS, also in 2009

In 2012, new AWS services focused on data storage; in that year alone the Redshift massive-scale data warehouse, the DynamoDB NoSQL database, and the Glacier data archival service were introduced. More recent key developments include the Aurora cloud-optimized relational database and the Lambda function-as-a-service component, both in 2014.

Major companies rely heavily on AWS for their computing and storage needs, not least of which is Amazon itself, which migrated its shopping services to it back in 2010. The US federal government has access to its own computing region, called GovCloud, for highly secured government applications.

By being a first mover in cloud providers, AWS was able to define the terminology and practices that many other cloud providers use, with their own variations. It continues to be highly active, experiencing more demand than even its originators had anticipated. While all of the major cloud providers do a good job of evolving their systems according to customer demand, Amazon usually makes the biggest impact when it unveils its latest offerings, and it remains the provider against which all others are compared.

References

- Timeline of Amazon Web Services (*https://en.wikipedia.org/wiki/Timeline_of_Amazon_Web_Services*)
- The myth about how Amazon's web service started just won't die (*http://www.networkworld.com/article/2891297/cloud-computing/the-myth-about-how-amazon-s-web-service-started-just-won-t-die.html*)

Google Cloud Platform

As the originator and popularizer of early Hadoop technologies like MapReduce, it is natural to consider *Google Cloud Platform* as a home for your own Hadoop clusters. Services such as BigQuery and BigTable provide direct access to big data systems based on those original technologies, but you can also host your own Hadoop clusters using other services.

Google Cloud Platform started out in 2008 as the Google App Engine service, a development environment backed by Google's infrastructure for needs such as persistent storage, CPU cycles, and user authentication. It was, and still is, focused on general web application development, although today it also focuses on hosting backends for mobile services.

The next separate service, Google Storage for Developers, was introduced in 2010; it is now called Google Cloud Storage, and works in a manner similar to AWS S3. The

BigQuery service for performing SQL-like queries on massive amounts of data followed in 2012.

Perhaps surprisingly, it was not until late 2013 that Google Compute Engine, Google Cloud Platform's answer to AWS EC2, was made available for general use. Google Cloud SQL followed quickly in early 2014, supporting cloud deployments of MySQL. Google Dataproc, unveiled in 2016, is a versatile service supporting Hadoop and Spark workloads.

The infrastructure supporting Google Cloud Platform is the same that powers Google's own services, most notably its internet search capability. Many major companies use Google Cloud Platform to run their own architectures.

There is a smaller variety of services under the Google Cloud Platform umbrella than under AWS, although they do cover the requirements for fielding Hadoop clusters. You may find that you must assemble some pieces of your system "by hand" at times, whereas in AWS there is a service or service feature that fills the gap. Despite that, Google Cloud Platform is under active development just as the other cloud provider systems are, and the generally cleaner design of Google Cloud Platform compared to AWS may be attractive to some. Fundamentally, though, the concepts used in AWS and Google Cloud Platform are quite compatible, and being familiar with one makes it easier to get going with the other.

References

- Google Cloud Platform blog (*https://cloudplatform.googleblog.com/*)
- Google Developers blog (*https://developers.googleblog.com/*)

Microsoft Azure

Microsoft's cloud provider offering, today called *Microsoft Azure*, started its life in 2008 as Windows Azure, a service for running .NET and other services on Windows inside Microsoft's infrastructure. Storage services for tables and general "blobs" were included, along with a service bus for queuing data between applications. Windows Azure became generally available in 2010.

Also made available in 2010, although announced a year earlier, was Azure SQL Database, a distributed database service based on Microsoft SQL Server.

The services in Azure continued to grow and advance, and finally in 2012 the ability to run images of Windows and Linux on persistent virtual machines was delivered. By 2014, given Azure's continuing expansion and shifting focus from being a platform-as-a-service to infrastructure-as-a-service, the provider was renamed to Microsoft Azure.

The mode of working with Azure has changed over time, and today one of its distinguishing features is its portal, a highly customizable and dynamic web interface to the large variety of Azure services. The current portal was made available in 2015.

Like AWS and Google Cloud Platform, Azure hosts its company's own large internet services, such as Microsoft Office 365, Bing, and OneDrive. Microsoft's long history of supporting large enterprises has led to many of them using Azure as their cloud provider. Azure also has excellent security accreditations and meets requirements for EU data protections, HIPAA, and US government FedRAMP. Among the major cloud providers, Azure has the widest geographic footprint.

Azure has similar services to both AWS and Google Cloud Platform when considering them at a high level, but its conceptual framework varies significantly, such that it is more difficult to translate ideas and designs from Azure to the other providers, or back again. Organizations that have innate familiarity with the Microsoft ecosystem may be drawn naturally to Azure. While it originally leaned heavily on Microsoft technologies such as Windows, SQL Server, and .NET, today it works just as well as a cloud provider for Linux-based architectures, which are paramount for Hadoop cluster support.

References

- Microsoft launches Windows Azure (*https://www.cnet.com/news/microsoft-launches-windows-azure/*)

- A Brief History of Azure (*http://www.slideshare.net/MattDeacon/a-brief-history-of-azure*)

- Windows Azure's spring fling: Linux comes to Microsoft's cloud (*http://www.zdnet.com/article/windows-azures-spring-fling-linux-comes-to-microsofts-cloud/*)

- Upcoming Name Change for Windows Azure (*https://azure.microsoft.com/en-us/blog/upcoming-name-change-for-windows-azure/*)

- Announcing Azure Portal General Availability (*https://azure.microsoft.com/en-us/blog/announcing-azure-portal-general-availability/*)

Which One Should You Use?

This chapter is indeed only a short overview of these three cloud providers, and you should take the time to learn about them through their own marketing and technical materials as well as trade articles and blog posts. War stories abound about how using cloud provider capabilities saved the day, and large and successful customers openly share how they are able to run their businesses in the cloud.

All of the providers offer free trials or credits in some form, so another important task in evaluating them is to try them out. While you will be limited in the scope of what you can field, hands-on experience tells you about how the providers work in ways that no web page can. Tasks you should try out to get a feel for a provider include:

- Allocating a new computing resource, or *instance* (see Chapter 3), and logging in to it
- Moving data from your local system to a cloud instance and back
- Downloading software to an instance and running it
- Navigating the provider's web console
- Saving data to and retrieving data from the provider's object storage service (see Chapter 5)

Pricing plays a huge role in selecting a cloud provider. Your organization may already have a business relationship with a cloud provider (Microsoft is most common here) that can be parlayed into discounts. The providers themselves are in robust competition with each other as well, so since Hadoop clusters can be deployed on any of them quite effectively, you can easily pit them against each other.

Since the cloud providers evolve and change so quickly, and to be fair to all of them, it is not possible to come up with a simple recipe for finding one that is best for you. Still, since your goal is to spin up Hadoop clusters, a suggestion that can be given here is to use this book as your guide, and take them each for a test drive. Here are some of the questions you'll want to find answers for:

- How easy is it to understand what the services do?
- Are the web interfaces easy to use?
- Is essential information easy to find?
- Does the provider make it simple to do tasks that are important to the organization?
- When there are problems, are they easy to fix? How capable is the provider support?
- Are the prices fair?
- Does the provider infrastructure meet security requirements?

If you are just starting out and need to get a basic understanding of cloud provider concepts in order to answer these questions and more, then continue on to Chapter 3, which starts you off with what an instance is. Otherwise, if you are ready to jump in and build a cluster, head to Part III, where you can get rolling on the cloud provider of your choice.

## PART II

Cloud Primer

This part provides an introduction to cloud provider concepts, including compute capabilities, networking, and storage. If you are already familiar with using a cloud provider, you may wish to skim the chapters in this part.

Cloud providers can use different terminology to refer to the same concept, or even offer different features that support the same concept. In these cases, the descriptions here begin by using the terminology for Amazon Web Services (AWS). Differences in other cloud providers are called out after the basic concept is described.

## CHAPTER 3

Instances

The core of a cloud provider's offerings is the ability to provision instances. An *instance* is similar in concept to a virtual machine, which is an emulation of a particular computer system. While historically virtual machines were thought of as running on a specific piece of hardware—perhaps a server in a company's machine room—a cloud instance is thought of as running somewhere unspecified within the cloud provider's vast infrastructure. Precisely where and how an instance is provisioned is often not revealed to you as a customer, although you do have some coarse-grained control (see "Regions and Availability Zones" on page 23 for one example). All that matters to you is that you ask for an instance, and the cloud provider brings it to life.

 Instances running in Azure are called "virtual machines."

The features of an instance, beyond its precise physical location, are up to you. You can choose from a variety of combinations of CPU power and memory, any of several operating systems, and different storage options, just to start with. Once the instance has been provisioned, you can access it over SSH through the networking capabilities of the cloud provider. From that point on, it acts and feels just like a real, physical machine. You have root access, so you can install applications, perform additional upgrades, start web servers or Hadoop daemons, and so on.

Your cloud provider account has limits that affect the number and size of instances you can provision. Those limits, along with the cost of running instances, influence how you design your cloud architecture. Given those limits, often the first step in the design process is determining which instance types to use.

Instance Types

Cloud providers offer instances in a multitude of combinations of features. These combinations usually differentiate themselves in terms of compute power, memory, storage capacity, and performance. To make selecting a combination easier, and also to enable the cloud provider to fit all its customers' instances together efficiently on its infrastructure, a cloud provider offers a set of fixed feature combinations, like a menu. Each of these *instance types* is defined for a purpose: heavy compute capability, vast storage, economy, or simply general-purpose use.

 Azure refers to instance types as "instance sizes."

While you are free to always select a top-of-the-line instance type with lots of everything, it will be among the most expensive of your options, and most of the time you will not need all of that power all the time.[1] It is much more efficient, and cheaper, to pick instance types that focus on what you need the instances for. Since a cloud provider makes it easy to provision new instances, you have the option of allocating more, cheaper instances, instead of staying with a smaller number of ultrapowerful ones.

Cluster technologies like Hadoop can flourish in this sort of environment. As your needs change over time, you can scale up or scale down the number of daemons you run for different components without worrying about the physical hardware. Moreover, Hadoop components do not require top-of-the-line instance specifications to work; they can perform well on mid-range instance types. Still, you should pick instance types that focus on the features that the components need.

Advice for selecting instance types for Hadoop clusters is provided in "Picking Instance Types" on page 187. In short, roles are defined for instances in a cluster, and then the needs for each role are discussed.

Cloud providers offer many different instance types, so it can be tricky to decide on which ones to use. It is somewhat easier, though, to choose where the instances will run.

---

[1] During the free trial period for cloud providers, you are usually restricted to only basic instance types with relatively meager specifications. Once you upgrade to a regular account, or after some amount of time, your options open up.

Regions and Availability Zones

An advantage of using a cloud provider is geographic distribution. A major cloud provider's infrastructure spans time zones and continents, running 24 hours a day. A data center can be constructed anywhere that has space, electricity, network connectivity, and people to maintain it. This enables you to set up your own systems in a distributed fashion, reaping all of the associated availability and performance benefits.

A cloud provider infrastructure is exposed as a set of divided, geographic areas called *regions*. For example, a cloud provider could define three regions in the continental United States (say, west, central, and east) along with two more in Europe and two in Southeast Asia. The number and coverage areas of cloud provider regions changes over time. A busy geographic area may be covered by multiple regions.

When you provision new instances, you select the region where they live. You may decide to pick the region you work in, so that network performance between you and the instance is quickest. Or, you may be setting up a failover system and decide to choose a region farther away. If you know that most of the traffic to your instance will be from customers, you may choose a region close to them. You may pick a region to satisfy legal requirements that apply to where your data may be stored.

Regions are one of the key factors in designing a large Hadoop cluster. While spreading a cluster far and wide across the world sounds attractive for availability, it takes much longer, and will cost more, for instances in different regions to communicate with each other. So, it's important to plan carefully to minimize cross-region communication while still getting the availability you need.

To help provide both availability and performance, a cloud provider defines one or more *availability zones* within a region. Availability zones are themselves independent within a region, but they have faster interconnections. This lets you set up a distributed architecture that sits within a single region and has good performance, yet has some measure of availability. While it is rare for an entire availability zone to fail, it is far rarer for an entire region to fail.

Azure does not support the concept of availability zones, but instead lets you define *availability sets*. An availability set contains instances that are spread out among multiple *fault domains*, each of which has separate power and network connections and therefore are housed in different hosts and racks.[2] So, rather than managing availability zones yourself for each individual instance in your architecture, you can group them into availability sets based on their roles.

Communication between instances in different availability zones generally costs more than between instances in the same availability zone, and this is one factor that will influence your cluster architecture. In general, you would not spread a Hadoop cluster across availability zones except to achieve high availability. Chapter 10 is dedicated to exploring high availability, and discusses the pros and cons of availability zones as a factor.

As you've seen, you have control over the specifications of an instance through selecting an instance type and some amount of control over where an instance runs. It's time to discuss how you can control an instance's existence once it has been started.

Instance Control

Just like a real machine, even when no one is connected to it, an instance still "exists" and keeps running. This makes instances perfectly suited for hosting daemons like those across the Hadoop ecosystem. The cloud provider monitors your instances, and you can set up alerts to be notified if any of your instances become unreachable or, in rare cases, die out.

If you know that you will not be using an instance for a while, you can *stop* it. Stopping an instance works like shutting off a physical machine; processes running on it are terminated normally and the operating system halts. A stopped instance is unreachable until it is started again, which works like turning a physical machine back on.

Why stop an instance instead of just leaving it running? One important reason is that your cloud provider charges your account much less, or not at all, for an instance while it is stopped, so it is economical to stop instances you aren't using. In addition, some operations on an instance, like changing its attached storage, can only be performed when the instance is stopped.

---

2 Fault domains may still reside in the same data center.

Azure continues to charge for instances that are stopped. You must also "deallocate" instances to suspend charging for instances. This is because Azure retains the compute and memory resources for your instances even when they are stopped.

Once an instance has served its purpose, it can be *terminated* or deleted. A terminated instance cannot be started up again; you need to provision a new instance to replace it. Once an instance is terminated, everything that was on its disks is lost, unless you have backed it up, either on your own or by using other cloud provider capabilities (see Chapter 5). Cloud providers stop charging for instances when they are terminated.

Terminating an instance causes a cloud provider to reclaim most or all of the resources associated with that instance, but stopping may also cause the provider to reclaim some resources, such as ephemeral storage (see "Block Storage" on page 47) or public IP addresses (see "Virtual Networks" on page 30). Check your provider's documentation for complete information. It may be the case that even stopping an instance participating in a Hadoop cluster will render it unusable when it is started again.

Temporary Instances

By default, once you allocate an instance, it is yours to control until you terminate it yourself; it will not be taken away from you unless some rare problem occurs at the cloud provider, and even then you usually receive a warning and some lead time to react.

Under some circumstances, however, you may decide to use a *temporary instance*, which can disappear after some time. While this seems like a bad idea in the general case, temporary instances can be useful for surging your capacity for a few hours, or for running some process that won't take long.

Still, though, why not just use ordinary instances all the time? The main reason is that cloud providers charge significantly less for temporary instances than for ordinary ones. Cloud providers almost always have excess capacity going unused, so temporary instances are a way to earn revenue on it, even at a discount, until the capacity can be allocated to ordinary provisioned instances.

In order to use temporary instances effectively, you must have automated means of bootstrapping them and pressing them into service. If you spend too much time getting them set up, they may disappear before you get a chance to do anything with them. Nevertheless, if that does happen, it's straightforward to rerun automation and try again with another temporary instance. This mode of retrying on temporary instances is not suitable for critical pieces of your system, but can save money elsewhere.

While it makes good sense to not under-utilize temporary instances, it makes good sense as well not to over-utilize them, especially for the sake of saving money. Temporary instances *will* disappear on you, sometimes when you least expect or want them to, and a quiet spell of weeks where temporary instances have been reliable and lingered for plenty of time can end surprisingly suddenly. So, use them, but use them wisely.

Azure does not offer temporary instances at this time.

Spot Instances

AWS calls its temporary instances *spot instances*.[3] There is a market for spot instances within AWS, driven by the price that customers are willing to pay for them. When demand for spot instances is low, the price is low; when demand goes up, so does the price. When you request spot instances, you select a price that you are willing to pay, anywhere from the current market price up to the fixed rate for ordinary instances.

The spot market determines not only the price for spot instances, but also how long they last. Once the spot price rises above your chosen price, your spot instances are reclaimed so that their resources can be used by those who bid higher (or for ordinary instances). So, you can choose a higher initial price for a higher probability of keeping your spot instances longer, but you may end up paying "too much" if the market price remains low.

Spot instances are particularly prone to overuse, since there is no predetermined time after which they will disappear. They can persist for days or weeks, and lull users into a false sense of stability. Don't be fooled; always treat them as if they could disappear at any moment.

Preemptible Instances

Google Cloud Platform calls its temporary instances *preemptible instances*. Unlike AWS, there is no market determining the price for a preemptible instance; there is a single offered price, which is lower than the price of a standard instance.

---

3 AWS documentation capitalizes the word "Spot." This book does not, reflecting how the term is commonly used to describe temporary instances from any cloud provider.

While market conditions in AWS determine when your spot instances are reclaimed, preemptible instances are *guaranteed* to be reclaimed within a day (24 hours), if not sooner. This does much to reduce the temptation to over-rely on them and promotes the practices of automating their configuration and keeping your cluster resilient to loss of instances.

Images

Besides its instance type, location, and lifecycle, another key feature of an instance is what it's actually running: its operating system type and version, the software packages that are available, and applications that are installed. These considerations are all bundled up into *images*. An image can be thought of as the plan for a virtual drive that your instance runs from. Conceptually it is just like a virtual machine image file: an encapsulated filesystem with a specific operating system and other software installed and ready to go.

When you provision an instance, you select the image that it should start from. Larger cloud providers can support hundreds or thousands of different images, some that they fashion themselves, but many more that are created by operating system vendors, vendors of other software, and in some cases even individuals. Cloud providers will propose a small set of stock images to help you get started, but you have the freedom to use any image you like.

Most images are free to use, especially those that bundle free operating systems. However, there are some that cost money to use, either as a fixed additional cost or a continual surcharge to running them. In addition, some images may host unlicensed, freshly installed (at the time the image was created) software that will prompt you for license details before your instances will start to fully function. Hadoop can be used on images that include free operating systems like Ubuntu and CentOS, or on those that require licenses, such as Red Hat Enterprise Linux.

One of the most important things you can do to make using Hadoop on a cloud provider easier is to create your own images. Instead of using a basic image for every instance and installing Hadoop components on them every time, even in an automated fashion, you can instead create a custom image with the components installed where you need them. Chapter 16 goes into detail about this process.

No Instance Is an Island

Instances provisioned by a cloud provider aren't of much use if no one can reach them. The next chapter discusses how instances are connected into a network so that you can reach them and they can reach other and other systems outside the cloud provider.

## CHAPTER 4

Networking and Security

An essential aspect of working with instances is configuring their network connectivity. While cloud providers start customers off with a basic, working network configuration, it's important to understand the ways to construct different network topologies, so that your clusters can communicate effectively internally, and back and forth with your own systems and with the outside world.

Network topology is of primary importance when setting up Hadoop clusters. Worker daemons like datanodes and node managers must be able to work with namenodes and resource managers, and clients must understand where to send jobs to run and where cluster data resides. You will likely spend more time designing and maintaining the network architecture of your clusters than the instances and images that serve as their building blocks.

Security considerations are intertwined with network design. Once network connections are made, you need to determine the rules by which they are used. Which parts of the network can talk to which other parts of the network? What can reach out to the internet? What can reach *in* from the internet? What ports should be exposed, and to whom?

This chapter covers a wide range of topics, and is more of an introduction to cloud networks and security than an application of them to Hadoop, although there are some pointers. Chapter 14 goes into much more detail about designing a network and security rules for a Hadoop cluster.

A Drink of CIDR

Before diving into the details of cloud provider network services, it's helpful to be familiar with *CIDR* (*Classless Inter-Domain Routing*) *notation*, a way of denoting a continuous range of IP addresses. The scopes of network partitions and the rules that apply to activity in them are defined using CIDR notation. In this book, the term "CIDR" or "CIDR block" is used to refer to an IP address range specified in CIDR notation.

An IP address range expressed in CIDR notation has two parts: a starting IP address and a decimal number counting the number of leading bits of value 1 in the *network mask*, which is as long as the IP address itself. An IP address lies within the range if it matches the starting IP address when logically ANDed with the network mask.

Here are some examples that illustrate how to interpret CIDRs:

- The range 192.168.0.0/24 represents the IP addresses from 192.168.0.0 to 192.168.0.255, for a total of 256 addresses.

- The range 172.16.0.0/20 represents the IP addresses from 172.16.0.0 to 172.16.15.255, for a total of 4,096 addresses. Note that the number of 1 bits in the network mask does not need to be a multiple of 4, although it commonly is.

- The range 192.168.100.123/32 represents only the single IP address 192.168.100.123. It is common practice to target a single IP address, in a security rule for example, using a /32 block.

For more about the role of CIDR in IP routing and allocation, see the Wikipedia article on Classless Inter-Domain Routing (*https://en.wikipedia.org/wiki/Classless_Inter-Domain_Routing*). Their usefulness in allocating IP addresses is why CIDR blocks are used to delimit virtual networks in the cloud.

Virtual Networks

Cloud providers establish *virtual networks* as the top-level containers where instances live. Each virtual network is separate from other virtual networks, and instances within a virtual network always communicate with each other more directly than with instances in other virtual networks or outside of the cloud provider.

A virtual network is just a basic, coarse-grained concept. To enable finer control of network topology, each virtual network is divided up into subnetworks or *subnets*. A subnet is not just a lower-level instance container; it also covers a range of *private* IP addresses. There are normally several subnets within a virtual network, each with a distinct range of private IP addresses.

RFC 1918 (*https://tools.ietf.org/html/rfc1918*) establishes three ranges of private IP addresses. Cloud providers use these ranges to define subnets. Any of these blocks, including just portions of them, can be used for a subnet:

- 10.0.0.0–10.255.255.255 (CIDR 10.0.0.0/8)
- 172.16.0.0–172.31.255.255 (CIDR 172.16.0.0/12)
- 192.168.0.0–192.168.255.255 (CIDR 192.168.0.0/16)

Amazon Web Services calls its virtual networks Virtual Private Clouds or VPCs. Each VPC has a private IP address range, and the address range for each subnet within a VPC must be a subset of the VPC's range. The subnet ranges do not have to completely cover the VPC range.

For example, a single virtual network could be designed to cover the entire 16-bit private IP address block of 192.168.0.0/16. One way to divide the network, as shown in Figure 4-1, is into four subnets, each covering a distinct quarter of the block: 192.168.0.0/18, 192.168.64.0/18, 192.168.128.0/18, and 192.168.192.0/18.

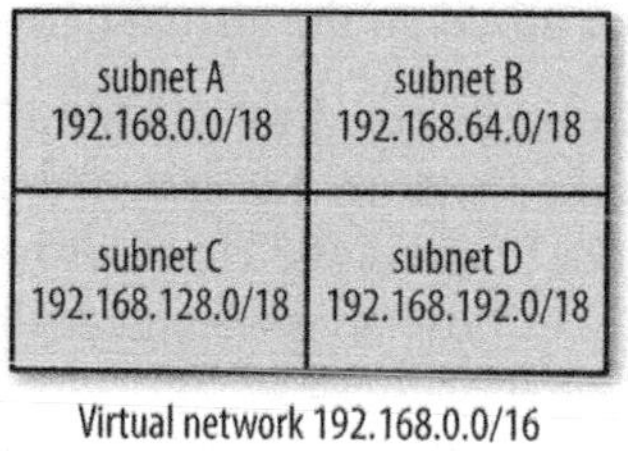

subnet A 192.168.0.0/18	subnet B 192.168.64.0/18
subnet C 192.168.128.0/18	subnet D 192.168.192.0/18

Virtual network 192.168.0.0/16

Figure 4-1. A virtual network with four subnets

After a virtual network is established, subnets must be created within it as homes for instances that will reside in the virtual network. Sometimes the cloud provider establishes one or more default subnets, and sometimes it is up to you to define them. The size of the private IP range of a subnet dictates its capacity for instances: for example, a range like 192.168.123.0/28 only supports 16 instances, while a range like 172.16.0.0/16 supports thousands. Instances that reside in the same subnet can communicate more quickly and easily than those in separate subnets, so sizing subnets appropriately is important for designing efficient clusters.

When you provision an instance on a cloud provider, you choose its subnet. The cloud provider assigns the instance an IP address from the remaining unused addresses in the subnet's range, and that IP address sticks with the instance until it is terminated.

The private IP address for an Azure virtual machine can either be static or dynamic. A dynamic private IP address, which is the default, is dissociated from the virtual machine even when it is stopped, while a static private IP remains across stops until termination. In order to avoid needing to reconfigure your Hadoop cluster after virtual machines are stopped and started, you will want to use static addresses.

Most of the time, a Hadoop cluster should reside within a single subnet, itself within one virtual network. Not only is this arrangement simplest, it is the least expensive and has the best performance. Chapter 10 explores other arrangements in terms of establishing high availability.

Private DNS

When an instance is provisioned inside a subnet, it is assigned not only a private IP address, but also a *private* DNS hostname. The hostname is automatically generated for you and registered with the cloud provider's internal DNS infrastructure. It may simply be a form of the public IP address or some random string, and thus have no meaning. The cloud provider also automatically configures each instance's network settings so that processes running on it can resolve private DNS hostnames successfully, both its own and those of others in the virtual network.

A private DNS hostname can be resolved to a private IP address *only* by instances within the virtual network of the instance it is assigned to. Other instances, including those in other virtual networks of the same cloud provider, must use a public DNS hostname or public IP address, if those are assigned at all.

In Azure, two virtual networks can be *peered*, so that instances in them can communicate using private IP addresses. The two networks must have private IP address ranges that do not overlap.

In practice, private DNS hostnames have limited usefulness in working with a Hadoop cluster; the private IP addresses work just as well, and are often shorter and therefore easier to work with. Given all the other things to think about when managing virtual networks and how instances are deployed within them, you may find that private DNS can essentially be ignored.

Public IP Addresses and DNS

While an instance is always assigned a private IP address, it may also be assigned a public IP address. The public IP address is not part of the instance's subnet's IP range, but is instead assigned from the block of IP addresses administered by the cloud provider. An instance with a public IP address is therefore addressable from outside the virtual network and, in particular, from the internet.

While having a public IP address is a prerequisite for an instance to have connectivity outside the virtual network, it does not mean that the instance *can* be reached, or itself reach out from the virtual network. That depends on the security rules that govern the instance and routing rules that apply to the subnet.

A cloud provider may also assign a public DNS hostname to an instance with a public IP address. The typical public DNS hostname is under the domain of the cloud provider and, like a private DNS hostname, often has no real meaning. Still, the cloud provider does establish resolution of the public DNS hostname to the public IP address for external clients, so it is usable.

If you have a DNS domain that you want to use for assigning public DNS hostnames to your instances, you can use the cloud provider's public DNS component to manage assignments (AWS Route 53, Google Cloud DNS, and Azure DNS). In the context of configuring and using Hadoop clusters, however, it's almost always sufficient to work with private DNS hostnames for instances. Save public DNS hostnames for those few gateway instances[1] that host public-facing interfaces to your system.

 Without a public IP address or public DNS hostname, an instance is not reachable from the internet. It is therefore much more difficult to accidentally expose such an instance through, for example, overly permissive security settings.

The private and public addresses for instances in a virtual network provide a logical means for finding where instances are. It is not as obvious how to understand where a virtual network and subnets within it are located.

Virtual Networks and Regions

The location of a subnet in a virtual network, or of an entire virtual network, is determined in different ways, depending on the cloud provider.

A subnet in AWS and Google Cloud Platform, besides determining the private IP address for an instance, also determines the region where the instance resides. In AWS, each subnet that you define is assigned to an availability zone, so instances in the subnet run in that availability zone, in the zone's region. In Google Cloud, the arrangement is slightly different: each subnet is associated with an entire region, but

---

1 See "Cluster Topologies" on page 204 for a description of gateway instances.

when you provision a new instance, you can select an availability zone in the subnet's region.

The association of regions with subnets in these providers make subnets the means by which you take geography into account when architecting the network topology for your clusters. There is a need to strike a balance between the fast, open communication possible between instances in a single subnet with the availability and reliability benefits of distributing instances across regions and therefore across subnets. Figure 4-2 shows an example virtual network demonstrating subnets in different locations.

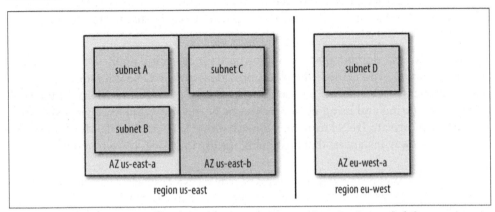

Figure 4-2. A virtual network spanning two regions and multiple availability zones

Region determination works differently in Azure. With this provider, each subnet and, in turn, each virtual network is associated with a resource group, and a resource group specifies the region for all its resources. So, setting up a cluster that spans regions is somewhat more challenging in Azure, since you will need multiple resource groups, which spreads out management.

Chapter 10 goes into detail about spanning clusters across availability zones and regions. The general advice is to never span regions, and rarely even span availability zones, due to the impact to performance and the high cost of data transfer, given the large amount of intracluster traffic that Hadoop generates. An architecture that keeps clusters confined to single regions, and even single availability zones, is much more cost effective.

Routing

Cloud networking is about much more than placing instances in the right IP address ranges in the right geographic regions. Instances need paths to follow for communication with other instances and with the world outside the cloud provider. These paths are called *routes*.

From the point of view of an instance, there are several possibilities for where a route leads. The shortest and simplest path is back to the instance's own subnet. There are also usually routes that lead to other subnets in the instance's virtual network. Some other routes lead outside the network, either to other virtual networks, or completely outside the cloud provider.

A route is comprised of an IP address range and a destination. The route declares that a resource whose IP address falls within its range can be reached by communicating with the route's destination. Sometimes the destination is the desired resource itself, a direct route; but sometimes it is a device, specialized instance, or cloud provider feature that handles establishing communication. In general, that sort of intermediary destination is called a *gateway*.

Here are some examples of routes, which are also illustrated in Figure 4-3:

- For IP addresses in the CIDR range 192.168.128.0/18, the destination is subnet C.
- For IP addresses in the CIDR range 10.0.0.0/8, the destination is the corporate VPN gateway.
- For any IP address (CIDR 0.0.0.0/0), the destination is the internet gateway.

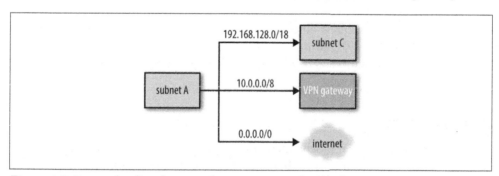

Figure 4-3. Routes leading from a subnet to various destinations

A cloud instance has a set of routes to look through, which are arranged into a *route table* or *routing table*. Given an IP address to communicate with, the route table is consulted, and the best match for the destination IP address is used. Sometimes there is only one route that satisfies the need, but sometimes there are multiple. In that case, generally, the route that most specifically matches the IP address is chosen.

Suppose that an instance has an associated route table listing the three example routes as shown in Figure 4-3. When a process on the instance attempts to initiate communication with 10.0.0.126, the instance's networking system consults the route table and looks for the best match. The IP address does not fall within the range for subnet C, so that route is discarded. The VPN route and the internet route both match; however, the VPN route is a better match, so that route is chosen.

If there is no match at all, then network communication will fail. That is why it is typical for there to be a catch-all (or default) route for CIDR 0.0.0.0/0 that leads to the internet, the idea being that any IP address not accounted for must be outside the cloud provider.

 Designing a cloud network architecture can appear daunting. A cloud provider gives you a lot of power and flexibility, but that carries complexity as well. Fortunately, when you create your first virtual network, the cloud provider sets up a reasonable default configuration for networking so you can get started quickly. For exploratory use the configuration is often acceptable, but before long you will want to look at routing and security rules to ensure they are set up for what you need, such as your first Hadoop cluster.

Routing is an important factor in building out a functioning Hadoop cluster. The daemons that comprise each service, like HDFS and YARN, need to be able to connect to each other, and the HDFS datanodes in particular need to be available for calls from pieces of other services. If all of a cluster's daemons are confined to a single subnet, then the cloud provider's default routing is enough; some providers can even handle routing across subnets automatically or with their defaults. For reaching out farther, such as across VPNs or to the internet, it usually becomes necessary to define some routes, as the defaults start out restrictive for the sake of security.

Each cloud provider provides routing services in a different way.

Routing in AWS

In AWS, a route table is an independent object that is associated with VPCs and subnets. Each VPC has a route table that is used as the default for subnets that do not have their own route tables.

The destination for each route is termed a *target*. There are a variety of targets available, some of which are described here:

- A "local" target points to the virtual network of the communicating instance. This covers not only that instance's own subnet, but other subnets in the same VPC.

- An internet gateway target provides access to the internet, outside the cloud provider. When a subnet has a route to the internet, it is called a *public subnet*; without one, it is called a *private subnet*. See "Public and Private Subnets" on page 197 for more detailed descriptions.

- A virtual private gateway links to your corporate network's VPN device, allowing access to resources within that network. To establish this connection, you must define a *customer gateway* in AWS representing the VPN device, create a virtual private gateway that links to it, and then define the IP address ranges covered by the gateway.

- A VPC peering connection allows for communication between VPCs using just private IP addresses.

- A network address translation (NAT) gateway provides access to the internet for private subnets. The gateway itself resides in a public subnet.

Routing in Google Cloud Platform

In Google Cloud Platform, each route is associated with a network, so all instances in the network may have use of it. Routes and instances are associated by tags: if a route has a tag, then it is associated with any instance with a matching tag; if a route has no tag, it applies to all instances in the network.

All of the routes defined for a network form the network's *route collection*, while all of the routes that are associated with an instance form that instance's routing table.

The destination for each route is termed its *next hop*. There are a variety of destinations available, some of which are described here:

- A subnet, or portion of a subnet, can be designated as the next hop by providing a CIDR block for its private IP addresses.

- An internet gateway URL for the next hop provides direct access to the internet, as long as the source instance has an external (public) IP address.

- The URL or IP address of a single instance can be the next hop. The instance needs to be configured with software that can provide connectivity to the ultimate desired destination. For example, the instance could use Squid as a proxy or perform NAT using iptables to provide internet access.

Google Cloud Platform provides a service called Cloud VPN to help manage connectivity between your corporate VPN device and your instances in virtual networks, as well as between virtual networks in Google Cloud Platform itself. A VPN gateway leading to a VPN tunnel is another possible next hop for a route.

Routing in Azure

In Azure, a route table is an independent object that is associated with subnets. A route table may be associated with multiple subnets, but a subnet can have only one route table.

Azure provides *system routes* for common needs, which are usually comprehensive enough that you do not need to define a route table at all. For example, system routes direct network traffic automatically within a subnet, between subnets in a virtual network, and to the internet and VPN gateways. If you define a route table for a subnet, its routes take precedence over system routes.

The destination for each route is termed its *next hop*. There are a variety of destinations available, some of which are described here:

- The local virtual network can be specified as the next hop for traffic between subnets.

- A virtual network gateway or VPN gateway for the next hop allows traffic to flow to other virtual networks or to a VPN.

- Naming the internet as the next hop provides direct access to the internet.

- A null route or black hole route can be used as the next hop to drop outgoing traffic completely.

Network Security Rules

If routing builds the roads for traffic between your instances, then security rules define the laws the traffic must obey. Cloud providers separate the definitions of the connections between instances from the definitions of how data may flow along those connections.

In a way, routing is a coarse-grained security measure: if there is no route defined between an instance and some destination, then absolutely no traffic can pass between them. When a route is established, however, then security rules provide a way to allow some kinds of traffic and disallow others.

As with routing, each cloud provider provides network security in different ways, but they share common concepts.

Inbound Versus Outbound

Inbound rules control traffic coming to an instance, while *outbound* rules control traffic leaving an instance. Most of the time, you will find yourself focusing on inbound rules, and allowing unrestricted traffic outbound. The implication is that you trust the activity of the instances that you yourself control, but need to protect them from traffic coming in from outside, particularly the internet.

Allow Versus Deny

An *allow* rule explicitly permits some form of network traffic, while a *deny* rule explicitly blocks it. If an allow rule and a deny rule conflict with each other, then usually the deny rule wins out. A common pattern is to establish an allow rule with a broad scope, and then use deny rules to pick out exceptions; for example, you could allow HTTP access from everywhere with one rule, and add deny rules that block IP ranges that are known to exhibit bad behaviors.

Some security rule structures do not use deny rules at all. Instead, they start from an initial implicit state of denying all traffic, and you add allow rules for only what you want to permit.

Network Security Rules in AWS

AWS provides two main mechanisms for securing your VPC.

Security groups

The most common mechanism used is *security groups*. A security group provides a set of rules that govern traffic to and from an instance. Each instance can belong to one or several security groups; a VPC also has a default security group that applies to instances that aren't associated with any groups themselves.

Each rule in a security group only allows traffic. If none of the security groups for an instance allows a particular kind of traffic, then that traffic is denied by default.

A rule in a security group can apply to either inbound traffic or outbound traffic. An inbound rule allows traffic into an instance over a protocol (like TCP or UDP) and port or port range from either another security group or a range of IP addresses. Similarly, an outbound rule allows traffic out from an instance to either another security group or to a range of IP addresses. Here are some examples of typical inbound and outbound security group rules:

- If you are running a web server on an instance, an inbound rule for TCP port 80 can allow access from your IP address, or the IP range for your corporate network, or the entire internet (0.0.0.0/0).

- To allow SSH access to an instance, an inbound rule should permit access for TCP port 22. It's best to restrict this rule to your own IP address, or those in your network.

- If a process running on an instance will need to access a MySQL server elsewhere, an outbound rule over TCP port 3306 will allow it. The destination could be the IP address of the MySQL server or, if the server is running in EC2, the server's security group.

Figure 4-4 shows how these rules appear in the AWS console. The image is a composite view of both the Inbound and Outbound tabs for a single security group.

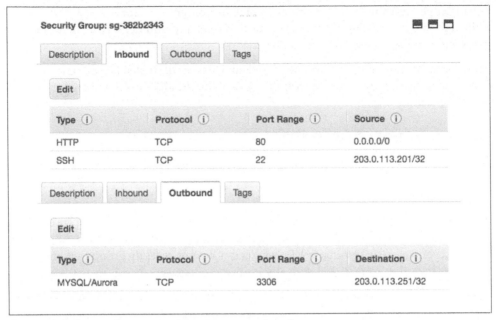

Figure 4-4. A security group with some example rules

Each VPC comes with a simple, default security group that allows outbound access to anywhere, but inbound access only from other instances in the same security group. This means that you need to set up SSH access from your local network before you can access instances provisioned there.

One convenient feature of security groups is that you only need to allow one side of a two-way connection. For example, it is enough to allow TCP port 80 inbound for a web server; since requests are allowed to flow in, AWS automatically permits responses to flow back outbound from the web server. This feature is not true of the other main mechanism for securing VPCs, network ACLs.

Network ACLs

Network ACLs are a secondary means of securing a VPC. Like security groups, they are comprised of a set of rules that govern network traffic. Unlike security groups, a network ACL is associated with a subnet, not individual instances. A subnet may only have one network ACL, or else it falls back to its VPC's default network ACL.

A network ACL rule can either allow or deny traffic. While all of the rules in a security group apply to every network access decision, the rules in a network ACL are evaluated in a numbered order, top to bottom, and the first matching rule is enforced. If none of the rules match, then the fixed, final default rule in every network ACL denies the traffic.

Each network ACL rule is an inbound rule or outbound rule, as with security group rules. A rule applies to a protocol and port range, but sources and destinations are only specified as IP address ranges, not as security groups.

Figure 4-5 lays out a simple network ACL that allows limited inbound SSH access and HTTP access, but no other network traffic. The image is a composite view of both the Inbound Rules and Outbound Rules tabs for the ACL.

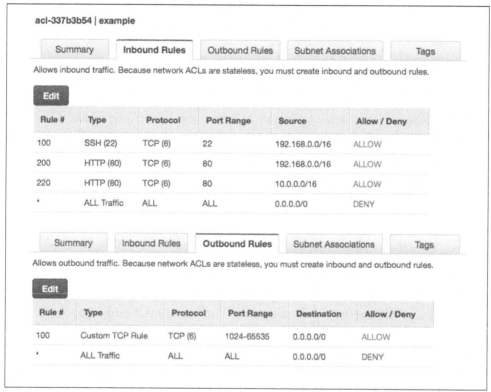

Figure 4-5. An ACL with some example rules

The inbound rules allow only SSH access from one IP address range and HTTP port 80 access from two IP address ranges. Any other inbound network access is blocked by the default final deny rule.

The outbound rules allow any traffic over nonprivileged TCP ports. This is necessary to permit outbound traffic for SSH and HTTP connections. Unlike security groups, network ACLs require you to allow both sides of two-way connections. Since it can be unpredictable what port a requesting process may use to connect out from its host, the network ACL rule here permits a wide range of ports.

To illustrate, here is an example of an HTTP client outside the virtual network performing an HTTP request to a server running inside the network. The simple ACL defined previously gates both the incoming request and outgoing response.

Inbound request from 10.1.2.3:12345 to port 80

- rule 100: does not apply (port range)
- rule 200: does not apply (source CIDR)
- rule 220: applies, so access is allowed

Outbound response from port 80 to 10.1.2.3:12345

- rule 100: applies, so access is allowed

Each VPC comes with a default network ACL that allows all traffic inbound and outbound. So, by default, your VPC does not make use of a network ACL for security, but it is still available for a second line of defense.

Network Security Rules in Google Cloud Platform

Google Cloud Platform supports *firewall rules* for governing traffic to instances in a network. Firewall rules are associated with the network itself, but they can apply to some or all of the instances in that network.

Each firewall rule only allows traffic. If none of the firewall rules for a network allow a particular kind of traffic, then that traffic is denied by default.

A firewall rule controls inbound traffic only. You can control outbound traffic from an instance using network utilities installed on the instance itself.

You can specify the source a firewall rule applies to as either a range of IP addresses, a subnet in the network, or an instance tag. When a subnet is specified, then the rule applies to all of the instances in that subnet as sources. An instance tag limits the applicability of a firewall rule to just instances with that tag.

Each firewall rule names a protocol (like TCP or UDP) and port or port range on the destination instances that it governs. Those instances can be either all of the instances in the network, or just instances with another instance tag, called a target tag.

Here are some examples of typical firewall rules. They are shown with some others in Figure 4-6:

- If you are running a web server on an instance, a rule for TCP port 80 can allow access from your IP address, or the IP range for your corporate network, or the entire internet (0.0.0.0/0). To narrow down where the firewall rule applies, you can tag the web server instance as, say, "webserver", and provide that tag as the target tag for the rule.

- To allow SSH access to an instance, a rule should permit access for TCP port 22. It's best to restrict this rule to your own IP address, or those in your network.

Name ^	Source tag / IP range / Subnetworks	Allowed protocols / ports	Target tags	Network
default-allow-icmp		icmp	Apply to all targets	default
default-allow-internal	10.128.0.0/9	tcp:0-65535, 2 more ▾	Apply to all targets	default
default-allow-ssh		tcp:22	Apply to all targets	default
example-allow-http	0.0.0.0/0	tcp:80	webserver	default
example-allow-ssh	203.0.113.201/32	tcp:22	Apply to all targets	default

Figure 4-6. Some firewall rules (some source IP ranges are obscured)

The default network that Google Cloud Platform supplies for you comes with a small set of firewall rules that allow all traffic within the network as well as SSH (TCP port 22), RDP (port 3389), and ICMP from anywhere. This is a reasonable default behavior, although it makes sense to adjust the rules to limit sources to just your own IP address or your own network. Any new networks you create, however, do not start out with any firewall rules, and so absolutely no inbound access is permitted. It is up to you to build out the necessary firewall rules to gain access.

One convenient feature of firewall rules is that you only need to allow one side of a two-way connection. For example, it is enough to allow TCP port 80 inbound for a web server; since requests are allowed to flow in, Google Cloud Platform automatically permits responses to flow back outbound from the web server.

There are a few automatic firewall rules that are enforced on all networks. Here are some of them:

- TCP port 25 (SMTP) is always blocked outbound from your network.
- TCP ports 465 and 587 (SMTP over SSL) are also always blocked outbound, except to SMTP relay services hosted on Google Apps.
- Network traffic using a protocol besides TCP, UDP, or ICMP is blocked unless the Protocol Forwarding feature of Google Cloud Platform is used to allow it.

 Check the latest Google Cloud Platform documentation (*https:// cloud.google.com/compute/docs/tutorials/sending-mail/*) for ways to send email from its instances, such as SMTP relays, that involve third-party email providers.

One final security rule deserves mention here. If an instance does not have a external IP address assigned to it, then it is not granted access to the internet. This rule is enforced even if a network route provides a path to an internet gateway URL. To reach the internet from such an instance, it's necessary to go through a gateway, using either NAT or a VPN.

Network Security Rules in Azure

Azure provides *network security groups* for controlling traffic into and out of either subnets or individual virtual machines through their network interfaces. A virtual machine can be subject to its subnet's network security group as well as its own.

A network security group holds a set of rules, each of which controls either inbound traffic or outbound traffic. An inbound rule allows or denies traffic into an instance over a protocol (like TCP or UDP) and port or port range from either a range of IP addresses, a default tag (defined next), or all sources. Similarly, an outbound rule allows or denies traffic out from an instance to either a range of IP addresses, a default tag, or all destinations.

A *default tag* is a symbolic representation for a set of IP addresses. For example, the virtual network tag stands in for the local virtual network and those connected to it. The internet tag represents the internet, outside of Azure's infrastructure and connected VPNs.

Here are some examples of typical inbound and outbound security group rules:

- If you are running a web server on an instance, an inbound rule for TCP port 80 can allow access from your IP address, or the IP range for your corporate network, or the entire internet using the internet default tag.

- To allow SSH access to an instance, an inbound rule should permit access for TCP port 22. It's best to restrict this rule to your own IP address, or those in your network.

- If a process running on an instance will need to access a MySQL server elsewhere, an outbound rule over TCP port 3306 will allow it. The destination could be the IP address of the MySQL server.

Figure 4-7 shows how these rules appear in the Azure portal.

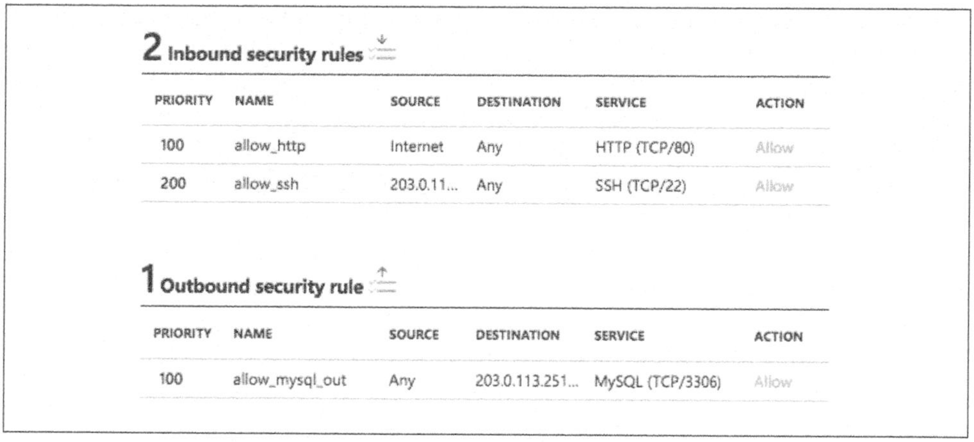

2 Inbound security rules ↓

PRIORITY	NAME	SOURCE	DESTINATION	SERVICE	ACTION
100	allow_http	Internet	Any	HTTP (TCP/80)	Allow
200	allow_ssh	203.0.11...	Any	SSH (TCP/22)	Allow

1 Outbound security rule ↑

PRIORITY	NAME	SOURCE	DESTINATION	SERVICE	ACTION
100	allow_mysql_out	Any	203.0.113.251...	MySQL (TCP/3306)	Allow

Figure 4-7. A network security group with some example rules

Rules are evaluated in priority order to determine which one holds sway. A lower number priority on a rule indicates a higher priority.

Every network security group has a default set of rules, which have lower priorities than any user-defined rules. They allow, among other things, all traffic from the same virtual network and all outbound traffic to the internet, but deny inbound traffic from anywhere but the virtual network. The rules can be overridden with user-defined rules.

Putting Networking and Security Together

As you have seen, there is a lot to think about when it comes to networking and security in a cloud provider. Getting started with them can feel like jumping into the deep end of a pool, or being dropped into a foreign land without a map. Here are some pointers to getting rolling.

Cloud providers do try to start you out with a sensible initial arrangement: a single virtual network with one or a few subnets, and default routing and security rules applied. Of all the concerns, routing tends to require the least amount of attention, as defaults and fallbacks define almost all of the necessary connections.

For small-to-medium Hadoop deployments, a single virtual network usually suffices. As described in the beginning of this chapter, it is useful to think of each virtual network as a container for your clusters. With subnets to provide any necessary divisions or regional variations, and ample IP addresses available, you may find you can go a long time before needing to define an entirely new network.

Routing and security rules become more important once traffic needs to be sent to or received from outside a virtual network. Keeping Hadoop clusters confined to single subnets or, at worst, single virtual networks eliminates most of the need to define routes and security rules. One important exception is allowing SSH access to some number of instances, which is described in the following chapters about getting started with each cloud provider. Another is opening up ports for applications running alongside clusters, or for web interfaces of Hadoop components. For these exceptions, the process is typically only defining a route if necessary and declaring a security rule that allows access.

What About the Data?

The purpose here of creating cloud instances, networking them together, and establishing routes and security rules is to stand up Hadoop clusters, and the purpose of these clusters is to work on data. The data moves through the network between instances, but where is it stored?

As you would expect, cloud providers offer ranges of storage options that include disks, databases, general object storage, and other services. Understanding how these storage options can be used is just as important for creating effective clusters as understanding networking and security.

## CHAPTER 5

Storage

Hadoop clusters are about working with data, usually lots and lots of data, often orders of magnitude larger than ever before. Cloud providers supply different ways to store that data on their vast infrastructure, to complement the compute capabilities that operate on the data and the networking facilities that move the data around. Each form of storage serves a different purpose in Hadoop architectures.

Block Storage

The most common type of storage offered by a cloud provider is the disk-like storage that comes along with each instance that you provision. This storage is usually called *block storage*, but they are almost always accessed as filesystem mounts. Each unit of block storage is called a *volume* or simply a *disk*. A unit of storage may not necessarily map to a single physical device, or even to hardware directly connected to an instance's actual host hardware.

Persistent volumes survive beyond the lifetime of the initial instances that spawned them. A persistent volume can be detached from an instance and attached to another instance, in a way similar to moving physical hard drives from computer to computer. While you wouldn't usually do that with physical drives, it is much easier to do so in a cloud provider, and it opens up new usage patterns. For example, you could maintain a volume loaded with important data or applications over a long period of time, but only attach it to an instance once in a while to do work on it.

Volumes that are limited to the lives of the instances to which they are attached are called *ephemeral* volumes. Ephemeral storage is often very fast and can be large, but it is guaranteed to be eliminated when an instance is stopped or terminated, at which time its data is permanently lost. In the context of Hadoop clusters, critical cluster-wide information like HDFS namenode data should reside on persistent storage, but information that is normally replicated across the cluster, like HDFS data copied in as the source for a job, *can* reside on ephemeral storage.

A volume is backed up by taking a *snapshot*, which preserves its exact state at an instant in time. It is common to take snapshots of a volume repeatedly over time, and cloud providers store snapshots in an incremental fashion so that they don't take up unnecessary space. If something goes wrong with a volume, perhaps due to data corruption or a rare hardware failure, then a new volume can be created from a snapshot and attached to an instance to recover. A snapshot can also be used as the basis for a new instance image, in order to generate many new identical volumes over time.

For security, the major cloud providers all support encryption at rest for data on persistent volumes. They all also automatically replicate persistent volumes, often across data centers, to avoid data loss from hardware failures.

Block Storage in AWS

The AWS component offering block storage is called Elastic Block Storage (EBS). When you provision an instance in EC2, you select an image for its root device volume, and the image determines whether that volume is a persistent volume in EBS or an ephemeral volume in the EC2 instance store. The root device volume houses the operating system and other files from the image. The physical hardware can use either magnetic or SSD storage.

After provisioning an instance, you can attach multiple additional EBS volumes, or you can swap out the EBS root device volume of an instance with another existing one. EBS volumes are resizable, although for older instance types one must be detached before it can be resized.

Some EC2 instance types support both EBS and ephemeral volumes, while others only support EBS. Those that support ephemeral volumes do so through drives that are attached to the physical hosts for the instances. Data on those ephemeral drives survive reboots of their associated instances, but not stoppages or termination. Each instance type specifies the maximum number and size of supported ephemeral volumes.

Block Storage in Google Cloud Platform

Persistent block storage for Google Compute Engine (GCE) instances are called persistent disks. When you provision an instance in GCE, a root persistent disk is automatically allocated to house the operating system and other files from the image selected for the instance.

After provisioning an instance, you can attach multiple additional persistent disks. Each persistent disk, including the root disk, can use either magnetic or SSD storage. Persistent disks can be resized at any time.

Any instance provisioned in GCE can be augmented with local SSDs, which are drives attached to the physical hosts for the instance. These drives are ephemeral storage; while data on them survives reboots of their associated instances, it is discarded when the associated instance stops or terminates. They come in a fixed size and only a limited number may be attached to an instance. Like persistent disks, local SSDs support at-rest encryption.

RAM disks are another block storage option for GCE instances. A RAM disk is a virtual drive that occupies instance memory. These are even more ephemeral than local SSDs, as their data does not even survive instance restarts; however, they can be very fast.

Block Storage in Azure

Every Azure virtual machine is automatically granted two *virtual hard disks* or VHDs: one based on an image hosting the operating system, and a second temporary disk for storing data that can be lost at any time, like swap files. Both of these disks are persistent, but the content of the temporary disk is not preserved if the virtual machine is migrated to different hardware.

Additional persistent VHDs can serve as data disks to store data that needs to last; they are either created by mandate from the virtual machine image or can be attached later. The operating system disk and data disks are resizable, but the associated virtual machine must be stopped first.

All VHDs are actually stored as *page blobs* within the storage account associated with your Azure account, and the replication strategy for the storage account determines how widely disk contents are backed up across data centers. See "Object Storage in Azure" on page 53 for further discussion about storage accounts.

Azure File Storage is another block storage service, dedicated to serving file shares over the Server Message Block protocol. A file share works like a mounted disk, but it can be mounted across multiple virtual machines simultaneously.

Finally, while not necessarily qualifying as a block storage service, Azure Data Lake Store (ADLS) stores files of arbitrary size in a folder hierarchy. The service is designed to satisfy the requirements of a Hadoop-compatible file system, so cluster services such as Hive and YARN can work with it directly.

Object Storage

Disk-like block storage is clearly essential for supporting instances, but there is still the problem of where to keep large amounts of data that should survive beyond the lifetime of instances. You may have a compressed archive of some massive data set that will be referenced across multiple instances, or even from outside the cloud provider. You may have a backup of some important analytic results or critical logs that must be preserved. Sometimes it is possible to dedicate a block storage volume to store these big chunks of data, but there still must be at least one instance running to access it, and often it can be tricky to share that volume across multiple instances.

As an alternative, cloud providers offer *object storage*. In object storage, each chunk of data is treated as its own entity, independent of any instance. The contents of each object are opaque to the provider. Instead of accessing a data object through a filesystem mounted on a running instance, you access it through either API operations or through URLs.

Cloud providers each offer their own object storage solution, yet they all share many common features.

Buckets

Data objects reside inside containers called *buckets*. A bucket has a name and is associated with one or more regions.

  Azure calls its buckets *containers*.

There are restrictions on bucket names, because a bucket's name is used as part of the URLs for accessing objects in the bucket. In general, you should avoid special characters, spaces, and other characters that can be problematic in URLs. A bucket name must be unique to your cloud provider account; the solutions for AWS and Google Cloud Platform also require them to be globally unique.

The region or regions associated with a bucket determine where in the world the objects in the bucket are stored. Hadoop clusters benefit in performance and cost by working with buckets that are in the same region as their instances. A bucket can be configured with replication to other regions, through provider-specific mechanisms, to geographically disperse data. This can be a valuable tool for expanding Hadoop architectures across regions; instead of clusters around the world all needing to reach back to a single region to access bucket contents, the bucket can be replicated to the clusters' regions for faster, cheaper local access.

A bucket does not have an internal hierarchy for object storage, but object naming can be used to create the appearance of one.

Data Objects

A data object in object storage is a single opaque unit from the cloud provider's point of view. Metadata in the form of key-value pairs can be associated with each object, to use as tags or as guides for searching for, identification of, and tracking of the data within.

The name of an object is used to locate it. As with buckets, there are restrictions on object names since they are also used in URLs. Although buckets are flat storage, objects can include forward slashes in their names to create the appearance of a directory-style hierarchy. The APIs, tools, and conventions for object storage interpret object names in a way that supports hierarchical access, often by treating common slash-delimited prefixes of object names as pseudodirectories.

An object has a *storage class*, which determines how quickly it can be accessed and, in part, its storage cost. The standard or default storage classes for cloud providers favor quick access over cost, and these classes tend to be the ones most useful for storing data Hadoop clusters will use. Other storage classes cost less but aim at access frequencies on the order of a few times each month or each year. While Hadoop clusters cannot effectively use objects in those storage classes directly due to their intentionally lower performance, they can be employed in associated archival strategies.

Most of the time, a data object is immutable. When an object needs to be updated, it is overwritten with a completely new version of it. Cloud providers are capable of storing past, versioned copies of objects so that they can be restored as necessary in the future.

 AWS and Google Cloud Platform object storage services automatically version each data object as it is updated. Azure's object storage service does not, but permits taking snapshots of data objects.

Each data object can have permissions associated with it, in order to restrict who may access it. The permissions scheme folds in with each cloud provider's own authorization systems.

Object Access

There are two main methods for accessing objects in object storage. The most flexible method is through the cloud provider's own API, which provides all of the access and management operations available. An API client can create new objects, update them, and delete them. It can manage access permissions and versioning as well.

Jobs running in Hadoop clusters can use APIs to work with objects, either directly or through common libraries. Some libraries provide a filesystem-like view of buckets, enough to allow access in many of the same ways that jobs would work with HDFS. This is a powerful capability, because it lets new clusters start their work right away by reading from durable, reliable object storage, instead of waiting to be primed by getting data copied up to their local HDFS storage. By the same token, clusters can save their final results back to object storage for safekeeping or access by other tools; once that happens, the clusters could be destroyed. So, object storage access enables the use of *transient* clusters, a pattern that is covered in more detail in Chapter 15.

The other main method for object access is through URLs. Each provider's object storage service offers a REST API for working with buckets and objects; perhaps the most salient capability is simply the ability to download an object with an HTTP GET request. Because of URL access, each bucket and object must be named to be compatible with URL syntax.

For example, an object named "my-dir/my-object" in a bucket named "my-bucket" could be accessed by the following URLs, depending on the cloud provider. Each provider supports a handful of different URL formats:

- AWS: *https://s3.amazonaws.com/my-bucket/my-dir/my-object*
- Google Cloud Platform: *https://storage.cloud.google.com/my-bucket/my-dir/my-object*
- Azure: *https://my-account.blob.core.windows.net/my-bucket/my-dir/my-object*

The following sections get into more detail about the differences in the object storage services offered by major cloud providers.

Object Storage in AWS

The AWS component offering object storage is called Simple Storage Service, or S3. It stores objects in buckets that are each associated with a single region that determines where objects are stored.[1] A bucket can be configured to replicate data to a bucket in a different region for redundancy.

S3 offers four storage classes, and a bucket may hold objects in any mix of classes:

- The *standard* storage class is aimed at fast, frequent data access.
- The *standard-ia* or *standard-infrequent access* storage class carries the same durability guarantees as the standard class. It costs less to store data in this class, but each retrieval has an associated fee.

---

1 The choice of region also influences how data may be accessed. See "Configuring the S3 Endpoint" on page 164 for more information.

- The *reduced redundancy storage* or *RRS* storage class is just as fast as the standard class but has lower durability guarantees. It costs less, and should be used for data that can be regenerated if necessary.
- The *Glacier* storage class is for nonrealtime, long-term, cheap data storage. Data must be "restored" from Glacier before it can be accessed.

The storage class for each object is selected when it is first created. Lifecycle configuration rules can be attached to buckets to automatically migrate data from more accessible to less accessible storage classes over time, so that less frequently accessed data can be stored more cheaply.

Object Storage in Google Cloud Platform

Google Cloud Storage is the service offering object storage for Google Cloud Platform. It stores objects in buckets, which are each associated with a location and a default storage class.

Google Cloud Storage offers four storage classes, and a bucket may hold objects in several classes:

- The *regional* storage class is aimed at fast, frequent data access, with storage confined to a single region determined by the bucket location.
- The *multi-regional* storage class is similar to ordinary regional storage, but data is replicated across multiple regions, determined by the bucket location. It costs somewhat more than regional storage.
- The *nearline* storage class carries the same durability guarantees as the regional and multi-regional classes. It costs less to store data in this class, but each retrieval has an associated fee.
- The *coldline* storage class is for long-term, cheap data storage. Retrieval for objects in coldline storage costs much more than for nearline storage.

The storage class for each object is selected when it is first created, or defaults to that of the bucket. Lifecycle policies can be attached to buckets to automatically migrate data from more accessible to less accessible storage classes over time, so that less frequently accessed data can be stored more inexpensively.

Object Storage in Azure

Azure has a few different forms of data storage. The service that is most pertinent to Hadoop clusters is Azure Blob Storage.

Azure Blob Storage stores objects, which are called *blobs*.[2] There are a few types of blobs:

- A *block blob* is an immutable, opaque data object.
- An *append blob* can have additional data appended to it, and can be used to receive a stream of data such as continuously generated logs.
- A *page blob* is used by Azure as the backing storage for disks.

Of the three types of blobs, the block blob is the type most useful for Hadoop clusters. Page blobs are used to store virtual machine disks, but it's not necessary to work with them directly.

Each blob is stored in a container. Each container, in turn, is associated with a *storage account* that is part of your Azure account. You can have multiple storage accounts, and each serves as a home for object storage containers and other forms of cloud storage offered by Azure. It is notable that the name for a storage account must be globally unique, but this means that container names only need to be unique within a storage account.

There are two kinds of storage accounts: general-purpose and blob. A blob storage account allows for specifying one of two access tiers for the objects stored within it:

- The *hot* access tier is aimed at fast, frequent data access. It has higher storage cost, but lower access and transaction costs.
- The *cold* access tier carries the same durability guarantees as the hot access tier. It costs less to store data in this tier, but it has higher access and transaction costs.

The storage account also determines the primary region where objects are stored, as part of the account's replication strategy. There are four replication strategies available:

- *Locally redundant storage*, or LRS, has the highest performance, but the lowest durability and is bound to a single data center in a single region.
- *Zone redundant storage*, or ZRS, goes further than LRS and spreads data out to multiple data centers, either in a single region or a pair of regions. However, it has limitations in when it can be used; in particular, a blob storage account cannot use ZRS.
- *Geo-redundant storage*, or GRS, is similar to ZRS in that it replicates data out to a secondary region.

---

2 The term "blob," which simply refers to a large chunk of data, has an interesting etymology (*https://en.wikipedia.org/wiki/Binary_large_object*).

- *Read-access geo-redundant storage*, or RA-GRS, works like GRS but also allows replicated data to be read from the secondary region.

The access tier and replication strategy for each object is determined by the storage account governing the container where the object is created. With some limitations and some costs, the access tier and replication strategy for a storage account can be changed over time.

Cloud Relational Databases

Although Hadoop breaks away from the traditional model of storing data in relational databases, some components still need their own databases to work their best. For example, the Apache Hive metastore database[3] is crucial for mapping non-relational data stored in HDFS into a relational model that allows for SQL queries. The Apache Oozie workflow scheduling system also requires a backing database. While these components and others often can work using embedded databases, supported by software like Apache Derby, they are only production-ready when their databases are stored on full-fledged servers. By doing so, those database servers can themselves be maintained, backed up, and even shared across components, as part of an overarching enterprise architecture.

It is also helpful in some situations to simply have relational databases store some data that Hadoop clusters use or refer to. Using Hadoop does not require completely abandoning other useful technologies. Analysis jobs can refer to tables in outside databases to find metadata about the information being analyzed, or as lookup or translation mechanisms, or for numerous other helpful purposes.

Finally, applications that work with Hadoop clusters may require their own relational databases. Perhaps authentication and authorization information resides in one, or the definitions of data views reside in another.

It is perfectly reasonable to use an ordinary cloud instance as the host for a database server. It is a familiar and comfortable arrangement for database administrators, and lets you carry over existing maintenance processes into the cloud. You have direct control over upgrades, downtime, backups, and so on, and additional applications can be installed alongside the server as necessary. There are images available for popular databases to make standing up a database server instance even easier.

However, cloud providers also offer native, abstracted services for supporting database servers. With these services, instead of requesting a compute instance, you request a database server instance, specifying the type, version, size, capacity, administrative user credentials, and many other parameters. The cloud provider handles

---

3 Chapter 11 covers setting up Hive in the cloud.

setting up the server and ensuring it is accessible to your virtual networks as you request. You do not have login access to the instance, but can access the database server process using all the usual client tools and libraries in order to define schemas and load and query data. The provider handles backups and ensures availability.

Hadoop components can easily use cloud relational databases. The servers have hostnames and ports, and you can define the users, accesses, and schemas each component requires. From the components' points of view, the servers host remote databases like any other.

Cloud Relational Databases in AWS

The AWS component offering cloud relational databases is called Relational Database Service, or RDS. Each *database instance* hosts a single database server, and is similar in concept to an EC2 instance, having an *instance class* that determines its compute power and memory capacity. Storage capacity is managed separately, ranging from gigabytes to terabytes.

Like ordinary instances, database instances run inside an availability zone associated with a subnet inside a VPC network, and security groups govern access. Moreover, a multi-AZ database instance can continuously replicate its data to another in a separate availability zone.

RDS also automatically takes care of performing periodic database backups and minor server software upgrades. It also handles automatically failing over a multi-AZ database instance in case of the loss of the primary database instance, due to an availability zone outage or a hardware failure.

RDS supports many popular database types, including MySQL, MariaDB, PostgreSQL, Oracle, and Microsoft SQL Server. It also offers Aurora, a MySQL-compatible database type that has some additional benefits, including the ability to establish a database cluster. For database types that require licenses, such as Oracle and Microsoft SQL Server, you have the option of bringing your own license (BYOL) or establishing instances that AWS has already licensed.

Cloud Relational Databases in Google Cloud Platform

Google Cloud SQL is the primary service offering cloud relational databases for Google Cloud Platform. A Cloud SQL instance hosts a database server in a specific region and availability zone, and like an ordinary instance has a *machine type* determining the number of virtual CPUs and the size of its memory. Storage capacity is specified separately and can be set to grow automatically as needed.

Network access to Cloud SQL instances can be granted by whitelisting the IP addresses of GCE instances, but an easier method is to use a Cloud SQL proxy, which provides an encrypted tunnel to a Cloud SQL instance. Client use of a proxy works just like ordinary database access, and the proxy can be configured with a list of Cloud SQL instances to support or perform automatic discovery.

A Cloud SQL instance can be set up for high availability, which causes the creation of a second instance serving as a failover replica. If the primary instance becomes unavailable, Google Cloud SQL automatically switches to the replica, redirecting the hostname and IP address accordingly. Google Cloud SQL also handles periodic database backups.

Only MySQL is supported by Google Cloud SQL.

Google Cloud Spanner

In beta at the time of writing, Google Cloud Spanner is another, new cloud relational database service that takes advantage of Google's robust global network to natively provide high availability while enforcing strong consistency. Cloud Spanner automatically maintains replicas across availability zones in the chosen region where an instance resides. What's more, it provides ways to control where related data is located through features like parent-child table relationships and interleaved tables.

Cloud Relational Databases in Azure

The Azure SQL Database service focuses primarily on the creation and maintenance of relational databases, as opposed to the servers that host them. A database belongs to a *service tier*, which defines the guaranteed amount of compute, memory, storage, and I/O resources available for database access. Each database runs on a server; multiple databases can reside on a single server.

A database server belongs to an Azure resource group,[4] which determines the region where the server resides. Firewall rules associated with a database server control which ranges of IP addresses are permissible for client access.

The service tier of a database can be updated over time in response to changing needs, but a more powerful approach is to use *elastic pools*. Resource usage is spread across all of the databases belonging to the pool, and administrative tasks can be conveniently performed *en masse*.

Azure SQL Database handles performing automatic backups, storing data both local to each database and in a separate data center. Long-term backups can be sent to a vault. You can also set up replication to several additional databases in other regions, any of which can be promoted to serve as a new primary database.

---

4 Azure resource groups are described in detail in "Creating a Resource Group" on page 89.

Azure SQL Database fully supports Microsoft SQL Server. However, newer services such as Azure Database for MySQL and Azure Database for PostgreSQL, support those open source databases in a similar fashion, including tiered guarantees on size and performance and automatic replication.

Azure Cosmos DB

Newly introduced at the time of writing, Azure Cosmos DB is a service for managing globally distributed databases that are either relational or nonrelational, using a common data storage model beneath. The service gives you some control over how data is partitioned and automatically scales storage to achieve the desired throughput. You can also choose from one of several consistency models to guide the timeliness of data availability. Behind the scenes, Cosmos DB spreads data globally to fit your desired associations, and you can control whether to focus service interactions on specific regions or across the world.

Cloud NoSQL Databases

It is in the same spirit of offering relational database services that cloud providers also offer services that provide nonrelational or "NoSQL" databases. These services are usually pushed to the margins when working with Hadoop clusters, since Hadoop's own data storage technologies take center stage. However, as with relational databases, NoSQL databases can be useful for ancillary applications associated with the cluster.

In general, the databases hosted by NoSQL database services are highly scalable both in size and geolocation, and offer high performance. The cloud provider handles administration and availability concerns, much like they do for relational databases. Access control is managed by the cloud provider's own identity and access management systems.

The primary drawback of NoSQL database services is that they are much more specific to each cloud provider. While any well-supported relational database supports SQL, each cloud provider's NoSQL database service has a way, or set of ways, of working with data that differs from other services, sometimes even those from the same provider. This can contribute to becoming tied to a single cloud provider, which may be undesirable from a competitive point of view. Also, Hadoop components rarely have use for a NoSQL database beyond whatever storage is set up within their clusters.

Still, NoSQL database services are a part of the storage services available from cloud providers, and they can find their place in some architectures. Here is a quick rundown of what is available at the time of writing:

- AWS offers the DynamoDB database service. Tables can be accessed through the AWS console or through a variety of client-side libraries.
- Google Cloud Platform offers two NoSQL database services. Cloud Datastore works well for frequent transactions and queries and has higher durability, while Bigtable emphasizes speed and supports access through the API for Apache HBase.
- Azure's DocumentDB service, now part of Azure Cosmos DB, stores databases containing collections of documents, and can be accessed through a RESTful protocol as well as the MongoDB API. Azure Table Storage, which is associated with storage accounts, works with entity-based data.

Where to Start?

This chapter has covered four distinct forms of storage supported by cloud providers: block, object, relational, and NoSQL. Each of these is provided by one or more cloud provider services, and those are just a part of those providers' suites of services. It can be a lot to take in, especially when figuring out how Hadoop clusters fit.

The two more important services to think about are block storage and object storage. Block storage is the most crucial, since it provides the disk volumes that instances need to run. Every cluster needs block storage as an underpinning, and fortunately it is reasonably straightforward to work with. Object storage is a powerful addition to your clusters, giving you a place to keep data that survives cluster lifetimes and even supporting direct use by some Hadoop components.

Relational database services are handy for supporting the Hadoop components and secondary applications that work with clusters, but are not as important as block and object storage, especially since you can host your own database servers on ordinary instances. NoSQL database services are the least important, being unnecessary for most cluster architectures, but potentially useful in some cases.

Understanding the three core concepts of instances, networking, and storage, you are ready to jump in and create clusters in the cloud. The next part of this book begins with individual chapters for three major cloud providers, in which you will prepare instances and virtual networks necessary for a simple cluster. You should focus on your cloud provider of choice, although it is informative to see how similar tasks work in other providers, so you may want to skim the chapters for the other providers:

- If you are using AWS, continue with Chapter 6.
- If you are using Google Cloud Platform, continue with Chapter 7.

- If you are using Azure, continue with Chapter 8.

Once you have worked through your cloud provider's chapter, Chapter 9 pushes forward with Hadoop installation, configuration, and testing, which works much the same no matter what provider you use.

## PART III

A Simple Cluster in the Cloud

In this part, you will stand up a simple Hadoop cluster running on the infrastructure of a cloud provider. The first three chapters in this part each focus on a separate cloud provider, so start with the one that you use. The chapters for the other providers can give you a sense of what it's like to use a different one, so they may also be of interest. The cluster that you create will have the same structure, regardless of the provider you choose.

The simple cluster built here is used as the basis for further exploration later on in the book.

## CHAPTER 6

Setting Up in AWS

In this chapter you'll create a simple Hadoop cluster running in Elastic Compute Cloud (EC2), the service in Amazon Web Services (AWS) that enables you to provision instances. The cluster will consist of basic installations of HDFS and YARN, which form the foundation for running MapReduce and other analytic workloads.

This chapter assumes you are using a Unix-like operating system on your local computer, such as Linux or macOS. If you are using Windows, some of the steps will vary, particularly those for working with SSH.

Prerequisites

Before you start, you will need to have an account already established with AWS. You can register for one for free.

Once you are registered, you will be able to log in to the *AWS console*, a web interface for using all of the different services under the AWS umbrella. When you log in, you are presented with a dashboard for all of those services. It can be overwhelming, but fortunately, for this chapter you only need to use one service: EC2. Find it on the home page in the console, as shown in Figure 6-1.

Over time, Amazon will update the arrangement of the console, and so the exact instructions here may become inaccurate.

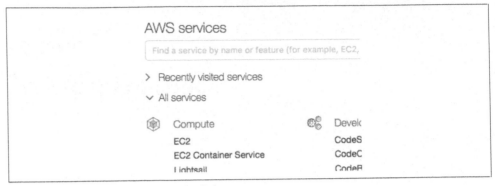

Figure 6-1. EC2 on the AWS console home page

Notice at the top of the page a drop-down menu, as shown in Figure 6-2, with a geographic area selected, such as N. Virginia, N. California, or Ireland. This indicates the AWS region where you are currently working. If the selected region is not the one you prefer, go ahead and select a different one using the drop-down. It is generally a good idea to use a region that is close to your location.

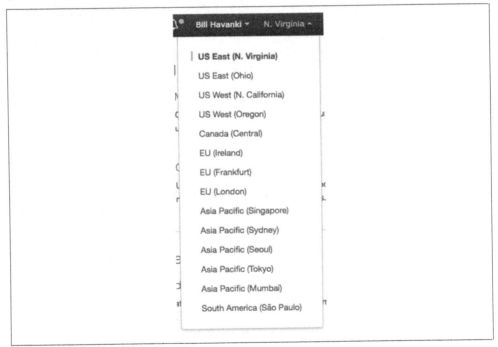

Figure 6-2. A drop-down menu for the AWS regions

Allocating Instances

In this section, you will launch the instances that will comprise a Hadoop cluster. You will also ensure that they have the right networking connections, and that you can connect to them over SSH.

Generating a Key Pair

Before provisioning instances in EC2, you must create a *key pair*. A key pair consists of a public key and a private key, to be used for SSH communication with your instances. If you are already familiar with asymmetric encryption technologies such as SSL/TLS, you will be comfortable with EC2 key pairs.

You can have AWS generate the key pair for you and download the private key. As an alternative, you can use a client-side tool like OpenSSL to create the key pair yourself, and then upload the public key to AWS. For now, you'll let AWS do the work.

To have AWS generate a key pair, log in to the AWS console and select EC2. A menu will appear on the left side of the page with options for working in EC2. Select Key Pairs in the menu. The main area of the page will show that you have no key pairs for the region yet. Click the Create Key Pair button to start the process of creating a new key pair, and follow the instructions.

When you are done, you will receive a PEM file that contains a private key. The phrase "BEGIN RSA PRIVATE KEY" starts the contents of the file. This is the key file you will use to SSH to your provisioned instances. Save the file in a safe place, using file permissions on your local computer to protect it (e.g., make it readable only by your account). A great place to store it is in the hidden *.ssh* directory in your home directory, which is normally used by OpenSSH for key storage and other sensitive files:

```
$ mv keyfile.pem ~/.ssh
$ chmod 600 ~/.ssh/keyfile.pem
```

Launching Instances

You're now ready to launch instances. For this simple cluster, you'll launch four instances: one "manager" and three "workers." The manager instance will host the HDFS namenode and the YARN resource manager, while the workers will host the HDFS datanodes and YARN node managers. A minimum of three workers is recommended, since the default HDFS replication factor is three.

The manager instance

Let's start by launching the manager instance. Select Instances from the EC2 menu. (Pick EC2 from the set of AWS services if you need to.) You'll see that you don't have any running instances yet; you'll change that. Click the Launch Instance button to start the process.

In the first step, you need to choose an image to base your instance on, as shown in Figure 6-3. In AWS, an image is called an *Amazon Machine Image* (AMI). A "Quick Start" set of AMIs is presented to you. The AMIs cover popular operating systems and architectures; they are updated periodically as new recommended images are made available. Find an AMI for Ubuntu Linux that uses virtualization type HVM and select it.

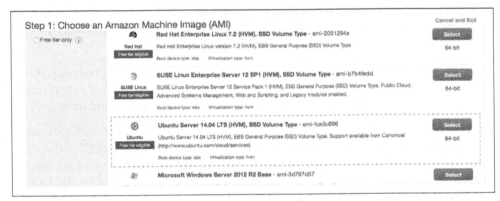

Figure 6-3. Some AMI choices

Free Tier

For the first year that you have an AWS account, you are eligible for the free tier (*https://aws.amazon.com/free/faqs/*), which lets you provision small instances on free operating systems without any cost. The free tier is great for exploring how to use AWS, but the instance types that fall within it are, sadly, too underpowered to host a Hadoop cluster that can do more than trivial work.

You do not need to use Ubuntu to deploy Hadoop in the cloud. It was chosen for the instructions here because it is popular and widely supported across all cloud providers. The steps for using a different Linux distribution can differ, especially in the system tools available and in package management.

Next, select an instance type for the manager. A subset of the available choices is shown in Figure 6-4. A manager instance often needs more powerful specifications than a worker. For this cluster, select an instance type in the General purpose family with at least four vCPUs and at least 8 GB of memory.[1] Over time, EC2 introduces new instance types with faster processing, better or more memory, or better storage capabilities, and these new types are preferred over older ones. Unless you have particular requirements that only an older instance type satisfies, you should favor new instances types.

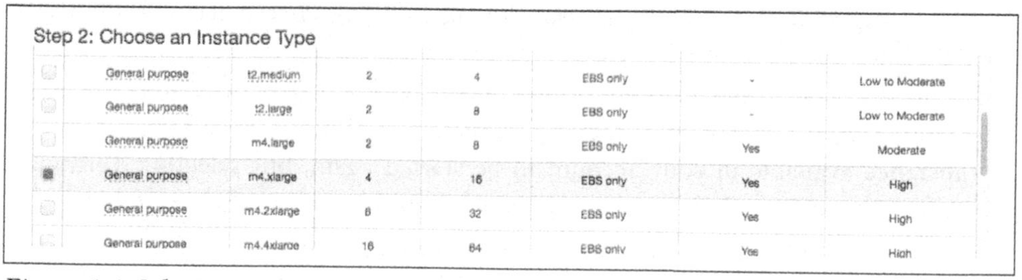

	Step 2: Choose an Instance Type						
	General purpose	t2.medium	2	4	EBS only	-	Low to Moderate
	General purpose	t2.large	2	8	EBS only	-	Low to Moderate
	General purpose	m4.large	2	8	EBS only	Yes	Moderate
	General purpose	m4.xlarge	4	16	EBS only	Yes	High
	General purpose	m4.2xlarge	8	32	EBS only	Yes	High
	General purpose	m4.4xlarge	16	64	EBS only	Yes	High

Figure 6-4. Selecting an EC2 instance type

Instead of clicking the tempting Review and Launch button, you need to work through the full set of steps for launching an instance to fully configure it. Click the Next: Configure Instance Details button to review networking choices and other information. The form for doing so is shown in Figure 6-5.

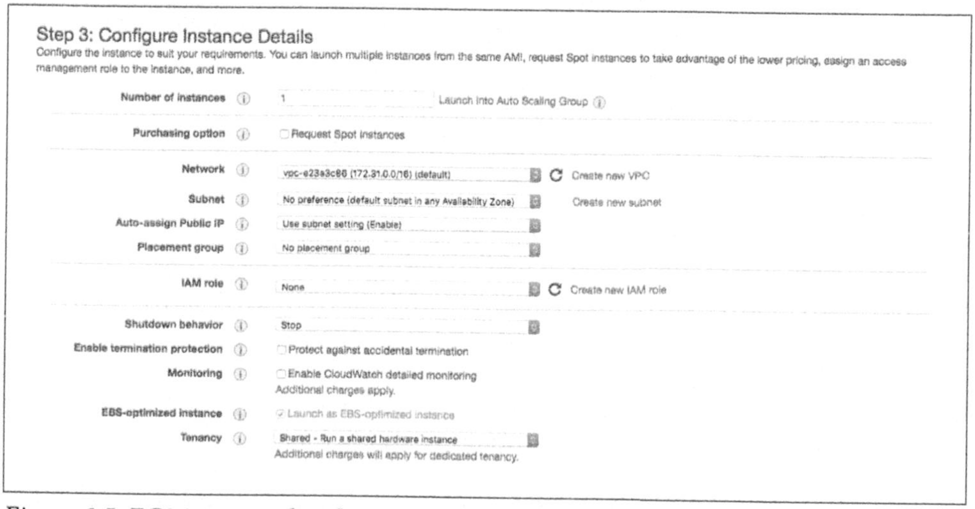

Figure 6-5. EC2 instance details

---

1 If you just created your AWS account, you may discover that you are not permitted to use such a powerful instance type right away. If so, go ahead and use a free tier instance type that at least has the minimum memory needed. The cluster will still work for experimentation.

There is a lot to digest here, but here are some highlights:

- The number of instances to launch defaults to one. That is fine for now, because only one manager is necessary for a simple cluster.

- A VPC has already been selected. Your AWS account is automatically set up with a VPC upon creation; if you are using a long-standing, shared account, there may be a few VPCs to choose from.

- The shutdown behavior defines what happens if you issue a system shutdown within your instance (e.g., `/sbin/shutdown`). The default of Stop leaves the instance available in your account to be started again, but selecting Terminate causes the instance to instead be destroyed. You should leave Stop selected.

- You can enable termination protection on instances so that they cannot be terminated without explicitly disabling the protection via the console as an extra step.

Since the cluster will have multiple instances talking to one another, configuration will be easier and performance will be much better if they are all close to each other in the network. So, select a specific subnet from the list of available subnets. A *subnet* is a segment of the overall address space in a VPC that resides within a single availability zone. Remember the subnet you choose now, so that the worker instances can be provisioned there as well.

Click Next: Add Storage to see options, as shown in Figure 6-6, for adding storage to the new instance.

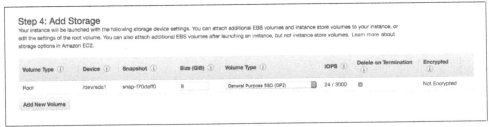

Figure 6-6. EC2 instance storage configuration

By default, an EC2 instance comes with a modest amount of dedicated storage mounted as its root volume. Increase the amount, if necessary, to at least 30 GB, so that there is ample room for installing what you need for your cluster. Resist the temptation to add more storage than you need: you will be charged per GB provisioned, not per GB utilized. Then click Next: Tag Instance to see the tag entry form as in Figure 6-7.

Figure 6-7. Setting EC2 instance tags

Tags are simple name-value pairs that are attached to instances. They are useful for organizing instances and noting their name, purpose, owner, or any other basic information. For this instance, enter a tag with key "Name" and value "manager". Click Next: Configure Security Group to set up security for the new instance using the form shown in Figure 6-8.

Figure 6-8. The default security group selection for EC2 instances

Here, you will define the permissions for network communications to and from the cluster through a security group. Start by selecting the "Create a new security group" radio button, and then entering "basic-security" for the group name. Supply any description you like. The renamed security group is shown in Figure 6-9.

The new security group defaults to having one incoming rule, allowing SSH access from any IP address, and is represented by the CIDR 0.0.0.0/0. While this can be acceptable for a case such as this where you are only trying things out, you should instead restrict access to only an appropriate range of IP addresses.

To restrict SSH access to your IP address alone, either replace the default CIDR address by selecting Custom IP and enter your IP address, or just select My IP to have your address autodetected. To instead restrict access to a range of IP addresses (e.g., your address may change over time, or you may switch local computers), select Custom IP and enter the appropriate CIDR address.

If you are on a local network that accesses the internet through a router performing network address translation (NAT), then be sure to use the IP address assigned to the router. The My IP auto-detection should select the correct IP address.

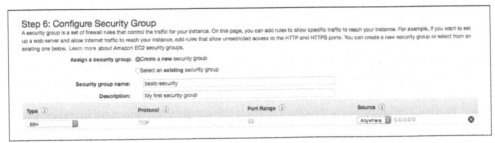

Figure 6-9. Updated security group configuration for EC2 instances

Click the Review and Launch button to see an overview of the instance you are about to launch. The chosen AMI, instance type, security group, and other details are available to look over. When you are satisfied, click the Launch button to complete the last step.

Before EC2 proceeds to launch your instance, you will be asked for a key pair to use for SSH access. Since you already created a key pair, select its name and click Launch Instances.

Your new instance will start to launch. You can monitor its progress by returning to the AWS console and selecting Instances from the EC2 menu. Once the instance state is shown as "running," you can attempt to connect to it over SSH, using the private key from your chosen key pair to authenticate. The username to use depends on the AMI you have chosen; sometimes "root" will work, but often it will be a different username; for Ubuntu, you can try "ubuntu" as the username. You can use either the public DNS name or public IP address to reach the instance; these can be found in the instance details when you select the manager instance from the list of running instances.

The AWS console can help you with your SSH command line for connecting to an instance. Select Instances from the EC2 menu, select the row for the instance you want to connect to, and click the Connect button. A dialog box will suggest an SSH command line, including a username that may work.

The worker instances

Once you can connect to the manager instance, you've completed the first step toward standing up a cluster. Now, repeat the preceding steps to launch the three worker instances. The procedure is almost the same, but there are important changes:

- You can choose a less powerful instance type for workers: for example, an instance type with only two vCPUs.
- When configuring instance details, change the Number of Instances to 3.
- Be sure to select the same subnet as the one hosting the manager instance. As mentioned earlier, this will make configuration of the cluster much easier.
- Use the value "worker" for the Name tag.
- Instead of creating a new security group, select the same security group that you created for the manager instance.

After the worker instances are launched, make sure you can SSH to each of them as well. At this point you have a set of instances that is able to run a Hadoop cluster.

Securing the Instances

Some of the work to secure the new instances was done when the security group for them was defined, but there is a little more to do.

If you took the recommended step of locking down SSH access in the "basic-security" security group created while allocating instances, then SSH between instances will not work. This is because the security group only allows SSH from your IP address (or IP address range), and nowhere else. So, the security group must be updated to allow wider SSH access. In fact, there will be more than just SSH traffic between instances once the cluster is running, so the best way to allow it all is to open up inbound traffic from anywhere in the security group itself.

Start by selecting Security Groups from the EC2 menu. Select the row for the "basic-security" group, and then select the Inbound tab for the group. Click the Edit button, and then Add Rule in the dialog box that appears. For the Type of the new rule, select "All traffic," and enter the security group ID or name in the Source field. Click Save, and the security group will be updated. At this point, it should be possible to SSH between any two instances in the security group.

Next Steps

At this point, there are instances destined to host a cluster running in EC2. To pause here, you can stop the new instances by selecting them in the list of running instances and then using the Actions button to select Instance State, and then Stop. You can start them later by using Start in the same menu.

Otherwise, proceed to Chapter 9 to install Hadoop and configure it, and then try it out with some basic MapReduce jobs.

## CHAPTER 7

Setting Up in Google Cloud Platform

In this chapter you'll create a simple Hadoop cluster running in Google Compute Engine (GCE), the service in Google Cloud Platform that enables you to provision instances. The cluster will consist of basic installations of HDFS and YARN, which form the foundation for running MapReduce and other analytic workloads.

This chapter assumes you are using a Unix-like operating system on your local computer, such as Linux or macOS. If you are using Windows, some of the steps will vary, particularly those for working with SSH.

 If you just worked through the previous chapter on AWS, you'll find that this chapter covers the same procedures, just under Google Cloud Platform. If you're more interested in using your AWS cluster, skip ahead to Chapter 9.

Prerequisites

Before you start, you will need to have an account already established with Google Cloud Platform. You can use your current Google account, or register for a separate account for free.

Once you are registered, you will be able to log in to the *Google Cloud Platform console*, a web interface for using all of the different services under the Google Cloud Platform umbrella. When you log in, you are presented with a dashboard providing a curated view of some of those services; a complete list is available from the "hamburger" menu accessible from the top-left corner. For this chapter, you will be focusing on GCE, whose dashboard tile is shown in Figure 7-1.

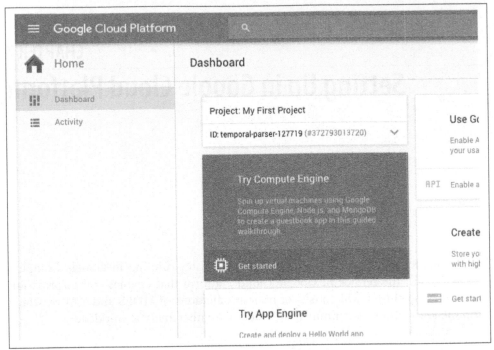

Figure 7-1. GCE on the Google Cloud Platform dashboard

 Over time, Google will update the arrangement of the console, and so the exact instructions here may become inaccurate.

Creating a Project

Work that you perform in Google Cloud Platform is always done within the context of a *project*. You can define projects yourself and switch between them. Each project defines a scope for instances, billing, security, default metadata, and so on. Perhaps most importantly, a project has a default region and availability zone for instances that are created within it. Google Cloud Platform will select a region that is near your location, but you can choose a different one yourself if you want.

To create a new project, use the project drop-down menu next to the search bar across the top of the dashboard to select "Create a project." The menu is shown in Figure 7-2.

Figure 7-2. Creating a new project

A cluster creation form, as shown in Figure 7-3, appears. This project can be called "My First Cluster". By selecting "Show advanced options," you can select a specific default region for the project. Click the Create button to create the new project. Once the project has been created, the dashboard switches to working within it. Now you have a space for allocating instances. Open the hamburger menu and select Compute Engine.

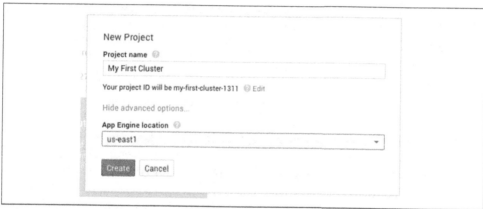

Figure 7-3. The "My First Cluster" project

Allocating Instances

In this section, you will launch the instances that will comprise a Hadoop cluster. You will also ensure that they have the right networking connections, and that you can connect to them over SSH.

SSH Keys

Before provisioning instances in Google Cloud Platform, you must provide it an *SSH key*. An SSH key is just the public key that forms half of a public/private key pair used for SSH communication with your instances. If you are already familiar with asymmetric encryption technologies such as SSL/TLS, you will be comfortable with SSH keys.

If you already have a key pair that you like to use, you can reuse it for Google Cloud Platform. If not, you can create a new one yourself using a client-side tool like OpenSSL. In either case, you will upload the public key to Google Cloud Platform. Then, the public key can be chosen to be recognized by the default login account on newly provisioned instances, enabling SSH access.

To create a new key pair, try using the *ssh-keygen* utility. You can run it with no arguments to work completely interactively, or use command-line options to supply most of what the utility needs. The following example generates a 2048-bit RSA key, saving the private key to a file named "gcp" and the public key to a file automatically named "gcp.pub" in the hidden *.ssh* directory, which is normally used by OpenSSH for key storage and other sensitive files:

```
$ ssh-keygen -b 2048 -t rsa -f ~/.ssh/gcp
```

 When ssh-keygen asks for a passphrase for the new private key, you can enter an empty string (press Enter or Return) to leave the key unprotected. This is a common practice done for convenience, so that the key can be used to connect via SSH without entering a passphrase every time. If you do this, though, be sure to protect the private key file by using file permissions (e.g., make it readable only by your account), so that it is less likely to be compromised.

With the key pair generated, you can upload the *public* key data to Google Cloud Platform. Select Metadata from the Google Cloud Platform menu, and then the SSH Keys tab in the main part of the page. The empty form for adding new keys is shown in Figure 7-4.

Click the "Add SSH keys" button to reveal a simple form for adding the data. Copy the contents of your public key file to your clipboard, as demonstrated in Figure 7-5, and paste them into the text area. Then click Save.

 Use the contents of the *public* key, not the *private* key. Google Cloud Platform never needs to know your private key to provide SSH access. If you accidentally paste your private key data into the form, assume that the key has been compromised and generate a new one.

Figure 7-4. The SSH Keys tab

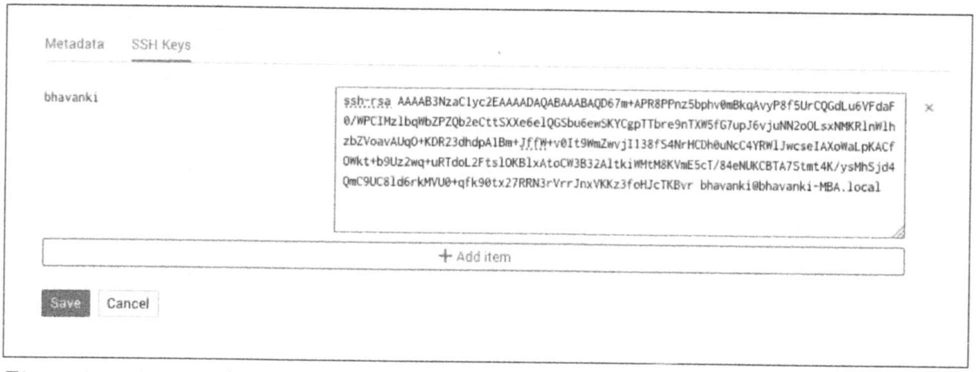

Figure 7-5. An SSH key

Creating Instances

You're now ready to create instances. For this simple cluster, you'll create four instances: one "manager" and three "workers." The manager instance will host the HDFS namenode and the YARN resource manager, while the workers will host the HDFS datanodes and YARN node managers. A minimum of three workers is recommended, since the default HDFS replication factor is three.

The manager instance

Let's start by creating the manager instance. Select VM instances from the Google Cloud Platform menu. You'll see, like in Figure 7-6, that you don't have any running instances yet; you'll change that. Click the "Create instance" button to start the process.

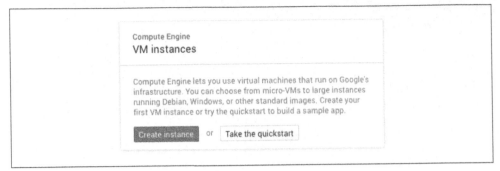

Figure 7-6. The first "Create instance" button

Free Trial

After signing up for Google Cloud Platform, you are eligible for a limited-time free trial (*https://cloud.google.com/free/docs/frequently-asked-questions*), during which you are granted a fixed amount of credit that can be used to provision instances. The free trial is great for exploring how to use Google Cloud Platform, but during the free trial you are limited in how many cores you can have active at once.[1] This prevents you from getting in over your head, but also disallows creating Hadoop clusters that can do more than trivial work. After the free trial ends, there is a permanent *free tier*, although resources that run under it are too underpowered for Hadoop.

A form appears, covering the basic information needed to create a new instance:

- Use the name "manager".
- Select an availability zone near your location. It does not need to be within the default region of your project.
- A manager instance often needs more powerful specifications than a worker. For this cluster, select an instance type in the standard family with at least four vCPUs and at least 8 GB of memory.[2]
- The boot disk hosts the operating system and file storage for the instance. Click the Change button to bring up a secondary form, as shown in Figure 7-7, where you can pick a different image and resize the disk. Select an Ubuntu image from

---

1 At the time of writing, the limit is eight, which is enough for a cluster of four instances with two cores each.

2 Such a powerful instance type may run up against your free trial core limit. Go ahead and use fewer vCPUs if you wish; the cluster will still work for experimentation.

---

the "Preconfigured image" tab, then increase the size, if necessary, to at least 30 GB, so that there is ample room for installing what you need for your cluster.

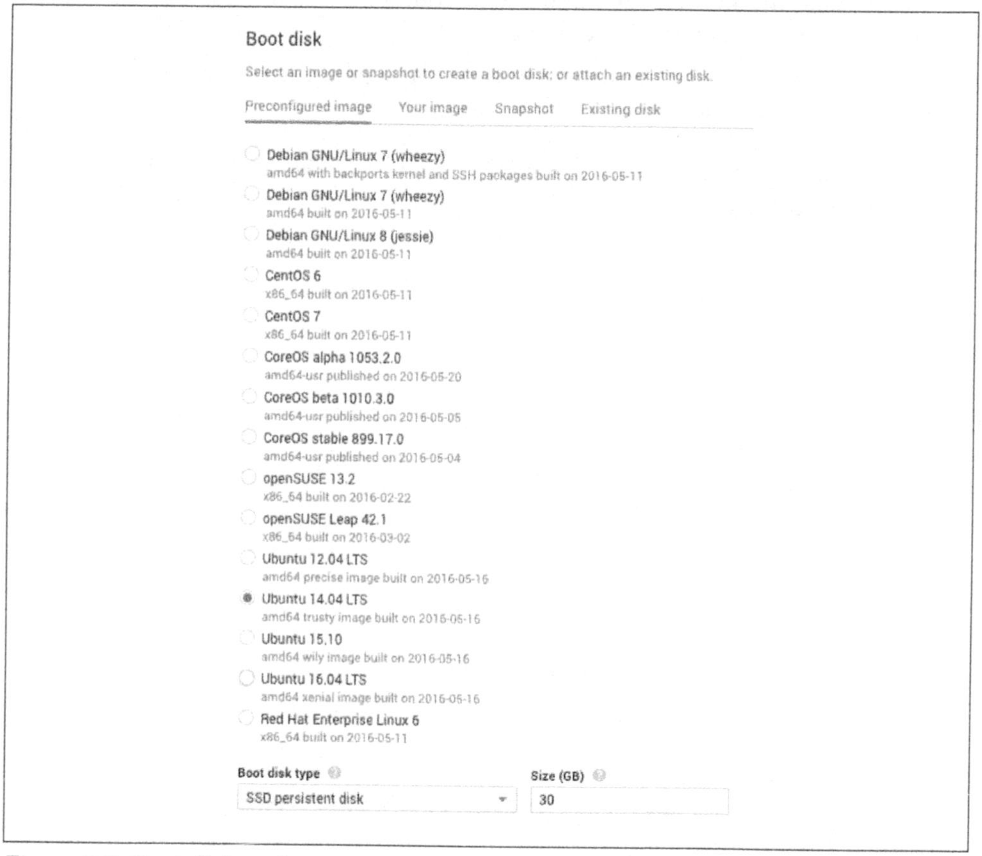

Boot disk

Select an image or snapshot to create a boot disk; or attach an existing disk.

Preconfigured image   Your image   Snapshot   Existing disk

○ Debian GNU/Linux 7 (wheezy)
    amd64 with backports kernel and SSH packages built on 2016-05-11

○ Debian GNU/Linux 7 (wheezy)
    amd64 built on 2016-05-11

○ Debian GNU/Linux 8 (jessie)
    amd64 built on 2016-05-11

○ CentOS 6
    x86_64 built on 2016-05-11

○ CentOS 7
    x86_64 built on 2016-05-11

○ CoreOS alpha 1053.2.0
    amd64-usr published on 2016-05-20

○ CoreOS beta 1010.3.0
    amd64-usr published on 2016-05-05

○ CoreOS stable 899.17.0
    amd64-usr published on 2016-05-04

○ openSUSE 13.2
    x86_64 built on 2016-02-22

○ openSUSE Leap 42.1
    x86_64 built on 2016-03-02

○ Ubuntu 12.04 LTS
    amd64 precise image built on 2016-05-16

◉ Ubuntu 14.04 LTS
    amd64 trusty image built on 2016-05-16

○ Ubuntu 15.10
    amd64 wily image built on 2016-05-16

○ Ubuntu 16.04 LTS
    amd64 xenial image built on 2016-05-16

○ Red Hat Enterprise Linux 6
    x86_64 built on 2016-05-11

Boot disk type   Size (GB)

SSD persistent disk   30

Figure 7-7. Boot disk options

 You do not need to use Ubuntu to deploy Hadoop in the cloud. It was chosen for the instructions here because it is popular and widely supported across all cloud providers. The steps for using a different Linux distribution can differ, especially in the system tools available and in package management.

The instance is ready to be created. While here, though, you can take a look through additional hidden options by selecting "Management, disk, network, SSH keys" near the bottom of the form. All of the defaults in these additional tabs are acceptable for this instance.

- You can see that Google Cloud Platform automatically selects a subnet for the instance. When you create a new project, Google Cloud Platform establishes a network for it automatically with a few subnets, one per region. The subnetwork selected here resides in the same region as the availability zone for the instance. If you update the network definition with additional subnets for the region, this form lets you select from those subnets.

- You could use the SSH Keys tab here to supply a public key, but since the project already has a default, it isn't necessary here.

With the manager instance fully specified as shown in Figure 7-8, click the Create button to start the instance creation process.

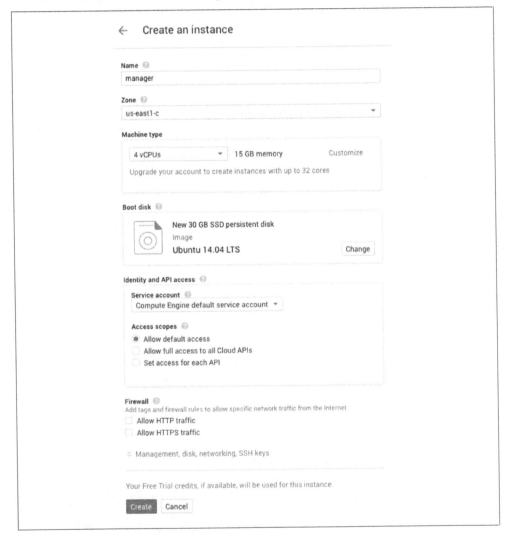

Figure 7-8. The manager instance

Your new instance will start to launch. You can monitor its progress on the Google Cloud Platform console by selecting "VM instances" from the Google Cloud Platform menu. Once the instance state is shown as running via a checkmark, you can attempt to connect to it over SSH, using the private key from your chosen key pair to authenticate. The username matches the username for your Google account. You can use the external IP address to reach the instance, which can be found in the list of instances in the console.

 The Google Cloud Platform console lets you connect to instances via SSH directly from the browser. Do this by selecting SSH from the Connect column in the list of instances. Google Cloud Platform generates a short-lived SSH key pair and configures a login account on the instance to recognize it, then connects you in a popup terminal window. The account created in this process does have sudo capability, so you can use it to fully explore the instance, including checking on what the standard account for the instance is.

The worker instances

Once you can connect to the manager instance, you've completed the first step toward standing up a cluster. On the VM instances dashboard page, you will see options across the top for creating an instance and an instance group. For efficiency, select Create Instance Group to begin the process of launching three worker instances at once.

The procedure here is similar to setting up the single manager instance, but there are important changes. Start off by using the name "worker-group-1" and selecting the same availability zone you selected for the manager.

Under "Creation method," leave "Use instance template" selected and select "Create an instance template" from the Instance Template drop-down. An *instance template* defines the parameters needed to automatically generate several instances at once, and the form that appears for defining a template, shown in Figure 7-9, works just like the similar part of the form for creating a single instance:

- Enter a template name "worker-template-1".

- If you wish, choose a less powerful instance type for workers: for example, an instance type with only 2 vCPUs.

- Select the same OS and root disk size.

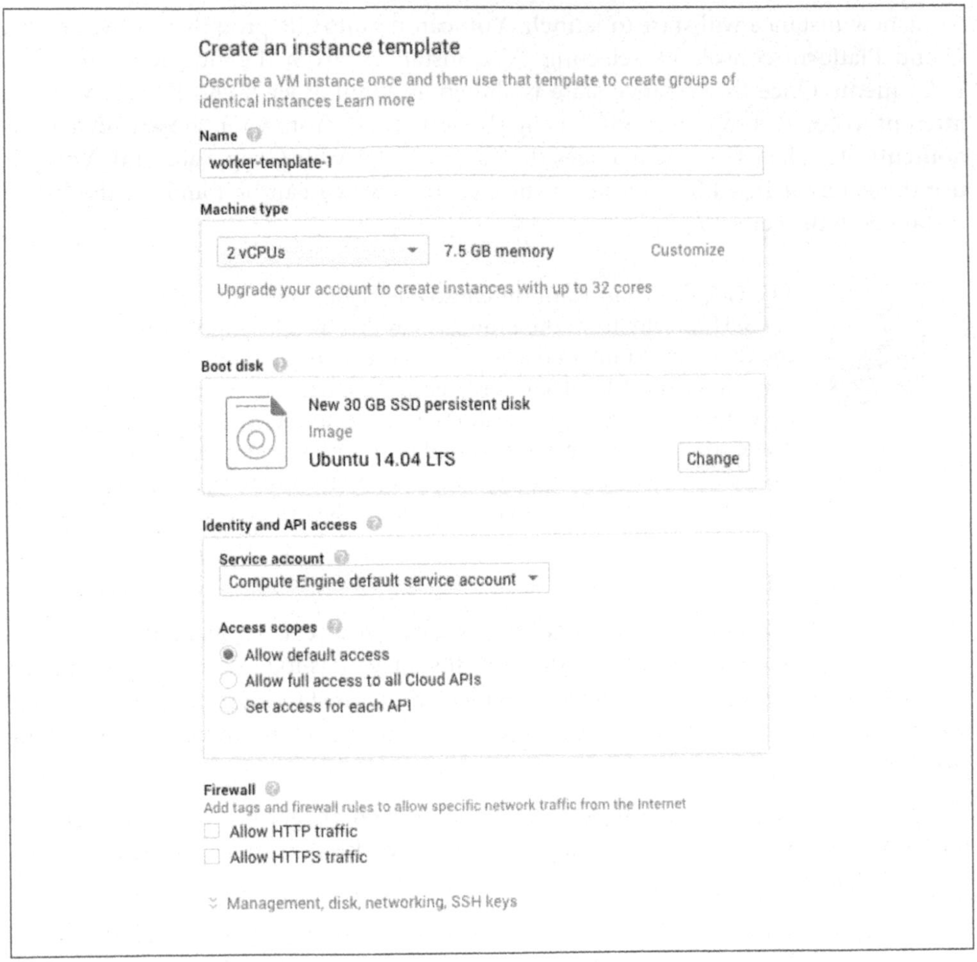

Create an instance template

Describe a VM instance once and then use that template to create groups of identical instances Learn more

Name

worker-template-1

Machine type

2 vCPUs ▼   7.5 GB memory   Customize

Upgrade your account to create instances with up to 32 cores

Boot disk

New 30 GB SSD persistent disk
Image
Ubuntu 14.04 LTS   Change

Identity and API access

Service account
Compute Engine default service account ▼

Access scopes
● Allow default access
○ Allow full access to all Cloud APIs
○ Set access for each API

Firewall
Add tags and firewall rules to allow specific network traffic from the Internet
☐ Allow HTTP traffic
☐ Allow HTTPS traffic

⌄ Management, disk, networking, SSH keys

Figure 7-9. The worker instance template

Back on the main form, as shown in Figure 7-10, change the "Number of instances" to 3. Then click Create.

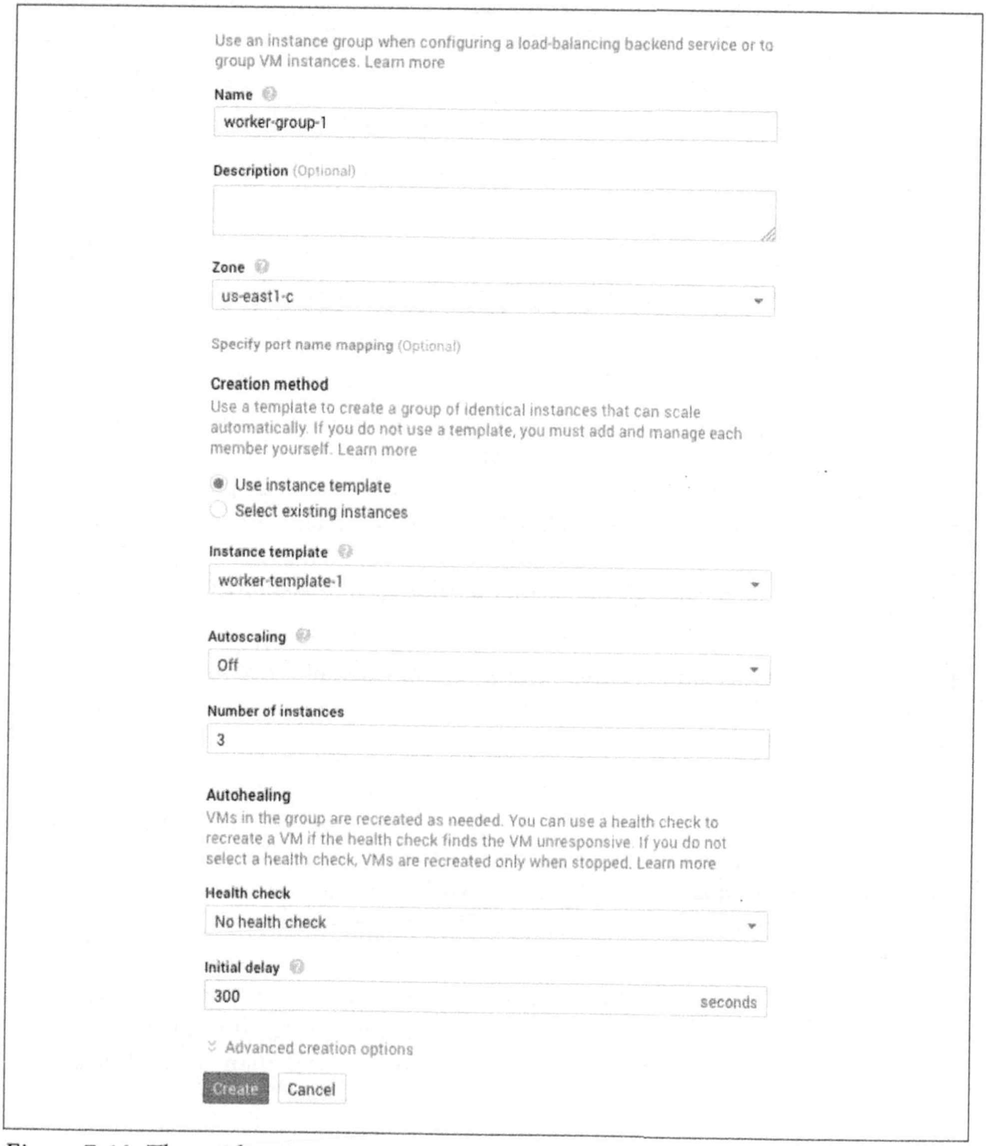

Use an instance group when configuring a load-balancing backend service or to
group VM instances. Learn more

Name ⓘ

```
worker-group-1
```

Description (Optional)

```


```

Zone ⓘ

```
us-east1-c                                            ▼
```

Specify port name mapping (Optional)

Creation method

Use a template to create a group of identical instances that can scale
automatically. If you do not use a template, you must add and manage each
member yourself. Learn more

◉ Use instance template
◯ Select existing instances

Instance template ⓘ

```
worker-template-1                                     ▼
```

Autoscaling ⓘ

```
Off                                                   ▼
```

Number of instances

```
3
```

Autohealing

VMs in the group are recreated as needed. You can use a health check to
recreate a VM if the health check finds the VM unresponsive. If you do not
select a health check, VMs are recreated only when stopped. Learn more

Health check

```
No health check                                       ▼
```

Initial delay ⓘ

```
300                                         seconds
```

⌄ Advanced creation options

[Create] Cancel

Figure 7-10. The worker instances

The VM instances dashboard page will show three new instances being provisioned.
Figure 7-11 shows a set of provisioned workers along with a manager. The name for
each of the workers is automatically determined by Google Cloud Platform, but they
are all prefixed with the instance group name. After the instances are running, make
sure you can SSH to each of them as well. At this point you have a set of instances
that is able to run a Hadoop cluster.

Figure 7-11. Instances running in GCE

Securing the Instances

You may have noticed that, besides selecting availability zones, no network choices needed to be made for provisioning instances. That is because GCE automatically placed the instances into the default network, which was already populated with subnets and firewall rules. Those firewall rules can be updated to improve the security posture of the cluster.

From the VM instances dashboard page, follow the link for the "default" network listed for any of the instances. (Alternatively, select Networking from the hamburger menu, then Networks, and follow the link for the "default" network.) The page for the default network, as shown in Figure 7-12, lists the subnets and firewall rules that are already in place.

The firewall rules defined for the default network do limit access from outside the network to only a few ports, but for those ports they allow access from anywhere, as can be seen from the IP range of 0.0.0.0/0 for the relevant rules. Make the following changes to the firewall rules to make the network more secure:

- Remove the RDP / port 3389 rule.
- Edit the ICMP and SSH / port 22 rules to restrict them to your IP address or organization's IP address range. To edit a rule, follow the link for its name and select Edit from the menu at the top of the page to bring up the rule editing form.

The IP range for a single IP address is expressed in CIDR notation by appending "/32" after the IP address, e.g., "203.0.113.123/32".

Figure 7-12. Default firewall rules

Note the firewall rule that allows traffic on any port from IP addresses in the subnet. This enables unfettered network connectivity between instances in the subnet including SSH and all the other ports used by Hadoop components. That is why an additional allow rule for that traffic isn't required; that helpful, permissive firewall rule takes care of it.

After updating the firewall rules, check to make sure that you can still connect to your instances via SSH as before. If you cannot, make sure that you used the correct IP address range in the edited rules.

Next Steps

At this point, there are instances destined to host a cluster running in GCE. To pause here, you can stop the new instances by selecting them in the list of instances and then clicking the Stop button in the options across the top of the list. You can start them later by using the Start button.

Otherwise, proceed to Chapter 9 to install Hadoop and configure it, and then try it out with some basic MapReduce jobs.

## CHAPTER 8

Setting Up in Azure

In this chapter you'll create a simple Hadoop cluster running in Azure. The cluster will consist of basic installations of HDFS and YARN, which form the foundation for running MapReduce and other analytic workloads.

This chapter assumes you are using a Unix-like operating system on your local computer, such as Linux or macOS. If you are using Windows, some of the steps will vary, particularly those for working with SSH.

 If you just worked through a previous chapter on AWS or Google Cloud Platform, you'll find that this chapter covers the same procedures, just under Azure. If you're more interested in using your AWS or Google Cloud Platform cluster, skip ahead to Chapter 9.

Prerequisites

Before you start, you will need to have an account already established with Azure. You can use your current Microsoft account, or register for a separate account for free.

Free Trial

After signing up for Azure, you are eligible for a limited-time free trial (*https://azure.microsoft.com/en-us/free/free-account-faq/*), during which you are granted a fixed amount of credit that can be used to provision resources. The free trial allows you to explore Azure, but the limited number of permitted cores per region may be so low that you are unable to field a Hadoop cluster. If so, contact Azure Support to request a limit increase.

Once you are registered, you will be able to log in to the *Azure portal*, a web interface for using all of the different services under the Azure umbrella. A view of the portal is shown in Figure 8-1. When you log in, you are presented with a default portal arrangement with a starter set of tiles; a complete list of services is available from the menu on the left side of the portal. You are free to rearrange the tiles to your liking.

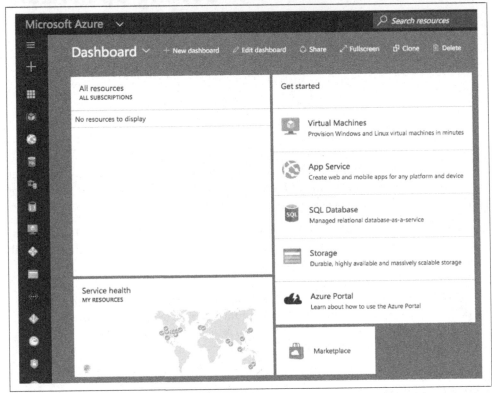

Figure 8-1. The default arrangement of the Azure portal

 Over time, Microsoft will update the default arrangement of the portal, and so the exact instructions here may become inaccurate. Also, as you work in Azure, the contents will change.

Creating a Resource Group

Working in Azure is about managing *resources*, which are things like virtual machines and virtual networks. Resources are grouped into *resource groups* so that they can share the same lifecycle and be tagged and controlled together. Each resource group is associated with a region, so all of the resources in the group are tied to that region. As a start to building a cluster in Azure, create a resource group for all of the cluster's resources.

To begin creating a resource group, select "Resource groups" from the portal menu. This opens a window within the portal, called a *blade*, which lists the resource groups. As shown in Figure 8-2, there are none at the moment, so click the "+ Add" button in the toolbar to create one.

Figure 8-2. A closeup of the Resource groups blade

A new blade appears, with a small form, as shown in Figure 8-3, to fill in about the resource group. Give it a name such as "my_first_cluster" and select a region for the "Resource group location." If you have just signed up for Azure, "Free Trial" is the only choice for the subscription; otherwise, pick the correct one. If desired, check the "Pin to dashboard" checkbox so that the resource group appears in the portal as a tile. Finally, click Create to complete the workflow.

Figure 8-3. The my_first_cluster resource group

Once Azure creates the resource group, a new blade will appear for it, with an empty list of resources. If you close this using the "X" at the upper right, you will see a new tile like the one shown in Figure 8-4 for the resource group in the dashboard, as long as you checked the "Pin to dashboard" checkbox.

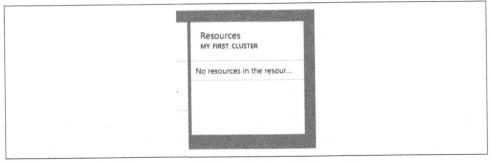

Figure 8-4. The my_first_cluster resource group in the portal

Creating Resources

Now it's time to fill up the resource group with the resources needed for a Hadoop cluster. The resources are:

- A virtual network, to house the cluster instances
- A storage account, as a home for the disk storage used by the cluster
- A network security group, to control network traffic to and from the cluster

In this chapter, the terms *virtual machine* and *instance* are used interchangeably.

There is a somewhat standard process for creating any resource: select the resource type from the portal menu to bring up a blade with a list of the resources, click the "+ Add" button to begin the process of creating the resource, and follow the steps provided, ending up back at the resource list. Because Azure creates resources asynchronously, the resource list might not show a new resource immediately, but it can be refreshed. Notifications keep you informed of progress.

The portal menu shows "favorite" resource types and other services, but all of them are available by following the "More services" option at the bottom of the menu. The menu contents can be customized by selecting and deselecting favorites, and the menu order can be rearranged by dragging items around. Do feel free to customize the menu for easier use.

 Creating these resources before any virtual machines that will comprise your cluster is one possible workflow. You can instead go ahead and create the first virtual machine, and Azure will generate a virtual network, storage account, and network security group for you. The instructions here show the supporting resources first to highlight how they are configured.

Start with creating a virtual network by selecting "Virtual networks" from the portal menu. Following the usual workflow, click the "+ Add" button above the empty list of virtual networks to reveal a form, as shown in Figure 8-5, for beginning the creation process:

- Give the virtual network a name such as "cluster_net".
- The default IP address space for the network is 10.0.0.0/16, which is more than enough.[1]
- Likewise, the first subnet in the network, named "default" with IP address space 10.0.0.0/24, will work fine for a cluster.
- Select the same subscription that you used for the resource group. You'll do this for each new resource, so it is not called out again here.

---

1 A /16 CIDR block such as this covers 65,536 addresses. For more about interpreting CIDR notation, see "A Drink of CIDR" on page 29.

- Select the resource group that you just created. This will also populate the location with the resource group's location. Again, this is a common step across resources and won't be repeated in these steps.

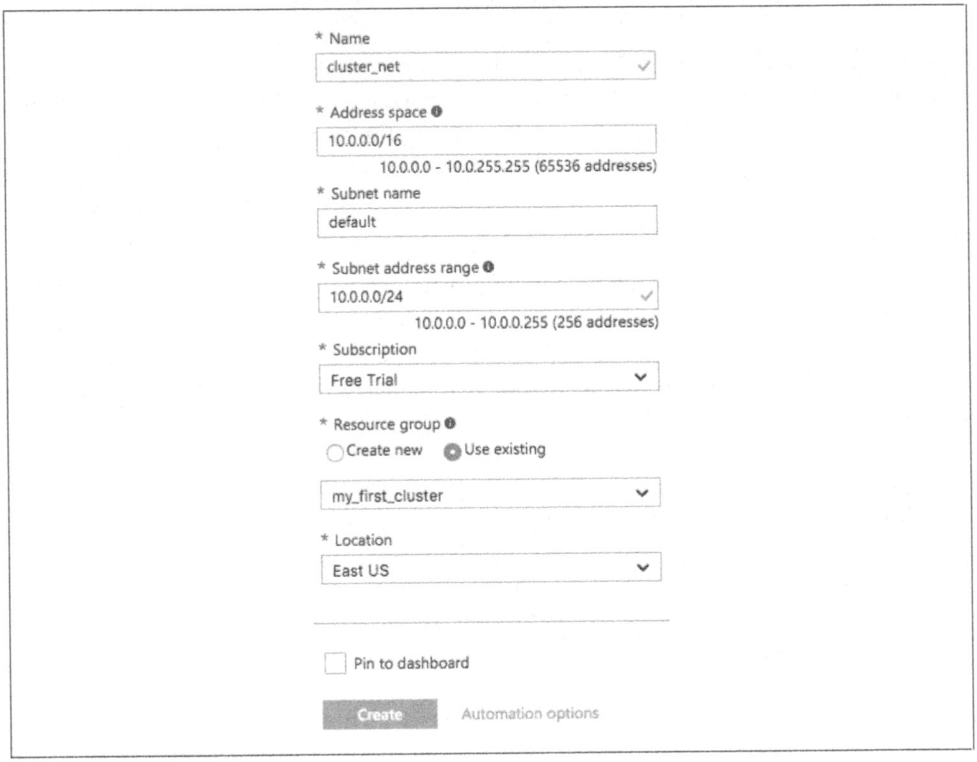

Figure 8-5. The virtual network

End by clicking the Create button. As with the resource group, and with other resources that you will make, you should see notifications that the resource is being created and then is ready. You can refresh the list of virtual networks to see it listed.

Next, create a storage account so that you can access Azure Storage services. This provides a home for the disks that will be attached to cluster instances. Start from the "Storage accounts" portal menu item and follow the usual workflow, using the form shown in Figure 8-6:

- Give the account a name. This must be globally unique across all Azure storage accounts, so short or obvious names might not be available.

- Select "Resource manager" for the deployment model.

- The correct account type is "General purpose," since this will be for virtual machine disks, as opposed to only blobs.

- Select Premium for performance. This directs the storage account to use SSDs for disks, instead of slower magnetic storage. Some virtual machine images require premium storage.

- For replication, select LRS (locally redundant storage) as the cheapest option. It may be the only option available. There are several options for data redundancy, which are discussed in "Object Storage in Azure" on page 53.

- Storage service encryption may be disabled.

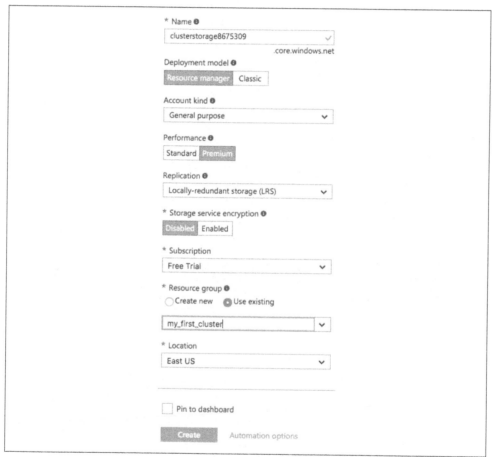

Figure 8-6. The storage account

Now for the network security group, starting from "Network security groups" in the portal menu and using the form shown in Figure 8-7, the only unique piece of information needed is a name, such as "cluster_nsg".

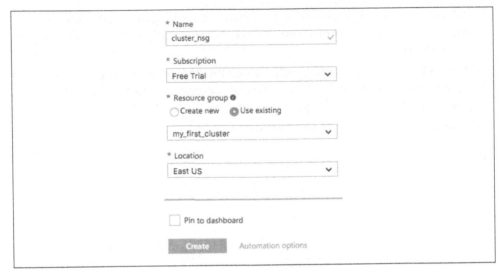

Figure 8-7. The network security group

With a network security group defined, add an inbound rule that permits SSH access from your local computer, so that you can connect directly to any of the cluster instances. Select the group from the list of network security groups, if necessary, to see a blade like the one shown in Figure 8-8, providing an overview of the group with its empty lists of inbound and outbound rules.

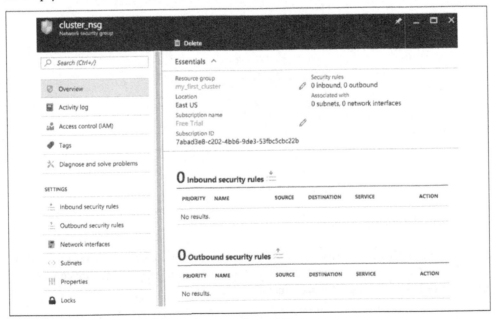

Figure 8-8. An overview of the new network security group

Select "Inbound security rules" from the blade menu to reveal a list of empty rules. Click the "+ Add" button above the list to create a new rule. Populate the new rule as shown in Figure 8-9:

- Give the rule a name such as "cluster_ssh".

- Pick a priority. The default of 100 represents the highest possible priority and is fine as a default.

- For a source, select "CIDR block," and provide an IP address range that includes your local computer.

- Select SSH for the service, and the protocol and port range are filled in automatically.

- Pick Allow for the action.

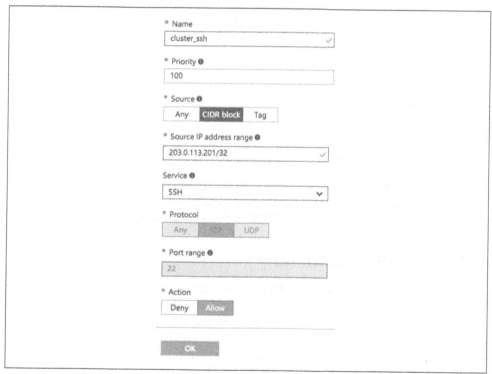

Figure 8-9. An inbound rule permitting SSH access

SSH Keys

Before provisioning instances in Azure, you need to generate an *SSH key*. An SSH key is just the public key that forms half of a public/private key pair used for SSH communication with your instances. If you are already familiar with asymmetric encryption technologies such as SSL/TLS, you will be comfortable with SSH keys.

If you already have a key pair that you like to use, you can reuse it for Azure. If not, you can create a new one yourself using a client-side tool like OpenSSL. In either case, the public key can be provided for the login account on newly provisioned instances, enabling SSH access.

To create a new key pair, try using the *ssh-keygen* utility. You can run it with no arguments to work completely interactively, or use command-line options to supply most of what the utility needs. The following example generates a 2048-bit RSA key, saving the private key to a file named "azure" and the public key to a file automatically named "azure.pub" in the hidden *.ssh* directory, which is normally used by OpenSSH for key storage and other sensitive files:

```
$ ssh-keygen -b 2048 -t rsa -f ~/.ssh/azure
```

When ssh-keygen asks for a passphrase for the new private key, you can enter an empty string (press Enter or Return) to leave the key unprotected. This is a common practice done for convenience, so that the key can be used to connect via SSH without entering a passphrase every time. If you do this, though, be sure to protect the private key file by using file permissions (e.g., make it readable only by your account), so that it is less likely to be compromised.

Creating Virtual Machines

With the preliminary work of establishing necessary support resources out of the way, you're now ready to create virtual machines. For this simple cluster, you'll create four instances: one "manager" and three "workers." The manager instance will host the HDFS namenode and the YARN resource manager, while the workers will host the HDFS datanodes and YARN node managers. A minimum of three workers is recommended, since the default HDFS replication factor is three.

The Manager Instance

Let's start by creating the manager instance, following the usual procedure: Select the Virtual machines item in the portal menu and click the "+ Add" button in the currently empty list of virtual machines, as shown in Figure 8-10.

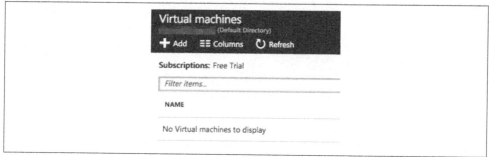

Figure 8-10. The initially empty list of virtual machines

A blade for the Azure Marketplace appears so you can select an image to base your instance on. Enter "ubuntu" in the search field to look for available Ubuntu images, and select a recent Ubuntu Server image. Remember which one you select, so you can re-use it for other cluster instances. Figure 8-11 shows a couple of options for Ubuntu versions.

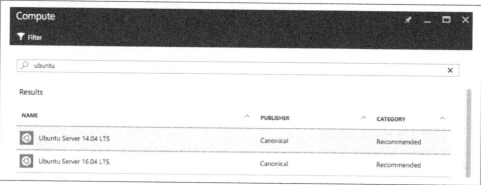

Figure 8-11. Search results for Ubuntu in the marketplace

 You do not need to use Ubuntu to deploy Hadoop in the cloud. It was chosen for the instructions here because it is popular and widely supported across all cloud providers. The steps for using a different Linux distribution can differ, especially in the system tools available and in package management.

The next blade asks for your deployment model, either Resource Manager or Classic. As shown in Figure 8-12, select the newer Resource Manager model, which lets you work with your cluster resource group, and click the Create button.

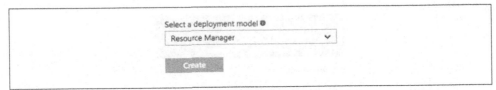

Figure 8-12. Selecting the Resource Manager deployment model

Next, a pair of blades appear to work through a wizard-like workflow for creating a new instance. The first step is a form, shown in Figure 8-13, for basic settings:

- Use the name "manager".
- Provider a username for the default account. These instructions assume the username is "ubuntu".
- Select "SSH public key" for the authentication type, and for the next field copy in the *public* key from your SSH key pair.

 Use the contents of the *public* key, not the *private* key. Azure never needs to know your private key to provide SSH access. If you accidentally paste your private key data into the form, assume that the key has been compromised and generate a new one.

- Select the "Use existing" radio button for the resource group and enter the name for your resource group.

Click OK to move to the next step.

Figure 8-13. The basic settings for the manager instance

Now select a size for the manager instance. A manager instance often needs more powerful specifications than a worker. For this cluster, select an instance size with at least four vCPUs and at least 8 GB of memory.[2] Figure 8-14 shows some available instance sizes, along with their monthly costs, at the time of writing.

---

2 Such a powerful instance size may not be available under a free trial subscription. Go ahead and select an instance size that at least has the minimum memory needed. The cluster will still work for experimentation.

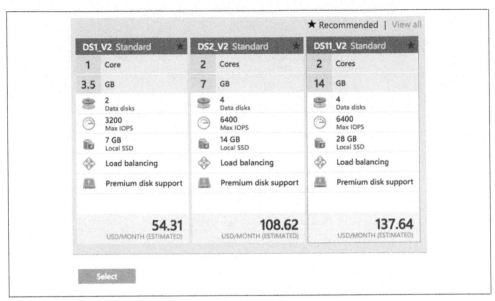

Figure 8-14. Some available instance sizes for a virtual machine

The next form, shown in Figure 8-15, is for "optional" settings, but for setting up a Hadoop cluster they are quite important:

- Select the storage account, virtual network, default subnet, and network security group that you created earlier. They may be automatically selected in the form.
- A new public IP address is suggested. Highlight the automatic selection and a pair of new blades appear, one for choosing a public IP address with the "Create new" option selected, and a second with a small form for defining the public IP address. A public IP address in Azure is a resource like any other, so you can establish one for the manager now. In the public IP address form, enter a name for the public IP address resource and select Static assignment.
- Monitoring diagnostics may be disabled.

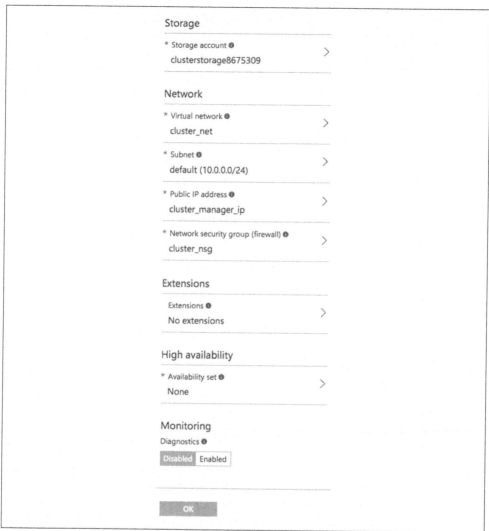

Figure 8-15. Optional settings for the manager instance

The last part of the workflow is just a summary, so you can verify your choices before Azure begins to create the virtual machine. An example summary is shown in Figure 8-16. Click OK one last time to start the creation process.

Figure 8-16. A summary of the manager instance settings

Azure automatically places a tile on the portal for the new virtual machine, which animates as the instance is created. You can select the tile to bring up a blade about the virtual machine and monitor its progress. You may notice that Azure automatically creates yet another resource, a *network interface*. This is analogous to a network adapter card in a physical machine, and links the virtual machine to its public IP address and virtual network.

When the virtual machine is created and running, the overview of the virtual machine describes its "Essentials," including the public IP address reserved for it. An example overview is shown in Figure 8-17. You can now attempt to connect to it over SSH, using the username and SSH key provided during the creation process.

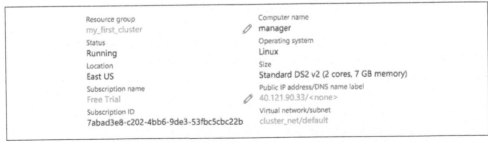

Figure 8-17. Essential information about the new manager instance

The Worker Instances

Once you can connect to the manager instance, you've completed the first major step toward standing up a cluster. Now, repeat the preceding steps to launch the three worker instances. The procedure is almost the same, but there are a couple of important changes:

- Use unique names for the instances, such as "worker1", "worker2", and "worker3".
- You can choose a less powerful instance size for workers: e.g., an instance size with only two vCPUs.

After the worker instances are launched, make sure you can SSH to each of them as well. At this point you have a set of instances that is able to run a Hadoop cluster.

Next Steps

The default rules of the network security group automatically permit connectivity between all of the instances, since they all belong to the same virtual network, and the explicit inbound rule in the group restricts SSH access appropriately, so there are no further steps needed to secure the instances.

To pause here, you can stop each new virtual machine; go to the list of virtual machines and select Stop in each one's action menu, which is denoted by an ellipsis (three periods). You can start them later by selecting Start in the same menu.

Otherwise, proceed to Chapter 9 to install Hadoop and configure it, and then try it out with some basic MapReduce jobs.

Standing Up a Cluster

Now that you have instances up and running in the cloud provider of your choice, they can be set up to run a Hadoop cluster. If you don't have instances at the ready and want to follow along, then go back to Chapter 6 for AWS, Chapter 7 for Google Cloud Platform, or Chapter 8 for Azure first, and then return here.

The JDK

Hadoop requires a Java runtime to work, and so Java must be installed on each of your new instances. A good strategy is to use the operating system package management capability already on the instances, e.g., yum on Red Hat Linux, apt on Ubuntu. Cloud providers ensure that these capabilities work within their infrastructures, sometimes even providing local mirrors or gateways to help.

Table 9-1 suggests packages to install for some operating systems. As new versions of Java are released, the package names will change.

Table 9-1. Suggested Java packages

OS	Package names
Debian or Ubuntu	openjdk-8-jdk or openjdk-7-jdk
Red Hat or CentOS	java-1.8.0-openjdk or java-1.7.0-openjdk

Instead of using a package available natively for your operating system, you can install an Oracle JDK by downloading an installation package directly from Oracle. Since you have root access to your instances, you are free to use whatever means you prefer to install Java.

After you have installed Java, make note of where the Java home directory is (i.e., what the `JAVA_HOME` environment variable should be set to). You will need to know this location later.

Hadoop Accounts

While Hadoop can run under the root account, it is better security practice to use nonprivileged accounts. For this simple cluster, create two ordinary user accounts on each instance for running HDFS and YARN. These instructions will assume that the usernames for the account are "hdfs" and "yarn". They will both belong to a new "hadoop" group. For even better security, instead of creating passwords for the new accounts, use an SSH key pair. One option is to copy in the *authorized_keys* file from the standard login account for the instance; that way, you can use the same private key to connect via SSH from your local computer to any of the accounts on the instances:

```
$ sudo groupadd hadoop
$ for u in hdfs yarn; do
> sudo useradd -G hadoop -m -s /bin/bash ${u}
> sudo mkdir /home/${u}/.ssh
> sudo cp ~/.ssh/authorized_keys /home/${u}/.ssh
> sudo chmod 700 /home/${u}/.ssh
> sudo chown -R ${u} /home/${u}/.ssh
> done
```

Passwordless SSH

The Hadoop distribution includes some helpful utility scripts that can connect to each instance in your cluster to start and stop everything for a service at once. To use these scripts, passwordless SSH must be established from the "hdfs" and "yarn" accounts on the manager instance to the same accounts on each of the worker instances, as well as for hopping from the manager instance back to itself.

While your cloud provider key pair can be used for passwordless SSH, it's better to keep its private key from being copied too widely. So, instead, generate new default SSH keys on the manager instance under each account, and then transfer the public keys to the corresponding accounts on the worker instances:

```
# on manager:
$ ssh-keygen -t rsa -b 2048 -f ~/.ssh/id_rsa -N ''
$ cat ~/.ssh/id_rsa.pub >> ~/.ssh/authorized_keys

# on each worker:
$ cat >> ~/.ssh/authorized_keys
# copy and paste public key contents
^D
```

The preceding commands accomplish transferring the public keys by just copying and pasting their contents through your SSH sessions. Another option, which is automatable, is to copy the public keys using SCP back to your local computer, and then copy them again from there to each worker instance. On a larger system, management tools like Chef or Puppet could be used to automatically distribute keys.

Now that the public keys have been distributed, connect via SSH from the "hdfs" and "yarn" accounts on the manager to the same accounts on each instance, including the manager itself, using each instance's private IP address. This is not only a useful check, but also gives you the chance to accept the key fingerprint for each instance and have it recorded in the SSH known hosts files of the manager accounts. Without doing so, automated scripts that use SSH might get stuck waiting for interactive confirmation of a fingerprint.

If the connections fail, verify the security rules governing the instances, and make sure to use the private keys generated for each Hadoop account, not the private key set up with the cloud provider.

Hadoop Installation

For now, the Hadoop cluster will only contain the basic Hadoop services HDFS and YARN. These instructions are based on the standard cluster setup instructions (*http://hadoop.apache.org/docs/current/hadoop-project-dist/hadoop-common/Cluster Setup.html*) and use the standard binary distribution from Apache. If you already have a tried-and-true set of steps for Hadoop installation, or if you prefer to use a customized or bundled distribution from a Hadoop vendor, you may be able to adapt these instructions.

To start, download a binary Hadoop distribution from *hadoop.apache.org* to each of your instances, under the standard login account. You can download to your local computer and then use SCP to transfer the distribution to each of your instances, or instead use curl or wget on each instance to download the distribution directly.

Apache uses a mirror system to offer distributions, so the simplest way to find a download URL is to visit the Hadoop download page (*http://hadoop.apache.org/relea ses.html*) to have it select a mirror, and then use the chosen mirror URL for your download command line.

Since multiple user accounts will be running Hadoop components, install it in a commonly accessible location. For this cluster you'll use */opt/hadoop* as that common location:

```
$ curl -O http://mirrorhost/path/to/hadoop-x.y.z.tar.gz
$ sudo tar xzfC hadoop-x.y.z.tar.gz /opt
$ sudo ln -s /opt/hadoop-x.y.z /opt/hadoop
```

Example commands in this chapter will use the version number x.y.z to stand in for the real Hadoop version number. Unless you have a specific need otherwise, you should simply use the latest release.

About now you may notice how often you need to repeat steps for every instance in your cluster. Once you are creating lots of clusters in the cloud, it's a good idea to use a tool that issues commands over SSH to multiple instances at a time. Chapter 17 discusses some options.

Now that Hadoop is installed, its *bin* directory can be added to the PATH environment variable for each of the Hadoop accounts:

```
# as hdfs and as yarn
$ echo "export PATH=\"/opt/hadoop/bin:\$PATH\"" >> ~/.profile
```

HDFS and YARN Configuration

Once Hadoop is installed across your cluster, it's time to configure it. The procedure here is much like configuring a Hadoop cluster on "real" hardware. Refer to the Hadoop documentation for all of the details, or consult texts like *Hadoop: The Definitive Guide* by Tom White (O'Reilly). The instructions here are simple ones, just to get the cluster going. Again, if you are used to configuring Hadoop clusters, go ahead and adapt what you normally do.

Many of these configuration steps require you to use sudo. The standard login account for your instances should be able to execute commands using sudo.

To avoid needing to type sudo before every command, use **sudo su -** in the standard instance login account to open a shell as root. Be careful, though, since you will have unrestricted access to the machine.

Unless otherwise stated, the configuration steps should be performed on every cluster node. Some that are only required on the manager node are called out.

The Environment

Create a script */etc/profile.d/hadoop.sh* that sets the HADOOP_PREFIX environment variable to point to the Hadoop installation. To have the script take effect, either log out and back in again, or source it in your current shell:

```
# as root
% echo "export HADOOP_PREFIX=/opt/hadoop" > /etc/profile.d/hadoop.sh
```

Redirection of a command run under sudo happens under the initial account, and not as root. That is why the preceding command requires you to be logged in as root. An alternative is to use the tee utility to write the file, but then discard standard output:

```
$ echo "export HADOOP_PREFIX=/opt/hadoop" | \
> sudo tee /etc/profile.d/hadoop.sh > /dev/null
```

Create a symlink at */etc/hadoop* that points to */opt/hadoop/etc/hadoop*, since you will be using that directory for the cluster's configuration:

```
$ sudo ln -s /opt/hadoop/etc/hadoop /etc/hadoop
```

Create the directories */var/log/hadoop* and */var/run/hadoop* for Hadoop logs and process ID files, and make them writable only by the Hadoop accounts:

```
$ for d in /var/log/hadoop /var/run/hadoop; do
> sudo mkdir $d
> sudo chgrp hadoop $d
> sudo chmod g+w $d
> done
```

On many Linux distributions, the contents of */var/run* are stored on a temporary filesystem and destroyed on reboot, causing the new */var/run/hadoop* directory to vanish. There are two options to cope with this. First, you can simply use a different directory for process ID files, such as */opt/hadoop/pids*, which resides on a nontemporary filesystem; however, this is a nonstandard approach. The other option is to employ a system initialization script, in accordance with the Linux distribution you are using, that creates */var/run/hadoop* on each boot. These instructions assume the latter approach.

Here is an example initialization script for Ubuntu and similar distributions, which can be saved as */etc/init.d/hadoop*:

```
#!/bin/sh

### BEGIN INIT INFO
# Provides:
# Required-Start: $remote_fs $syslog
# Required-Stop: $remote_fs $syslog
# Default-Start:  2 3 4 5
# Default-Stop: 0 1 6
# Short-Description: Create Hadoop directories at boot
### END INIT INFO

case "$1" in
  start)
    mkdir -p /var/run/hadoop
    chown root:hadoop /var/run/hadoop
    chmod 0775 /var/run/hadoop
```

```
    ;;
esac
```

The script can be activated through either of the following commands:

```
# activate with fixed start priority of 98
$ update-rc.d hadoop defaults 98
# activate using dependencies in INIT INFO comments
$ /usr/lib/lsb/install_initd hadoop
```

Next, edit */etc/hadoop/hadoop-env.sh* and make the following changes:

- Set the path for JAVA_HOME. Where this is depends on how you chose to install Java. If you used your platform's package manager, try seeing where */usr/bin/ java* or */etc/alternatives/java* links to.

- Set HADOOP_LOG_DIR and HADOOP_PID_DIR to point to */var/log/hadoop* and */var/run/hadoop*, respectively:

```
export JAVA_HOME=/path/to/jdk
export HADOOP_LOG_DIR=/var/log/hadoop
export HADOOP_PID_DIR=/var/run/hadoop
```

Edit */etc/hadoop/yarn-env.sh* and set the paths for YARN_CONF_DIR and YARN_LOG_DIR to point to */etc/hadoop* and $HADOOP_LOG_DIR, respectively. Also append a Java option to the YARN_OPTS variable so that YARN daemons prefer to listen over IPv4:

```
export YARN_CONF_DIR=/etc/hadoop
export YARN_LOG_DIR="$HADOOP_LOG_DIR"
YARN_OPTS="$YARN_OPTS -Djava.net.preferIPv4Stack=true"
```

XML Configuration Files

Edit */etc/hadoop/core-site.xml* and configure the fs.defaultFS property with the address of your manager instance. Use the private IP address of the manager instance in the URL. You can find the private IP address for an instance by locating it in your cloud provider's console.

You can also configure the hadoop.tmp.dir property with a different location for Hadoop's temporary file storage. HDFS, for one, uses this location as the basis for where namenode and datanode data is kept. The default value for the directory resides under */tmp*, which is cleared out when instances are restarted.[1] If you want to be able to stop and start your cluster, you should change this location. The value /home/${user.name}/tmp directs Hadoop to use a temporary directory under each Hadoop account's home directory. You could select other persistent locations as

---

[1] The */tmp* directory may map to persistent storage, but can still be cleared out by the operating system on reboot.

well, perhaps those that map to large persistent disks. "Stopping and Starting Entire Clusters" on page 192 discusses the practice of stopping and starting Hadoop clusters in more detail.

```
<property>
  <name>fs.defaultFS</name>
  <value>hdfs://203.0.113.101:8020</value>
</property>
<property>
  <name>hadoop.tmp.dir</name>
  <value>/home/${user.name}/tmp</value>
</property>
```

For Azure only, edit */etc/hadoop/hdfs-site.xml* and disable the requirement that datanodes have a resolvable IP address. Azure does not establish reverse DNS lookup for private IP addresses by default:

```
<property>
  <name>dfs.namenode.datanode.registration.ip-hostname-check</name>
  <value>false</value>
</property>
```

Edit */etc/hadoop/yarn-site.xml* and make the following changes:

- Configure the `yarn.resourcemanager.hostname` property for your manager instance. Use its private IP address here as well.

- Configure the `yarn.nodemanager.aux-services` property with the value "mapreduce_shuffle". This enables YARN node managers to perform the shuffle stage of MapReduce jobs:

```
<property>
  <description>The hostname of the RM.</description>
  <name>yarn.resourcemanager.hostname</name>
  <value>203.0.113.101</value>
</property>
<property>
  <name>yarn.nodemanager.aux-services</name>
  <value>mapreduce_shuffle</value>
</property>
```

Create the file */etc/hadoop/mapred-site.xml*; the easiest way is to copy the empty template file for it:

```
$ sudo cp /etc/hadoop/mapred-site.xml.template /etc/hadoop/mapred-site.xml
```

Then, add the `mapreduce.framework.name` property with the value "yarn" so that the cluster will use YARN for executing MapReduce jobs. Also set the `yarn.app.mapreduce.am.staging-dir` property to the */user* directory in HDFS; this will allow users running MapReduce jobs to write staging data into their home directories in HDFS, which will have the necessary permissions:

```
<property>
  <name>mapreduce.framework.name</name>
  <value>yarn</value>
</property>
<property>
  <name>yarn.app.mapreduce.am.staging-dir</name>
  <value>/user</value>
</property>
```

Finishing Up Configuration

Edit */etc/hadoop/slaves* and replace its contents with a list of the private IP addresses for the worker instances. This only needs to be done on the manager instance. This file is used by Hadoop's helper scripts to find each worker.

Startup

The cluster is ready to start. Begin by formatting HDFS as usual. Log in to the manager instance as the "hdfs" user for the step:

```
# as hdfs
$ hdfs namenode -format mycluster
```

Now start up HDFS and YARN using the helper scripts, also on the manager instance. This uses the passwordless SSH set up earlier to connect to the manager itself and each worker to start the daemons. If you did not try out the connections manually and accept the key fingerprints for each instance, then you will see the interactive prompts emitted by these scripts; just type "yes" for each one you see and they should continue executing:

```
# as hdfs
$ $HADOOP_PREFIX/sbin/start-dfs.sh
# as yarn
$ $HADOOP_PREFIX/sbin/start-yarn.sh
```

 For brevity, configuration and startup of the MapReduce Job History Server is omitted; the cluster will function without it. To set it up, establish a "mapred" user in the "hadoop" group, just like the "hdfs" and "yarn" users, and follow the standard instructions to configure and start the server.

SSH Tunneling

Now that all of the daemons are started, you can check their statuses through their web interfaces. However, connecting directly will not work, because the security rules governing the instances block access from outside to the necessary ports. You can open up access to those ports from your IP address by adding new rules, but a better

---

option is to use *SSH tunneling*, which maps a local port on your computer to a remote port on another computer through SSH. Using SSH tunnels lets you leave only the SSH port open to anything outside the security group, and encrypts the traffic as a bonus.

You can create SSH tunnels using the standard SSH client. Run commands like these to establish tunnels from the local ports 50070 (for the namenode web interface) and 8088 (for the resource manager web interface) to the same ports on your manager instance. Use the public IP address or, if it is available, the public DNS name for your manager instance to establish the connection from your local computer. For the remote end of the tunnel, "localhost" works for the namenode, but you must use the same IP address for the resource manager as configured for the `yarn.resourcemanager.hostname` configuration property in *yarn-site.xml*.

```
$ ssh -i /path/to/cloud_provider_key.pem -n -N \
> -L 50070:localhost:50070 userid@manager.cloud-provider.example &
$ ssh -i /path/to/cloud_provider_key.pem -n -N \
> -L 8088:203.0.113.101:8088 userid@manager.cloud-provider.example &
```

Consult the man page for `ssh` for more information about setting up SSH tunnels. Tunneling is also covered in more detail in Chapter 14.

Now, in your browser, navigate to *http://localhost:50070* and *http://localhost:8088* to see your namenode and resource manager ready for work. The web interfaces are being served from the manager instance, but tunneled through SSH to your browser.

Running a Test Job

After all of that work, it should be gratifying to see your cluster in action. The Hadoop distribution comes with many example programs bundled in an examples JAR. You can use any of those on your new cluster. One easy one to try is the "pi" example, which calculates the value of pi using a MapReduce algorithm.

MapReduce jobs in the cluster will write their history information to */user/history* in HDFS, so that directory needs to be established before any jobs are run. Using the "hdfs" user, create it with wide-open permissions but owned by the "mapred" user and the "hadoop" group:

```
# as hdfs
$ hdfs dfs -mkdir -p /user/history
$ hdfs dfs -chmod -R 1777 /user/history
$ hdfs dfs -chown mapred:hadoop /user/history
```

Now, you can run the example under any account on an instance. For the account you choose, create a home directory in HDFS, using the hdfs account. Then go ahead and run the example:

```
# as hdfs
$ hdfs dfs -mkdir -p /user/userid
$ hdfs dfs -chown userid /user/userid

# as the user account
$ export PATH=/opt/hadoop/bin:$PATH
$ export HADOOP_CONF_DIR=/etc/hadoop
$ hadoop jar \
> /opt/hadoop/share/hadoop/mapreduce/hadoop-mapreduce-examples-x.y.z.jar \
> pi 10 100
```

You should see the MapReduce job submitted to YARN and visible in the resource manager web interface. If not, then it is possible that you are not configured to use YARN for MapReduce, and the job is being run locally; check over the configuration, especially *yarn-site.xml* and *mapred-site.xml*.

After a short runtime and some output describing the progress of the job, you should see an answer like this. Yours may vary:

```
Estimated value of Pi is 3.14800000000000000000
```

Congratulations, you have created a functional Hadoop cluster in the cloud! You should feel free to try running more example programs or other analyses through it. Even though it is running in the cloud, using it is much like using an on-premises cluster.

What If the Job Hangs?

If the example job never gets started, but gets stuck waiting for an application master (AM) to be allocated, it's usually a sign that there may not be enough memory on the node managers for allocating the container needed for the application master process. The default configurations for YARN are higher than what you often have to work with in smaller cloud deployments. Try setting these configuration properties:

- In */etc/hadoop/yarn-site.xml*, set `yarn.nodemanager.resource.memory-mb` to something low; for example, 1,024 for a worker instance with 8 GB of memory. The default value of 8,192 is too high for such an instance.

- In */etc/hadoop/mapred-site.xml*, set `yarn.app.mapreduce.am.resource.mb` to the same value.

If this does not work, consult the documentation about tuning YARN configurations for MapReduce. They provide advice, and even worksheets, for coming up with appropriate configuration property settings for your cluster.

Running Basic Data Loading and Analysis

The example job does exercise your new cluster, but might not be representative of the type of work a cloud-based cluster will perform. The next test of the cluster will get a little closer to real life by running a couple of simple MapReduce jobs that read in text data from Wikipedia and then, following the tradition of new Hadoop clusters everywhere, count words in it.

Wikipedia Exports

Wikipedia offers on-demand and pregenerated exports of all of its data in XML format. You can export the complete information for a single article, or for a category of articles, on demand. Wikipedia also periodically posts large, complete dumps of many wikis in the Wikimedia family. These exports are well suited for analysis in a Hadoop cluster.

Visit *https://dumps.wikimedia.org/* to see the available pregenerated dumps.

Analyzing a Small Export

While it is tempting to grab a complete Wikipedia dump, it is better to start with a smaller one, and then scale up. Since the XML format is the same for any dump, the same jobs will work on any of them.

Generating the export

Visit *https://en.wikipedia.org/wiki/Special:Export*, which lets you export one or more articles from the English Wikipedia site. Collect a set of page titles that you want to export and enter them manually, or select a category. In Figure 9-1, the category is "Member states of the United Nations," which returns around 200 articles. Remove any subcategory entries, and be sure to check the boxes to include only the current revision of each article and to save as a file. Then click the Export button to receive the exported data as XML.

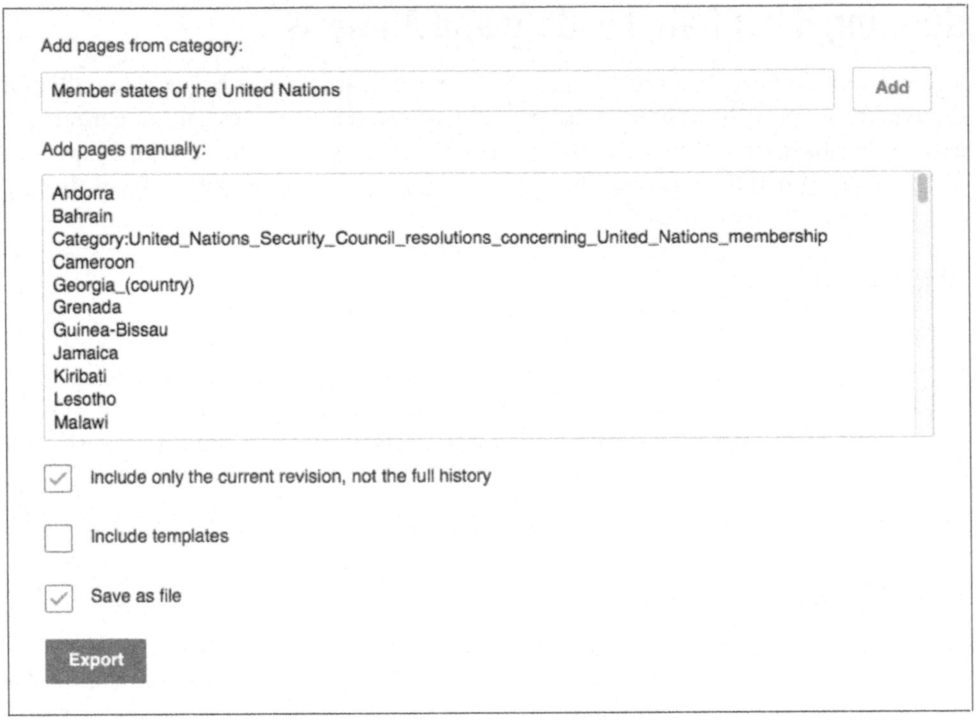

Figure 9-1. Wikipedia export page

The export will serve as the source data for analysis, so it needs to be copied into HDFS in the cluster. Copy the file up to the manager instance using scp; be sure to use the same private key that works for SSH access. Then, on the manager instance, use the hdfs utility to copy the XML into the home directory for the same user account used earlier to run the pi example:

```
# on the computer where the export was downloaded
$ scp -i /path/to/cloud_provider_key.pem Wikipedia-20160701000000.xml \
> userid@manager.cloud-provider.example:.
# on the manager instance
$ hdfs dfs -copyFromLocal Wikipedia-20160701000000.xml /user/userid
```

The MapReduce jobs

For this analysis, two MapReduce jobs will be used. The first one will scan the XML and extract each article's title and page contents, saving them into HDFS; this can be seen as a very basic *extract-transform-load* or *ETL* process, although real-life ETL is often much more involved. The second one will evaluate each article's text to count words in it, much like the standard Hadoop word-count example.

Examples 9-1 and 9-2 show the important parts of the Java source[2] for the loader job, which consists of a driver class and a mapper class. This is a map-only job with no reducers required. The driver sets up the job to stream the XML data from the file provided as the first argument, runs it through a mapper, and sends the output data to sequence files in an HDFS directory specified by the second argument.

Example 9-1. Wikipedia loader job driver code

```
JobConf conf = new JobConf(getClass());
conf.setJobName("WP dump loader");

// Set the mapper class, but skip the reduce phase
conf.setMapperClass(WikipediaDumpLoaderMapper.class);
conf.setNumReduceTasks(0);
// The object key/value pairs are text
conf.setOutputKeyClass(Text.class);
conf.setOutputValueClass(Text.class);

// Stream XML into the job
conf.setInputFormat(StreamInputFormat.class);
StreamInputFormat.addInputPath(conf, new Path(args[0]));
// Use the XML record reader, with each page as one record
conf.set("stream.recordreader.class",
         "org.apache.hadoop.streaming.StreamXmlRecordReader");
conf.set("stream.recordreader.begin", "<page>");
conf.set("stream.recordreader.end", "</page>");
// Emit sequence files
conf.setOutputFormat(SequenceFileOutputFormat.class);
SequenceFileOutputFormat.setOutputPath(conf, new Path(args[1]));

JobClient.runJob(conf);
return 0;
```

Example 9-2. Wikipedia loader job mapper code

```
private enum Counter { ARTICLES }

private DocumentBuilder db;

@Override
public void configure(JobConf conf) {
  try {
    db = DocumentBuilderFactory.newInstance().newDocumentBuilder();
  } catch (ParserConfigurationException e) {
    throw new IllegalStateException("XML parser configuration is bad", e);
  }
```

---

2 Find the complete source at: *https://github.com/bhavanki/moving-hadoop-to-the-cloud*.

```
    }

    @Override
    public void map(Text key, Text value, OutputCollector<Text, Text> output,
                    Reporter reporter) throws IOException {
      try {
        // Parse the page of XML into a document
        Document doc = db.parse(new InputSource(new StringReader(key.toString())));

        // Extract the title and text (article content) from the page content
        String title = doc.getElementsByTagName("title").item(0).getTextContent();
        String text = doc.getElementsByTagName("text").item(0).getTextContent();

        // Emit the title and text pair
        output.collect(new Text(title), new Text(text));
        reporter.getCounter(Counter.ARTICLES).increment(1L);
      } catch (SAXException e) {
        throw new IOException(e);
      }
    }
}
```

MapReduce veterans may notice that this job uses the old Java MapReduce API. This is because `StreamInputFormat` is currently only available under that API. An alternative design would use Hadoop Streaming to load the XML data.[3]

The `StreamInputFormat` is configured to simply send each article's content to the mapper as the key; the value sent to the mapper is always an empty string. Other than those details, the job is straightforward.

Once these classes are packaged into a JAR, the job is ready to run. Using `scp`, copy the JAR to the manager instance under your user account, and run it using the `yarn` command-line utility:

```
$ yarn jar basic-loader-1.0.0.jar com.mh2c.WikipediaDumpLoaderDriver \
> Wikipedia-20160701000000.xml wikitext
```

As before, you will see signs of progress as the job is run on the cluster. When the job completes, there will be one or more sequence files in a directory in HDFS (the preceding example uses the *wikitext* directory in the user's HDFS home directory). You should also see the custom "ARTICLES" counter reporting the total number of articles parsed. If you like, you can peek at a sequence file to check that article text is present; while a sequence file is binary, it will have large areas of plain text that are easy to discriminate:

```
$ hdfs dfs -ls wikitext
$ hdfs dfs -cat wikitext/part-00000
```

---

3 Or Spark (see Chapter 12).

It's time for the second job, also written in Java, which performs the word count. This job works like any other word-count job, except that it reads from sequence files instead of ordinary text files. Examples 9-3, 9-4, and 9-5 show the key portions of the code for the job.

Example 9-3. Wikipedia word-count job driver code

```
JobConf conf = new JobConf(getClass());
conf.setJobName("WP word count");

// Set the mapper and reducer classes, and use the reducer as a combiner
conf.setMapperClass(WikipediaWordCountMapper.class);
conf.setReducerClass(WikipediaWordCountReducer.class);
conf.setCombinerClass(WikipediaWordCountReducer.class);
// The object key/value pairs are text words and integer counts
conf.setOutputKeyClass(Text.class);
conf.setOutputValueClass(IntWritable.class);

// Read in sequence files
conf.setInputFormat(SequenceFileInputFormat.class);
SequenceFileInputFormat.addInputPath(conf, new Path(args[0]));
// Emit ordinary text files
conf.setOutputFormat(TextOutputFormat.class);
TextOutputFormat.setOutputPath(conf, new Path(args[1]));

JobClient.runJob(conf);
return 0;
```

Example 9-4. Wikipedia word-count job mapper code

```
private static final IntWritable ONE = new IntWritable(1);
private Text wordText = new Text();

@Override
public void map(Text key, Text value, OutputCollector<Text, IntWritable> output,
                Reporter reporter) throws IOException {
  // Split the text content of the article on whitespace
  String[] words = value.toString().split("\\s+");
  // Count each word occurrence
  for (String word : words) {
    wordText.set(word);
    output.collect(wordText, ONE);
  }
}
```

Example 9-5. Wikipedia word-count job reducer code

```
private IntWritable sumIntWritable = new IntWritable();

/**
 * key = word
 * values = counts
 */
@Override
public void reduce(Text key, Iterator<IntWritable> values,
                   OutputCollector<Text, IntWritable> output, Reporter reporter)
  throws IOException {

  // Total up the incoming counts for the word
  int sum = 0;
  while (values.hasNext()) {
    sum += values.next().get();
  }
  // Emit the word count
  sumIntWritable.set(sum);
  output.collect(key, sumIntWritable);
}
```

The old Java MapReduce API is used here, for consistency with the loader job, but this code could easily be rewritten to use the new API instead. Run the job to perform the word count:

```
$ yarn jar basic-loader-1.0.0.jar com.mh2c.WikipediaWordCountDriver \
> wikitext wikiwordcount
```

The results are in one or more files in HDFS under the *wikiwordcount* directory. The mapper code used here is intentionally simple; differing letter case and punctuation are not accounted for, so the results could be cleaned up with some improvements:

```
$ hdfs dfs -ls wikiwordcount
$ hdfs dfs -cat wikiwordcount/part-00000
```

Both of these MapReduce jobs are quite simple, and could have been combined into a single job, but they make clearer examples when separated. Also, the results of the first job could be saved off and used as the starting point for other analyses later, saving the work of parsing XML in each run. In a cloud architecture, you have the choice of saving valuable intermediate data long term in object storage services (see "Object Storage" on page 49), which lets you trade off the cost of repeated computation for the cost of increased data storage. As computation time increases, the option of reducing it by cheaply storing useful data products becomes more attractive.

Go Bigger

With the Wikipedia export jobs available and working in your cluster, you have a starting point for further exploration. The "Member states of the United Nations" example used an export of around 200 articles, which at the time of writing weighed in at 26 MB, but larger exports should work just as well. The only limitation is the amount of room available in HDFS, since the XML data needs to be loaded there first for the loader job to work on it. If you are low on room in HDFS, or find that your workers run out of disk space when spilling data, either add worker instances or increase the available block storage for the existing workers.[4]

The trickiest part of working with a large export is getting it from Wikipedia into HDFS. In this chapter, the file was downloaded to the local computer, copied to the manager instance, and then copied into HDFS. This approach may not work well for, say, the complete export of English language Wikipedia, which exceeds 20 GB, compressed, as of this writing.

It is feasible to download a large file directly to an instance, and then copy the file from there into HDFS. The disk where the large file resides can be kept as the "golden copy" of the data, and attached to instances when the file stored on it is needed.

A more advanced approach involves uploading a large file to the cloud provider's object storage service, and then configuring Hadoop to access the file from there. The exact mechanics of this approach vary with the cloud provider, and there can be multiple ways to pull it off. Some possibilities:

- Under AWS, download the file to an EC2 instance, and use the S3 command-line client to upload the file into S3. Then, use Hadoop's s3a protocol to access the file directly as an HDFS volume, or use the `distcp` tool to copy the file from S3 into local HDFS.

- Under Google Cloud Platform, use the Google Cloud Storage Transfer Service to load the file directly from Wikipedia into a bucket in Cloud Storage.[5] Then, install the Google Cloud Storage Connector into your cluster and access the file directly as an HDFS volume.

- Under Azure, download the file to a virtual machine, and use the Azure CLI to upload it to either Azure Blob Storage or Azure Data Lake Store (ADLS). Then, install the Azure Blob Storage module or the Azure Data Lake Store module into your cluster and access the file directly as an HDFS volume.

---

4 Increasing volume storage can be easy or difficult, depending on the cloud provider.

5 With the correct content type set for the file, Cloud Storage should decompress it when it is accessed.

Chapter 11, which covers adding Apache Hive to your cluster, describes how to use the s3a filesystem connector to directly access data residing in S3 for use in Hive queries.

Depending on the capabilities of the job, you may not need to decompress a large file before storing it in HDFS or cloud provider object storage services. Avoiding decompression saves not only on HDFS capacity, but also storage costs and potential data transfer costs. However, as usual, compressed files can hamper the performance of MapReduce or other analytic jobs performed on them, and you may find you need to change over a file from, say, gzip compression to a splittable compression algorithm such as LZO. This affects the time it takes for data to be ready for work and modestly increases storage costs. Consider these trade-offs in your data flow.

Check your cloud provider's documentation and examples to see what options you have for working with files and the provider's storage features. As new features are introduced, you may discover better patterns to move your large files around.

## PART IV

Enhancing Your Cluster

After working through Part III, you should have a simple, functional Hadoop cluster running on a cloud provider. While this can be satisfying, you may want to push it further, and that's what this part of the book is all about. Each chapter starts from the simple cluster and adds more capabilities to it, so that it works more like a real-world cluster. You can pick and choose which chapters to dive into based on your interests.

## CHAPTER 10

High Availability

A Hadoop cluster running in the cloud has some intrinsic reliability built in, due to the robustness of the cloud provider. Their data centers are built with reliable power sources and network connections. They also accommodate the constant parade of failing motherboards, memory chips, and hard drives that come with running huge numbers of servers. Often, when these "normal" hardware failures occur, your instances and infrastructure components are automatically migrated over to alternative resources. Sometimes, you won't even notice that anything went wrong.

Still, there are some failures a cloud provider can't hide from its customers. Disks can become corrupted due to either software or hardware failures. Although rare, network hiccups or power outages at a cloud provider data center can cause instances, or even whole availability zones, to disappear for some amount of time. Even some of those "normal" hardware failures can't be automatically handled every time.

Given that the risk of cluster failures is not completely eliminated by running on a cloud provider, it is reasonable to have a strategy in place to reduce their impact.

Running in the cloud, if a cluster fails, it's completely feasible to simply spin up a new one to take its place. As long as the data the cluster was operating on is preserved, for example, in cloud provider storage services, a new cluster can be created in the same or a different availability zone, or even a different region in extreme cases, to pick up where the failed cluster left off. This is one of the strategies that makes little sense when working with physical hardware, but that can be advantageous when working with a flexible and resilient cloud provider infrastructure.

If you prefer keeping clusters around for a while, perhaps because other systems depend on them being available constantly, then another strategy is to set up *high availability* (HA). An HA cluster involves running redundant copies of some Hadoop components in order to eliminate single points of failure. By keeping cloud provider infrastructure and features in mind, you can set up HA clusters that are even more robust than those in an ordinary, single data center.

This chapter does not completely describe Hadoop HA. Please consult Hadoop documentation for more information.

Planning HA in the Cloud

The most important Hadoop components in a cluster to set up for HA are HDFS and YARN, so those will be focused on here.

HDFS HA

There are two options for configuring HA for HDFS: using conventional shared storage (NFS) or using the Quorum Journal Manager. This chapter explores using the Quorum Journal Manager, which involves running several journalnode daemons as well as a second namenode. Automatic failover, using ZooKeeper, is also covered.

When a non-HA cluster is configured, it only has a single namenode, which of course runs in some availability zone in some region. When converting a cloud cluster to HA, a second namenode is added, as well as a set of at least three journalnodes. An important decision to make is whether to place the second namenode, and some of the journalnodes, in other availability zones or other regions.

While it is possible to run the new daemons in a different region, there are practical reasons why this should be avoided. First, network connectivity between regions is much slower than between availability zones within a region. Second, cloud providers often charge for data transfer between regions, increasing the cost for HA clusters. Finally, management of all of HDFS within a cluster is much easier when all of its instances run within one region.

There is a performance cost to spreading clusters across availability zones. Because clusters grow to hold more data and jobs running on them become more complex, the cost increases, and it can get to the point where jobs will tend to time out. In "Benchmarking HA" on page 139, some techniques for testing cluster performance are discussed; they can help guide your decision on using multiple availability zones for HA.

Figure 10-1 shows an HA deployment that is confined to a single availability zone. Figure 10-2 shows an HA deployment that spans two availability zones, with one namenode and several journalnodes in each zone.

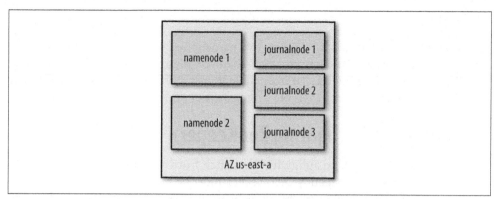

Figure 10-1. An HA deployment of HDFS within a single availability zone

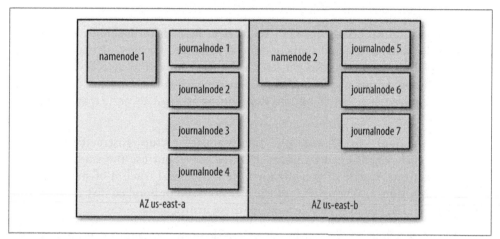

Figure 10-2. An HA deployment of HDFS in two availability zones. Many journalnodes are required so that there are at least three in each zone.

What about the datanodes?

HA configuration for HDFS does not require doing anything special for datanodes; it focuses on the critical data used by the namenode and on having a second namenode running. However, the loss of an availability zone causes a loss of datanodes within it as well, which can lead to data being lost or being unreachable for a time.

When configuring a cluster for HA, then, consider spreading datanodes across availability zones too, keeping in mind potential performance problems. New datanodes added to new availability zones will, as usual, gradually receive replicated copies of HDFS data, until they are fully participating in the cluster.

YARN HA

Just as HDFS HA is enabled by running two namenodes, one active and one standby, YARN HA is enabled by running two resource managers, one active and one standby. As with the namenodes, it is possible to install the second resource manager in a different availability zone than the original (first) one.

Installing and Configuring ZooKeeper

In order for an HA cluster to automatically switch from a formerly active namenode or resource manager to a standby, ZooKeeper must be running on the cluster. Zoo-Keeper is a distributed, highly reliable coordination system. It is used to enable many different capabilities in a Hadoop cluster, and automatic failover for HDFS and YARN HA is one of them.

A distributed ZooKeeper deployment requires at least three daemons, and as with journalnodes and the second namenode and resource manager, it may be spread across availability zones. ZooKeeper itself is "smart" enough to detect when its own daemons disappear, and it can continue functioning when that happens, so no special steps are required after installing and configuring it for it to participate in an HA cluster.

These instructions are based on the standard setup instructions (*http://zookeeper.apache.org/doc/trunk/zookeeperStarted.html*) and use the standard binary distribution from Apache. If you already have a tried-and-true set of steps for Zoo-Keeper installation, or if you prefer to use a customized or bundled distribution from a Hadoop vendor, you may be able to adapt these instructions.

Prepare for installing ZooKeeper by creating a dedicated account for it on each host that will be running ZooKeeper, just like those for HDFS and YARN (see Chapter 9). These instructions will assume that the username for the account is "zk" and that the account belongs to the "hadoop" group. SSH key pairs are used for logging in.

```
$ sudo useradd -G hadoop -m -s /bin/bash zk
$ sudo mkdir /home/zk/.ssh
$ sudo cp ~/.ssh/authorized_keys /home/zk/.ssh
$ sudo chmod 700 /home/zk/.ssh
$ sudo chown -R zk /home/zk/.ssh
```

If you have a cluster with three workers like the one set up in Chapter 9, then those can be the targets for ZooKeeper installation as well. You may want to create an account on the manager instance as well for hosting a control script, described later on in this section.

Download a binary ZooKeeper distribution from *zookeeper.apache.org* to each of your instances, under the standard login account. In keeping with the use of */opt/hadoop* as the installation location for Hadoop, install ZooKeeper to */opt/zookeeper*:

```
$ curl -O http://mirrorhost/path/to/zookeeper-x.y.z.tar.gz
$ sudo tar xzfC zookeeper-x.y.z.tar.gz /opt
$ sudo ln -s /opt/zookeeper-x.y.z /opt/zookeeper
```

 Example commands in this chapter will use the version number x.y.z to stand in for the real ZooKeeper version number. Unless you have a specific need otherwise, you should simply use the latest stable release.

This ZooKeeper system will be running "replicated" with a quorum of servers. Each of them receives the same configuration file, so it's enough to create the file on one worker instance and copy it to the others. (The file should be named */opt/zookeeper/ conf/zoo.cfg*.)

```
tickTime=2000
dataDir=/var/lib/zookeeper
clientPort=2181
initLimit=5
syncLimit=2
server.1=203.0.113.102:2888:3888
server.2=203.0.113.103:2888:3888
server.3=203.0.113.104:2888:3888
```

In the preceding example, the private IP addresses of the worker instances are used in the file. It also names */var/lib/zookeeper* as its data directory, so create that on each worker as well:

```
$ sudo mkdir /var/lib/zookeeper
$ sudo chgrp hadoop /var/lib/zookeeper
$ sudo chmod g+w /var/lib/zookeeper
```

Each server requires a file named */var/lib/zookeeper/myid* containing its numeric ID from the configuration file (e.g., 1, 2, or 3 for the preceding file). This file, therefore, must be created uniquely on each worker.

The last part of configuring ZooKeeper is setting its log directory. If it is not set, it defaults to the current directory, which in this configuration is the home directory of the "zk" account. You may want it to instead log to */var/log/zookeeper*, again to be similar to Hadoop. If so, create that directory on each worker, and set the ZOO_LOG_DIR environment variable in */opt/zookeeper/bin/zkEnv.sh* (before the script evaluates it):

```
# commands to make the log directory
$ sudo mkdir /var/log/zookeeper
$ sudo chgrp hadoop /var/log/zookeeper
$ sudo chmod g+w /var/log/zookeeper

# then, editing zkEnv.sh
export ZOO_LOG_DIR=/var/log/zookeeper
```

ZooKeeper is ready to start. This can be done by running */opt/zookeeper/bin/ zkServer.sh* on each worker instance; unfortunately, ZooKeeper does not ship with a distributed start script like the Hadoop distribution does. But it doesn't take anything complicated. See Example A-1 for a script that covers the basics.

In order to use the example script, the account running it must have passwordless SSH access to each worker. One option is to create a "zk" account on the cluster manager instance and establish access from there, just like for the "hdfs" and "yarn" accounts.

Once all the ZooKeeper servers are running, you can check the status of each one by running *zkServer.sh*, or the example script in Example A-1, with the `status` subcommand. One server should report it is the leader, and the others should report they are the followers:

```
# Using the example script "zk"
$ ./zk status
Checking ZooKeeper status
ZooKeeper JMX enabled by default
Using config: /opt/zookeeper/bin/../conf/zoo.cfg
Mode: follower
ZooKeeper JMX enabled by default
Using config: /opt/zookeeper/bin/../conf/zoo.cfg
Mode: leader
ZooKeeper JMX enabled by default
Using config: /opt/zookeeper/bin/../conf/zoo.cfg
Mode: follower
```

ZooKeeper is now running alongside your Hadoop cluster and ready to play its part in enabling HA.

Adding New HDFS and YARN Daemons

With ZooKeeper in place and ready to perform automatic failover, the additional HDFS and YARN daemons can be installed on the cluster, and the entire cluster configured for HA. Start by noting the availability zone(s) where the current namenode and resource manager are running, and identify which other zone or zones will host the second instances of those daemons.

The Second Manager

For a cluster set up with a single manager instance that hosts both the namenode and resource manager, as was done in Part III, the most straightforward path is to create a second manager instance. Follow the procedure you used to prepare the first manager instance, depending on which cloud provider you use, to prepare a second one. Give it a unique name, say, "manager2". If desired, select a different availability zone for the new manager instance.

In AWS, subnets do not span availability zones, and so the second manager instance in a separate availability zone must reside in a different subnet from the first one, which complicates cluster architectures. In Google Cloud Platform, this is not the case; a subnet may span availability zones. In Azure, instead of using a different availability zone, add the new manager instance to an availability set also containing the first one.

There are more efficient ways of essentially cloning or copying existing instances, which will be covered in Chapter 16.

Install Hadoop on the second manager instance and start to configure it like the first one, as covered in Chapter 9:

- Install a JDK and Hadoop as before.
- Set up the "hdfs" and "yarn" accounts, as well as "zk" if you are using a control script for ZooKeeper as described earlier.
- Set up passwordless SSH access from the Hadoop accounts on the new manager instance to all of the workers, as well as to itself. In the event that the first manager is unavailable, say, because its instance fails, then control of the cluster will pass to this new instance, and so it should be capable of starting and stopping daemons. The second manager instance does not need to use the same SSH key pair as the first one, but it can.
- Make the same directories and changes to the Hadoop environment scripts (like *hadoop-env.sh*) as before. You can copy the scripts from the first manager to the second, since the needed changes are identical. This does not include the XML configuration files, however, which need changes to set up HA.

HDFS HA Configuration

Now for the main part of this effort: configuring HDFS HA. Stop your existing cluster before proceeding, so that the Hadoop daemons aren't running while changes are being made to their configuration.

Edit */etc/hadoop/hdfs-site.xml* on the *first*, original master instance and make the following changes:[1]

- Configure the `dfs.nameservices` property with your cluster's name. These instructions assume a cluster name of "myfirstcluster"; replace this name with your own in other configuration properties.

- Configure the `dfs.ha.namenodes.myfirstcluster` property with a list of namenode IDs. There should be two since there are two manager instances in your cluster. These instructions use "nn1" and "nn2".

- Configure the `dfs.namenode.rpc-address.myfirstcluster` and `dfs.namenode.http-address.myfirstcluster` sets of properties with the private IP addresses of the manager instances.

- Configure the `dfs.namenode.shared.edits.dir` property with a `qjournal://` URI pointing to each of the worker instances in your cluster. Each worker will host a single journalnode.

- Specify the standard `ConfiguredFailoverProxyProvider` class with the `dfs.client.failover.proxy.provider.myfirstcluster` property.

- Configure the `dfs.journalnode.edits.dir` property with the path that journalnodes should use for storing their data. In these instructions, */var/data/jn* will be used.

- Configure the `dfs.ha.fencing.methods` property with at least the do-nothing value "shell(/bin/true)". Even though fencing isn't strictly required under the Quorum Journal Manager, automatic failover will not work without something set for it.

- Configure the `dfs.ha.automatic-failover.enabled` property with the value "true". As one might expect, this enables automatic HDFS failover:

```
<property>
  <name>dfs.nameservices</name>
  <value>myfirstcluster</value>
</property>
<property>
  <name>dfs.ha.namenodes.myfirstcluster</name>
  <value>nn1,nn2</value>
</property>
<property>
  <name>dfs.namenode.rpc-address.myfirstcluster.nn1</name>
  <value>203.0.113.101:8020</value>
```

---

1 The instructions in Chapter 9 did not include any modifications to *hdfs-site.xml*, so your file probably has no configuration properties to start with.

```xml
    </property>
    <property>
      <name>dfs.namenode.rpc-address.myfirstcluster.nn2</name>
      <value>203.0.113.105:8020</value>
    </property>
    <property>
      <name>dfs.namenode.http-address.myfirstcluster.nn1</name>
      <value>203.0.113.101:50070</value>
    </property>
    <property>
      <name>dfs.namenode.http-address.myfirstcluster.nn2</name>
      <value>203.0.113.105:50070</value>
    </property>
    <property>
      <name>dfs.namenode.shared.edits.dir</name>
      <value>qjournal://203.0.113.102:8485;203.0.113.103:8485;
            203.0.113.104:8485/myfirstcluster</value>
    </property>
    <property>
      <name>dfs.client.failover.proxy.provider.myfirstcluster</name>
      <value>org.apache.hadoop.hdfs.server.namenode.ha.
            ConfiguredFailoverProxyProvider</value>
    </property>
    <property>
      <name>dfs.journalnode.edits.dir</name>
      <value>/var/data/jn</value>
    </property>
    <property>
      <name>dfs.ha.fencing.methods</name>
      <value>shell(/bin/true)</value>
    </property>
    <property>
      <name>dfs.ha.automatic-failover.enabled</name>
      <value>true</value>
    </property>
```

Copy */etc/hadoop/hdfs-site.xml* over to the new manager instance, so that both of them have the same HA settings. Also copy it to the worker instances, so that they are aware of HA being in place.

Don't forget to create the journalnode data directory that was configured in *hdfs-site.xml*. It should be writable by the "hdfs" account, since that account will run the journalnodes. The directory only needs to be created where the journalnodes are running:

```
$ sudo mkdir -p /var/data/jn
$ sudo chgrp hadoop /var/data/jn
$ sudo chmod g+w /var/data/jn
```

Next, edit */etc/hadoop/core-site.xml* on all of the instances, and any other instances that serve as clients for Hadoop, and make the following changes:

- Change the `fs.defaultFS` configuration property from the URI for the single namenode to the HA URI.
- Configure the `ha.zookeeper.quorum` property with a list of the private IP addresses and ports for the ZooKeeper instances. Since ZooKeeper will arbitrate automatic failover, the system needs to be pointed to where its servers are running:

```
<property>
  <name>fs.defaultFS</name>
  <value>hdfs://myfirstcluster</value>
</property>
<property>
  <name>ha.zookeeper.quorum</name>
  <value>203.0.113.102:2181,203.0.113.103:2181,203.0.113.104:2181</value>
</property>
```

Start the ZooKeeper servers if they are not running, and initialize their HA state:

```
# as zk, if needed
$ ./zk start
# as hdfs
$ hdfs zkfc -formatZK
```

It is time to transition the cluster to HA, now that configuration is complete. Start by manually starting the journalnodes on each of the worker instances:

```
# as hdfs on worker instances
$ $HADOOP_PREFIX/sbin/hadoop-daemon.sh start journalnode
```

After the journalnodes are running, the namenodes can be started. First, on the original, first manager instance, initialize the namenode's shared edits directory and start the namenode. Then go to the new, second manager instance and initialize and start it as well:

```
# as hdfs on the original manager instance
$ hdfs namenode -initializeSharedEdits
$ $HADOOP_PREFIX/sbin/hadoop-daemon.sh start namenode

# as hdfs on the new manager instance
$ hdfs namenode -bootstrapStandby
$ $HADOOP_PREFIX/sbin/hadoop-daemon.sh start namenode
```

At this point, HDFS is not fully running: the namenodes and journalnodes are up, but nothing else. The easiest way to get everything running again is to start HDFS as usual, with the helper script. You may notice that this not only starts datanodes, but also the ZooKeeper failover controller (zkfc), which is required for automatic failover to work:

```
# as hdfs on a manager instance
$ $HADOOP_PREFIX/sbin/start-dfs.sh
```

Moving forward, the *start-dfs.sh* script is all you need to start and stop all of the HDFS daemons; once HA is configured, it handles starting journalnodes and zkfc processes.

HDFS is now running in an HA configuration. You can verify this by looking at the web interface for each of the two namenodes. If you are using SSH tunnels to reach the namenodes, note that since HA configuration required specifying private IP addresses for their HTTP addresses, the remote host specified for the tunnels must match those private IP addresses, instead of just "localhost". One of the namenodes should be listed as active, the other as standby. If this is not the case, check to make sure that ZooKeeper is running correctly and that the ZooKeeper failure controller processes are working properly.

Another way to find out which namenode is active is to use the hdfs haadmin command. In the following example output, as expected, one of the namenodes is listed as active, the other as standby:

```
$ hdfs haadmin -getServiceState nn1
active
$ hdfs haadmin -getServiceState nn2
standby
```

YARN HA Configuration

Configuring HA for YARN takes less work than for HDFS. As with configuring HDFS, stop the YARN daemons before configuring for HA. Edit */etc/hadoop/yarn-site.xml* on the *first*, original master instance and make the following changes:

- Configure the yarn.resourcemanager.ha.enabled property with the value "true".

- Configure the yarn.resourcemanager.cluster-id property with your cluster's name. These instructions assume a cluster name of "myfirstcluster"; replace this name with your own in other configuration properties.

- Configure the yarn.resourcemanager.ha.rm-ids property with a list of resource manager IDs. There should be two since there are two manager instances in your cluster. These instructions use "rm1" and "rm2".

- Configure the yarn.resourcemanager.ha.id property with the ID of the resource manager on the instance; for the first manager instance, use "rm1".

- Configure the set of yarn.resourcemanager.hostname properties with the private IP addresses of the manager instances. Eliminate or comment out the single, non-HA yarn.resourcemanager.hostname property.

- Configure the `yarn.resourcemanager.zk-address` property with a list of the private IP addresses and ports for the ZooKeeper instances.
- Configure the `yarn.resourcemanager.ha.automatic-failover.enabled` and `yarn.resourcemanager.ha.automatic-failover.embedded` properties each with the value "true". As one might expect, this enables automatic resource manager failover using the embedded elector:

```
<property>
  <name>yarn.resourcemanager.ha.enabled</name>
  <value>true</value>
</property>
<property>
  <name>yarn.resourcemanager.cluster-id</name>
  <value>myfirstcluster</value>
</property>
<property>
  <name>yarn.resourcemanager.ha.rm-ids</name>
  <value>rm1,rm2</value>
</property>
<property>
  <name>yarn.resourcemanager.ha.id</name>
  <value>rm1</value>
</property>
<property>
  <name>yarn.resourcemanager.hostname.rm1</name>
  <value>203.0.113.101</value>
</property>
<property>
  <name>yarn.resourcemanager.hostname.rm2</name>
  <value>203.0.113.105</value>
</property>
<property>
  <name>yarn.resourcemanager.zk-address</name>
  <value>203.0.113.102:2181,203.0.113.103:2181,203.0.113.104:2181</value>
</property>
<property>
  <name>yarn.resourcemanager.ha.automatic-failover.enabled</name>
  <value>true</value>
</property>
<property>
  <name>yarn.resourcemanager.ha.automatic-failover.embedded</name>
  <value>true</value>
</property>
```

Copy */etc/hadoop/yarn-site.xml* over to the new manager instance and update the `yarn.resourcemanager.ha.id` property with the value "rm2" in that copy. Also copy the file to the worker instances, so that they are aware of HA being in place, but remove the `yarn.resourcemanager.ha.id` property.

YARN is ready to be restarted. Unfortunately, its helper script does not have the ability to start both resource managers, so it's necessary to start one of them directly:

```
# as yarn on one manager
$ $HADOOP_PREFIX/sbin/start-yarn.sh

# as yarn on the other manager
$ $HADOOP_PREFIX/sbin/yarn-daemon.sh start resourcemanager
```

YARN is now running in an HA configuration. You can verify this by looking at the web interface for the active resource manager. The same caveat applies here as with HDFS: SSH tunnels must point their remote ends to the private IP addresses of the resource managers, and not "localhost".

It is possible that only the active resource manager is reachable over a tunnel. The standby resource manager returns to the browser an HTTP redirect to the active resource manager, and if the redirect uses a DNS name that is not resolvable on your local computer, the request will fail. This doesn't indicate a problem with YARN HA.

To find out which resource manager is active, use the yarn rmadmin command. In the following example output, as expected, one of the resource managers is listed as active, the other as standby. If this is not the case, check to make sure that ZooKeeper is running correctly:

```
$ yarn rmadmin -getServiceState rm1
active
$ yarn rmadmin -getServiceState rm2
standby
```

Testing HA

Perhaps the best part of running an HA cluster is testing it out. If everything has been configured correctly, then it should be possible to stop a namenode or resource manager and still have a functional cluster.

The first step is to ensure that the reconfigured cluster is still working. Running the pi example from "Running a Test Job" on page 113 again should succeed as it did before:

```
$ hadoop jar \
> /opt/hadoop/share/hadoop/mapreduce/hadoop-mapreduce-examples-x.y.z.jar \
> pi 10 100
```

If it doesn't work, any of a wide variety of problems could be at the root of the failure. Start by making sure that all of the daemons for HDFS and YARN are running, as well as the ZooKeeper servers. Check their logs in /var/log/hadoop for signs of any errors. See if HDFS on its own is working correctly before looking at YARN, which builds on top of it.

As you have seen, configuring HA is involved, and it is very easy to make a typographical error or forget a critical configuration property. Check over the configuration files, especially *core-site.xml* and *hdfs-site.xml*, on all of the instances to make sure they are correct.

Once you are able to run a job through the HA cluster, it's time to put it through its paces. Here are some things to try:

- Stop the active resource manager. The standby resource manager should automatically take over, and the pi example should run without any trouble:

    ```
    # as yarn on the manager instance with the active resource manager
    $ yarn rmadmin -getServiceState rm1
    active
    $ yarn rmadmin -getServiceState rm2
    standby
    $ $HADOOP_PREFIX/sbin/yarn-daemon.sh stop resourcemanager
    stopping resourcemanager
    $ yarn rmadmin -getServiceState rm2
    active
    ```

- Stop the active namenode. The standby namenode should automatically take over:

    ```
    # as hdfs on the manager instance with the active namenode
    $ hdfs haadmin -getServiceState nn1
    active
    $ hdfs haadmin -getServiceState nn2
    standby
    $ $HADOOP_PREFIX/sbin/hadoop-daemon.sh stop namenode
    stopping namenode
    $ hdfs haadmin -getServiceState nn2
    active
    ```

- Using the console for your cloud provider, stop the manager instance hosting the active namenode and active resource manager. This emulates, to a degree, the unanticipated termination of a manager instance in your cluster, and is much more severe than merely stopping a daemon. Be sure to only *stop* the instance, not terminate it, or else the work you put into its configuration will be lost.

Improving the HA Configuration

The HA cluster set up in this chapter works well enough, but there are additional changes that could be made to it to make it even more robust. Here are some suggestions for further exploration of HA clusters in the cloud.

A Bigger Cluster

It's recommended that the HDFS journalnodes be running on more robust instances than the worker instances; manager instances are a great choice. Allocate a third manager instance with Hadoop installed, and reconfigure the cluster to host journalnodes on the three manager instances.

Even though the second manager instance may be in a separate availability zone from the first manager instance, all of the datanodes are still in that original availability zone. Try allocating additional worker instances in the second availability zone and add them to the cluster, so that it could potentially survive the loss of an entire zone.

The cluster built up in this chapter is only running three ZooKeeper servers. Since ZooKeeper is vital for automatic failover, it is a good idea to run more servers. New servers could be run on the manager instances, or on additional worker instances that also host more datanodes and node managers. It's vital, though, to only run an odd number of ZooKeeper servers, so that a majority can be reached when the quorum makes decisions.

Complete HA

The instructions in this chapter did not cover all HA configurations, including namenode fencing and work-preserving recovery for resource managers. Those additional measures can be added to an HA cluster in the cloud just as they normally would be.

Namenode fencing using SSH implies that passwordless SSH to the "misbehaving" manager instance is possible from the other manager instance, so be sure to configure the fencing method with a private key that is already authorized for that SSH connection. Since either manager instance could be the one being fenced, keys need to be set up for either direction.

A Third Availability Zone?

If two availability zones can be good, wouldn't three be even better? Unfortunately, that is not the case. Both HDFS HA and YARN HA currently only support two namenodes and resource managers, respectively, so it is not possible today to field a third instance of those. You can add more datanodes, node managers, ZooKeeper servers, and more to a third availability zone, and the cluster should still hang together. Expanding too far, however, will not only increase the cost of the cluster but also further hurt performance as data moves across even more availability zones.

Benchmarking HA

Depending on your choices, the HA cluster implemented in this chapter may span two availability zones. Network traffic between availability zones is not as fast as within an availability zone, and so a cluster spread across availability zones can have poorer performance. While it is certainly better to have an HA cluster that continues to function during an availability zone failure, the performance penalty paid during the times when nothing has gone wrong could more than offset the benefit.

The best thing to do, then, is to run some benchmarks on the cluster. If its performance suffers, then either there are configuration tweaks to be made, or perhaps spanning availability zones is not worth it.

The best benchmarks are those that resemble the "real" workloads that will be run on the cluster. Here, benchmarks that ship with the Hadoop distribution are used. While they are general, they are well understood and have been used for years to measure cluster performance. You can use the same methodology with your own benchmarks.

The benchmarks described in this section were run using Hadoop 2.7.2 on an HA cluster just like the one developed in this chapter. The cluster ran on t2.large instances with 30 GB root volumes in AWS, in the us-east-1 region.

MRBench

The main concern about spreading cluster instances across availability zones is the increased time for them to communicate with each other. So, a good benchmark to try out first is MRBench, which focuses on MapReduce performance, and thereby communication between instances, instead of HDFS performance, which focuses on each instance's connection to its block storage.

For the following test results, MRBench was run with these parameters:

- 30 runs
- 3 maps
- 10 input lines

MRBench is a small benchmark, but it can be run many times in succession to get an average runtime:

```
$ hadoop jar \
> /opt/hadoop/share/hadoop/mapreduce/hadoop-mapreduce-client-jobclient-2.7.2.jar \
> mrbench -numRuns 30 -maps 3 -inputLines 10
```

 A long-standing bug in MRBench kept it from correctly obeying its -baseDir option. If you add the option and find that the benchmark tries to write to the /benchmarks/MRBench directory in HDFS anyway, then create the /benchmarks directory in HDFS with global write permissions and try again.

The benchmark was run under the following conditions:

1. The active namenode and resource manager are in the same availability zone (zone 1) as the datanodes, while the standby daemons are in a separate zone (zone 2); the job is run from zone 1.

2. The same as the first condition, except the active namenode is in zone 2.

3. The active namenode and resource manager are in zone 2; the job is run from zone 1.

4. The same as the first condition, except the job is run from zone 2.

5. The same as the first condition, except the standby namenode and resource manager are not running. This is similar to a non-HA cluster, although there are additional daemons running, such as the journalnodes and ZooKeeper servers.

The average job times for the test runs are listed in Table 10-1.

Table 10-1. Average job times for MRBench

Condition	Average time (ms)
1	20863
2	20860
3	20789
4	20858
5	20858

For this set of runs, you can see that the average job time does not vary significantly across the different test conditions.

Terasort

The Terasort benchmark tests both HDFS and MapReduce performance by sorting large amounts of data. It exercises HDFS as well as MapReduce, but it is much larger than MRBench, so it is useful to try it out.

For these runs, `teragen` was first executed to generate 5 GB of test data. Jobs were run under the "ubuntu" user account:

```
# run as the ubuntu user
$ hadoop jar \
> /opt/hadoop/share/hadoop/mapreduce/hadoop-mapreduce-examples-2.7.2.jar \
> teragen 50000000 /user/ubuntu/terasort-input
```

Then, `terasort` was run under the same conditions described for MRBench. In between each run, the previous run's output was deleted from HDFS and removed from the trash:

```
# as ubuntu
$ hdfs dfs -rm -r -skipTrash /user/ubuntu/terasort-output
$ hadoop jar \
> /opt/hadoop/share/hadoop/mapreduce/hadoop-mapreduce-examples-2.7.2.jar \
> terasort /user/ubuntu/terasort-input /user/ubuntu/terasort-output
```

 No tuning was performed on the cluster before running Terasort. Cluster tuning is a critical part of configuring real-world clusters, and the right settings can dramatically improve performance both on benchmarks like Terasort and on real workloads. So, interpret the results here as those of a cluster with an out-of-the-box configuration.

The CPU times for each run are listed in Table 10-2.

Table 10-2. Job times for Terasort

Condition	CPU time spent (ms)
1	416260
2	422250
3	416510
4	414970
5	415460

As was the case with MRBench, there were no significant differences in total CPU time across the test conditions.

Grains of Salt

What do the preceding results mean? Not too much, to be honest. There are a huge number of variables that can affect cluster performance, including:

- The number and instance types of cluster instances
- The version of Hadoop in use and the services running
- Cloud provider configuration, especially networking
- Current load and outages at the cloud provider
- The choice of cloud provider
- The nature of the workload

One conclusion that can be drawn from them is that it is possible to have an HA cluster that performs consistently under different configurations of active, standby, or inactive namenodes and resource managers. Whether this is true for your own clusters can only truly be determined by running tests on them.

One final, important principle to remember is that, while outages in cloud providers are rare, they can and will happen. Your clusters and applications should be structured in such a way that they can withstand those inevitable problems. By configuring high availability to automatically deal with outages, and running tests on your clusters' performance, you can implement a reliable and resilient cloud cluster architecture.

## CHAPTER 11

Relational Data with Apache Hive

So far, the clusters established in the cloud using the instructions in this book have only been capable of running classic MapReduce jobs. Of course, the Hadoop ecosystem offers many other ways to work with large amounts of data, and one of the most attractive is viewing it as relational data that can be queried using Structured Query Language (SQL). For decades before the advent of Hadoop and similar cluster architectures, data analysts worked with large data sets in relational databases, and for many use cases that is still appropriate today. Hadoop components such as Apache Hive allow those with experience in relational databases to transition their skills over to the big data world.

As you might expect, a Hadoop cluster running on a cloud provider can support these components. What's more, the cloud providers have features that the components can take advantage of, and the components themselves have ways to explicitly use cloud provider features to enhance their capabilities.

The content in this chapter starts off with installing Hive into a cloud cluster. The instructions assume that you have a cluster set up in the configuration developed in Chapter 9 but, as usual, you should be able to adapt the instructions to your specific situation.

Planning for Hive in the Cloud

The most important pieces of Hive to consider are the Hive server (HiveServer2[1]), a server process that accepts requests from other Hive clients, and the Hive metastore, which houses information about the objects and structures comprising Hive data-

---

1 In this book, Hive will run using the newer HiveServer2 server process and the Beeline client, as opposed to the older Hive CLI.

bases, tables, and partitions. A typical configuration has at least a single Hive server running on a manager node, alongside the HDFS namenode and YARN resource manager.

The Hive metastore, which maps HDFS data into relational data models, can live either "locally" within Hive itself or "remotely" on a separate database server. The instructions here start with a local metastore, since that is a quick way to check that Hive is working, but then go on to set up a remote metastore fronted by a Hive metastore server.

Installing and Configuring Hive

These instructions are based on the standard Hive installation instructions (*https://cwiki.apache.org/confluence/display/Hive/AdminManual+Installation*) and use the standard binary distribution from Apache. If you already have a tried-and-true set of steps for Hive installation, or if you prefer to use a customized or bundled distribution from a Hadoop vendor, you may be able to adapt these instructions.

Prepare for installing Hive by creating a dedicated account for it, just like those for HDFS and YARN (see Chapter 9). These instructions will assume that the username for the account is "hive" and that the account belongs to the "hadoop" group. SSH key pairs are used for logging in. Since Hive components only run on the manager node, it's not necessary to establish a "hive" account on workers or to have password-less SSH established across the cluster for the account:

```
$ sudo useradd -G hadoop -m -s /bin/bash hive
$ sudo mkdir /home/hive/.ssh
$ sudo cp ~/.ssh/authorized_keys /home/hive/.ssh
$ sudo chmod 700 /home/hive/.ssh
$ sudo chown -R hive /home/hive/.ssh
```

Download a binary Hive distribution from *hive.apache.org* to your manager instance, under the standard login account. In keeping with the use of */opt/hadoop* as the installation location for Hadoop, install Hive to */opt/hive*:

```
$ curl -O http://mirrorhost/path/to/apache-hive-x.y.z-bin.tar.gz
$ sudo tar xzfC apache-hive-x.y.z-bin.tar.gz /opt
$ sudo ln -s /opt/apache-hive-x.y.z-bin /opt/hive
```

 Example commands in this chapter will use the version number x.y.z to stand in for the real Hive version numbers. Unless you have a specific need otherwise, you should simply use the latest stable releases.

Now that Hive is installed, it can be configured. The instructions here are simple ones, just to get Hive going. Again, if you are used to configuring Hive clusters, go ahead and adapt what you normally do.

Fortunately, Hive's default configuration is set up to use a local metastore. Take a look at */opt/hive/conf/hive-default.xml.template* to see what the default configuration entails:

- The `hive.metastore.warehouse.dir` property points to where data that Hive operates on lives in HDFS. Its default value is */usr/hive/warehouse*, which works fine. These instructions will assume that default, but for something different, set this property in *hive-site.xml*.

- The `javax.jdo.option.ConnectionURL` and `javax.jdo.option.Connection DriverName` properties point to a local database running under Apache Derby (*https://db.apache.org/derby/*), a lightweight embedded relational database engine, as the metastore. Initially Hive will use that metastore, but later in this chapter Hive will be reconfigured to use a remote metastore.

- The `hive.metastore.uris` property is empty, which indicates to Hive that the metastore is local.

- The `hive.exec.scratchdir` property points to */tmp/hive*, also in HDFS like the warehouse directory, as Hive's scratch directory. This default works as well, and these instructions use it.

There are still some changes to make, however. Hive does not ship with a copy of */opt/hive/conf/hive-site.xml*, so create it:[2]

```
# as root
% cat > /opt/hive/conf/hive-site.xml
<?xml version="1.0" encoding="UTF-8" standalone="no"?>
<?xml-stylesheet type="text/xsl" href="configuration.xsl"?>
<configuration>
</configuration>
^D
```

These instructions require that impersonation (*https://cwiki.apache.org/confluence/ display/Hive/Setting+Up+HiveServer2#SettingUpHiveServer2-Impersonation*) be disabled in Hive, so that queries run as the user running the Hive server and not the querier. (A more secure installation would leave impersonation on and set permissions appropriately.) To do so, set the `hive.server2.enable.doAs` property in *hive-site.xml* to "false". Hive's instructions also recommend disabling filesystem caches to avoid memory leaks when impersonation is disabled, so also set the

---

2 You can instead copy *hive-default.xml.template* to *hive-site.xml*.

`fs.hdfs.impl.disable.cache` and `fs.file.impl.disable.cache` properties to "true":

```
<property>
  <name>hive.server2.enable.doAs</name>
  <value>false</value>
</property>
<property>
  <name>fs.hdfs.impl.disable.cache</name>
  <value>true</value>
</property>
<property>
  <name>fs.file.impl.disable.cache</name>
  <value>true</value>
</property>
```

As the "hdfs" user on the manager instance, create the required warehouse and scratch directories in HDFS, and set their permissions. Here, the *tmp* directory is opened up because the Hive server must write to it and will fail to start correctly if it cannot:

```
# as hdfs
$ hdfs dfs -mkdir /tmp
$ hdfs dfs -mkdir -p /user/hive/warehouse
$ hdfs dfs -chmod 777 /tmp
$ hdfs dfs -chown -R hive:hadoop /user/hive
```

Hive uses Apache Log4J 2 for its own logging. Since the rest of the Hadoop components in the cluster are logging to *var/log*, Hive should as well. Start by creating a *var/log/hive* directory that the "hive" user can write to:

```
$ sudo mkdir /var/log/hive
$ sudo chgrp hadoop /var/log/hive
$ sudo chmod g+w /var/log/hive
```

Then put the Log4J properties file in place for Hive and edit the value of `property` `.hive.log.dir` to point to *var/log/hive*:

```
$ sudo cp /opt/hive/conf/hive-log4j2.properties.template \
> /opt/hive/conf/hive-log4j2.properties
$ sudo vi /opt/hive/conf/hive-log4j2.properties # and edit property.hive.log.dir
```

Startup

Hive is ready to start. Set up the "hive" account to work with Hive by setting the HIVE_HOME and other environment variables, and by adding Hive's *bin* directory to the PATH:

```
# as hive
$ export HADOOP_HOME=/opt/hadoop
$ export HIVE_HOME=/opt/hive
$ export PATH=${HIVE_HOME}/bin:${HADOOP_HOME}/bin:$PATH
$ export HADOOP_CONF_DIR=/etc/hadoop
```

Use *schematool* to initialize the local metastore, and then start the Hive server:

```
# as hive
$ $HIVE_HOME/bin/schematool -dbType derby -initSchema
$ $HIVE_HOME/bin/hiveserver2 &
```

 If, while working with Hive, the server fails to start and logs errors saying that "direct SQL is disabled," it is because you did not start it from the same directory in which it was first started, and it cannot locate the local metastore. Find the *metastore_db* directory and start the Hive server from there.

As was the case with the HDFS namenode and YARN resource manager, you can check on the status of the Hive server through its web interface, but security rules governing the manager instance block access from the outside to the necessary port. Establish an SSH tunnel (see "SSH Tunneling" on page 112 for a refresher) from the local port 10002 to the same port on your manager instance:

```
$ ssh -i /path/to/cloud_provider_key.pem -n -N \
> -L 10002:localhost:10002 userid@manager.cloud-provider.example &
```

Now, in your browser, navigate to *http://localhost:10002* to see your Hive server ready for work.

Running Some Test Hive Queries

To make sure Hive is working properly, you can run some basic queries using the Beeline CLI. For now, run it from the "hive" account on the manager instance, since its environment is already set up for Hive. You can also try these steps from a separate account.

```
$ beeline -u jdbc:hive2://localhost:10000
```

Make a simple table and run some queries on it. This example creates a test table with a single column, inserts a row, and runs some SELECT queries. You should see evidence of Hive issuing MapReduce jobs, starting with the first SELECT query:

```
CREATE TABLE test (value INT)
ROW FORMAT DELIMITED
FIELDS TERMINATED BY '\t'
STORED AS TEXTFILE;

SELECT COUNT(*) from test;

INSERT INTO test VALUES (123);

SELECT * FROM test;

!quit
```

For something a little more interesting, try working with the MovieLens database using the instructions in Apache Hive documentation (*https://cwiki.apache.org/conflu ence/display/Hive/GettingStarted#GettingStarted-MovieLensUserRatings*).[3] The data-sets are distributed as ZIP files, so to extract them you will need the *unzip* utility; use your operating system's package manager to install it.

If the data load and count query work, you should see a correct result for the row count:

```
SELECT COUNT(*) FROM u_data;
...
OK
+---------+--+
|   c0    |
+---------+--+
| 100000  |
+---------+--+
```

At this point, Hive is working on your cluster and running MapReduce jobs in the cloud to satisfy queries. The next step, needed for a more robust Hive installation, is to switch to a remote metastore. Fortunately, your cloud provider can help you with setting up a database server where the metastore can live.

Switching to a Remote Metastore

The result of the previous instructions is a Hive server using a local metastore. To switch to a remote metastore, begin by stopping the Hive server and cleaning out the warehouse in HDFS. This will get Hive back into an empty state:

---

3 The MovieLens database contains ratings of movies entered by users of the MovieLens website. For full details, visit the MovieLens database (*https://grouplens.org/datasets/movielens*).

```
# as hive
$ kill hive-server-pid
# as hdfs
$ hdfs dfs -rm -r /user/hive/warehouse
$ hdfs dfs -mkdir -p /user/hive/warehouse
$ hdfs dfs -chown -R hive:hadoop /user/hive
```

A remote metastore requires a database server. The instance hosting the database should be separate from any of the cluster instances, so that it can be managed independently. While you can launch a new instance and manually install a database server, it's much easier to use your cloud provider's database hosting features. See "Cloud Relational Databases" on page 55 for an overview; here is a quick rundown:

- Under AWS, you can use RDS to stand up a database server, choosing from several supported engines. RDS handles backups, availability, and patching automatically.

- Under Google Cloud Platform, you can use Google Cloud SQL to stand up a MySQL database server. The server can be configured with automatic backups, high availability, and automatic failover.

- Under Azure, you can use Azure SQL database to stand up a Microsoft SQL Server database server, or Azure Database for MySQL or Azure Database for PostgreSQL to stand up one of those types of database server. The server is automatically backed up across data centers and can be explicitly replicated.

These instructions cover setting up a MySQL database server to host the remote metastore, since MySQL is supported across all three cloud providers. There are no special requirements on the database server, so you can follow your provider's standard instructions. The steps here work with AWS RDS, but even if you use Google Cloud Platform or Azure, it is worth looking through them to guide you.

It may be tempting to use an existing, on-prem database server for the remote metastore. While it is possible, it is a very bad idea. Not only will performance be much worse between the server and the rest of your cluster, but you will be charged for data moving into and out of the cloud provider infrastructure. See Chapter 13 and Chapter 14 for more about how the choices in where you position cluster components affects price and performance.

In the AWS console dashboard, select the RDS service. Be sure to select the same region where your cluster resides as well. Just like when working with EC2, the RDS dashboard presents a menu on the lefthand side of the page, as shown in Figure 11-1. Select Instances in the menu.

Figure 11-1. RDS dashboard

The main area of the page will show that you have no RDS instances. Click the Launch Instance button to start the process of creating a new RDS instance. Your first choice is which engine to use; pick the MySQL tab from the available options, as shown in Figure 11-2, and click Select for MySQL. You may be presented with a choice of using Amazon Aurora, an in-house, compatible variant of MySQL; these instructions stick with MySQL itself.

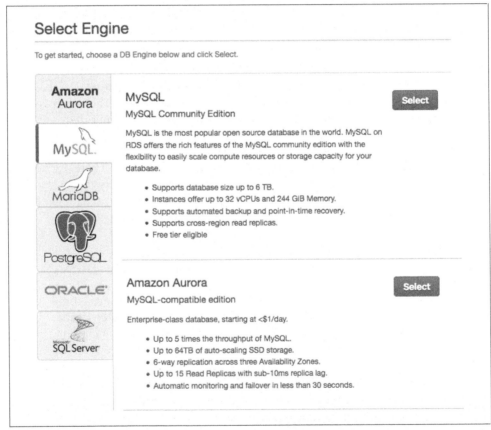

Figure 11-2. RDS engines

Your next decision is whether to set up a production-ready database or one suited for development and testing. See Figure 11-3 for an example of this prompt. Since the cluster is being used for testing and exploration, select Dev/Test.

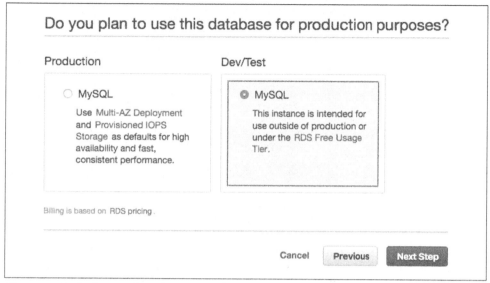

Figure 11-3. A choice of production or development database

The next page, part of which is shown in Figure 11-4, presents options for the specifications of the new RDS instance:

- Select the latest available version of MySQL for the Database Engine Version.
- The DB instance class may be the smallest available, since this is an exploratory installation of the remote metastore. Feel free to pick a larger instance if you plan to do more work in Hive. Similarly, a multizone deployment isn't necessary.
- The metastore does not require a lot of space, so the maximum permitted under the AWS Free Tier should be more than enough.

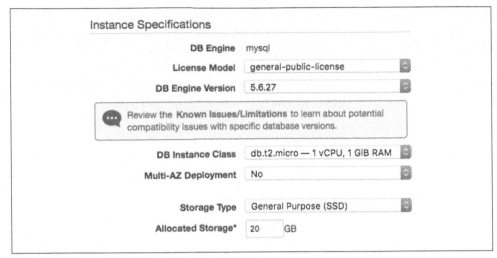

Figure 11-4. RDS instance specifications

Below the instance specifications is a separate form, shown in Figure 11-5, for naming the instance and providing its root username and password. Be sure to record your choices here, so that you can connect to it to create the metastore database.

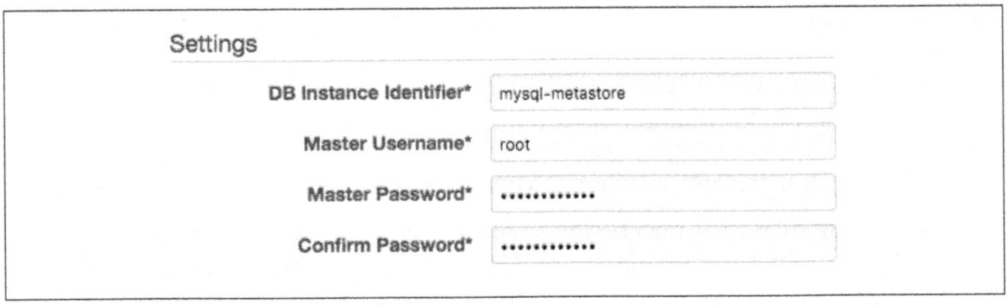

Figure 11-5. RDS instance settings

Next, describe where the new instance will reside in your network. Use the same VPC, subnet, and availability zone as your manager instance for the best performance and lowest cost. Also select the same security group that your cluster belongs to, so that communications between the metastore and the cluster are unimpeded. The instance does not need to be publicly accessible, because Hive is running inside the cloud provider as well. Figure 11-6 shows the network and security form filled out with these settings.

Network & Security   ⟳

VPC*	Default VPC (vpc-⬛⬛⬛⬛) ⬍
Subnet Group	default ⬍
Publicly Accessible	No ⬍
Availability Zone	us-east-1c ⬍
VPC Security Group(s)	Create new Security Group basic-security (VPC) default (VPC) example (VPC)

Figure 11-6. RDS instance network and security settings

The remaining items on the page can be left as they are. RDS can create an initial database, but to show more about how the remote metastore is created and managed, these instructions opt not to use that feature. Click the Launch DB Instance button to complete this last step. When RDS reports that the instance is being created, click View Your DB Instances to return to the list of instances.

Once the database server is available, determine its hostname or IP address.[4] The next step is to create the metastore database; Hive ships with a MySQL script for this purpose.

 The Hive schematool can be used as an alternative way to establish the metastore database; consult the Hive documentation (*https:// cwiki.apache.org/confluence/display/Hive/Hive+Schema+Tool*) for details.

To connect to the database server, install the MySQL client on the manager instance that hosts the Hive server, using the operating system's package manager. Then, run the SQL script included with the Hive distribution to create the metastore database:

```
$ cd /opt/hive/scripts/metastore/upgrade/mysql
# use chosen root username here
$ mysql -h mysql-hostname.cloud-provider.example -u root -p
Enter password: # enter chosen root password here
mysql> create database metastore;
mysql> use metastore;
mysql> source
/opt/hive/scripts/metastore/upgrade/mysql/hive-schema-x.y.z.mysql.sql;
# many queries are run
```

---

4 RDS does not divulge IP addresses for database servers, so use the assigned hostname.

```
mysql> create user 'hive'@'%' identified by 'hive';
mysql> grant all privileges on metastore.* to 'hive'@'%';
mysql> \q
```

The preceding MySQL commands create a "hive" user inside MySQL with access to the metastore database. Change the password in the create user command if desired. The new user can log in from any remote address, which is acceptable for testing and when security rules block access from most sources; in a production setting, you may wish to restrict access to a small range of remote addresses as an extra line of defense.

 The cd command is necessary because the SQL script that is sourced itself sources another script in the current directory. This limitation was fixed in issue HIVE-6559 (*https://issues.apache.org/ jira/browse/HIVE-6559*) but appears to have regressed.

As an extra check, you can reconnect to the database server as the "hive" user and see that the metastore tables have been created:

```
$ mysql -h mysql-hostname.cloud-provider.example -u hive -p
Enter password:
mysql> use metastore;
mysql> show tables;
# list of tables appears
mysql> \q
```

Next, Hive must be reconfigured to use the new database server for the metastore. Edit */opt/hive/conf/hive-site.xml* and make the following additions:

- Add the javax.jdo.option.ConnectionURL property, set to the JDBC URL of the metastore database.

- Add the javax.jdo.option.ConnectionDriverName property, set to "com.mysql.jdbc.Driver".

- Add the javax.jdo.option.ConnectionUserName and javax.jdo.option .ConnectionPassword properties with the username and password for the database user added while creating the metastore database.

- Add the hive.metastore.uris property with a Thrift URI for the manager instance that hosts the Hive server. This same instance will also host the metastore server:

```
<property>
  <name>javax.jdo.option.ConnectionURL</name>
  <value>jdbc:mysql://mysql-hostname.cloud-provider.example/
        metastore</value>
</property>
<property>
```

```
  <name>javax.jdo.option.ConnectionDriverName</name>
  <value>com.mysql.jdbc.Driver</value>
</property>
<property>
  <name>javax.jdo.option.ConnectionUserName</name>
  <value>hive</value>
</property>
<property>
  <name>javax.jdo.option.ConnectionPassword</name>
  <value>hive</value>
</property>
<property>
  <name>hive.metastore.uris</name>
  <value>thrift://203.0.113.101:9083</value>
</property>
```

Hive needs access to the MySQL JDBC driver in order to communicate with the remote metastore database server. Either install the driver JAR file, called Connector/J, using the manager instance's operating system package manager, or download a copy from the official download page (*http://dev.mysql.com/downloads/connector/j/*). Copy the JAR file to */opt/hive/lib/mysql-connector-java.jar*.

Hive is now configured for a remote metastore. Start the Hive metastore server, and then the Hive server once more. Use the same port for the metastore server that is configured in *hive-site.xml*, and direct its log to */var/log/hive* alongside the Hive server's log:

```
# as hive
$ $HIVE_HOME/bin/hive --service metastore -p 9083 > /var/log/hive/metastore.log &
# wait for the metastore server to come up
$ $HIVE_HOME/bin/hiveserver2 &
```

Once the servers are up, you can try the same tests that were performed for the local metastore. This time, Hive is reaching out to the remote metastore on the database server maintained by the cloud provider, with all the benefits of performance and reliability that come along with it.

The Remote Metastore and Stopped Clusters

If you stop your cluster instances, you may also wish to turn off the database server hosting the remote metastore. Google Cloud SQL allows you to stop a database instance, but if you are using RDS or Azure SQL, then you do not have the option to just stop a database server; you can only terminate it. In that case, go ahead and terminate the instance, but take one last snapshot or backup of the server contents. When it comes time to start the cluster again, create a new database instance that restores from the final snapshot. You may need to reconfigure Hive if the new database server's hostname or IP address differs from the old one's.

Hive Control Scripts

Hive does not ship with convenience scripts for starting and stopping its servers. See Example A-2 and Example A-3 for some simple ones that should work well, at least as starting points.

Hive on S3

So far, Hive has operated on data that was explicitly loaded into HDFS. The data is distributed across datanodes in the cluster, and metadata about how it can be interpreted as relational data tables is kept in a remote database server; all of the instances are running in the cloud. This is a common and reasonable way of working with Hive data. But you can go further, specifically in how the data is stored.

Cloud providers have object storage solutions, as described in "Object Storage" on page 49. Instead of pulling data into HDFS before analyzing it, you can keep the data in object storage and reference it there as Hive external tables.

This section describes how to configure Hive to work with data on the AWS object storage service, S3.

Configuring the S3 Filesystem

The first step in working with S3 under Hadoop is to configure the cluster to use a Hadoop S3 filesystem. When such a filesystem is enabled, you can address objects and folders in S3 like files and directories in HDFS. S3 cannot act exactly like a filesystem, due to its weaker guarantees on consistency, but it can work as one in many situations, including as a source for file-like data.

Why Not Use S3 for Everything?

If you can access data in S3 like a Hadoop filesystem, you may wonder why you shouldn't just use S3 for all file storage, forgoing HDFS completely.

The primary reason is that S3 does not adhere to POSIX-like constraints on how a filesystem should behave. Newly created files may not be immediately visible after creation, and deleted files may still be available for some time after deletion. These behaviors and others are why S3, and other object stores like it, are called *eventually consistent*. Because of the delays in some changes made in S3, it is not suitable for storing transient or highly variable data, like that saved in the middle of a workflow. Its strengths include storage of read-only data and archival use.

An attempt to compensate for S3's eventual consistency, called *S3Guard*, is underway at the time of this writing. It pairs up an external, consistent database with S3 access

---

> to improve consistency overall. See the Hadoop issue tracking its development at "HADOOP-13345" (*https://issues.apache.org/jira/browse/HADOOP-13345*).

Over time, Hadoop has supported three separate S3 filesystem implementations: the original S3 block filesystem or "s3", the S3 native filesystem or "s3n", and the latest "s3a" filesystem. The instructions here focus on s3a, since s3 has already been removed from Hadoop and s3n is deprecated.

The s3a filesystem implementation ships with Hadoop but is not active by default.[5] Activating it involves adding the library directory where the implementation and supporting JAR files reside to the Hadoop classpath.

On each cluster instance, edit */etc/hadoop/hadoop-env.sh* and add the following line, which places the necessary directory into the Hadoop classpath:

```
export HADOOP_CLASSPATH=$HADOOP_CLASSPATH:$HADOOP_HOME/share/hadoop/tools/lib/*
```

Then, again on each cluster instance, edit */etc/hadoop/mapred-site.xml* and add the `mapreduce.application.classpath` property. This property controls the classpath available to MapReduce tasks, which is independent from the Hadoop classpath. The value shown in the following code includes the default classpath as well as the directory containing the s3a filesystem implementation. (The following XML is edited for fit.)

```
<property>
  <name>mapreduce.application.classpath</name>
  <value>$HADOOP_MAPRED_HOME/share/hadoop/mapreduce/*,
        $HADOOP_MAPRED_HOME/share/hadoop/mapreduce/lib/*,
        $HADOOP_MAPRED_HOME/share/hadoop/tools/lib/*</value>
</property>
```

These new settings do not take effect until HDFS and YARN are restarted, but there are more settings to add.

Adding Data to S3

One way to check that the s3a filesystem is working properly, once it is fully configured, is to place some data into S3 and then attempt to look at it using the HDFS client. Since you are already familiar with the MovieLens data, that data can work for this test.

In the AWS console dashboard, select the S3 service. The welcome page for S3 appears, with a button for creating your first bucket. Click that button, and use the dialog box shown in Figure 11-7 to name your bucket. Remember that the bucket

---

5 As of Hadoop 2.7.

name is globally unique, so more obvious names are most likely already taken. Select the region where your cluster resides, and then click Create to create the bucket.

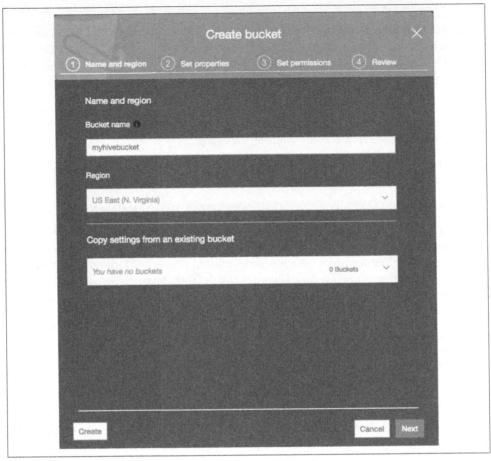

Figure 11-7. Creating an S3 bucket

Remember the region that you chose for your bucket, as that may influence how you must configure Hadoop later on.

Select the bucket from the S3 dashboard. The bucket is currently empty, so add a folder by clicking the Create Folder button. Enter the name "ml-100k" for the folder, and it will be created and displayed as shown in Figure 11-8.

Figure 11-8. A folder in an S3 bucket

Now the file containing the MovieLens data can be uploaded. Download the ZIP file containing the data to your local computer and unzip it. The file "u.data" in the contents contains the data set, and it's that file that should be uploaded to S3.

Back in the S3 console, select the folder you just created to navigate into it, and then click the Upload button. In the upload dialog, click the Add Files button, and navigate to the "u.data" file on your local computer and select it for addition. Then click the Upload button in the dialog to begin the file upload. It should complete in a few seconds, and the file should appear in the bucket as shown in Figure 11-9.

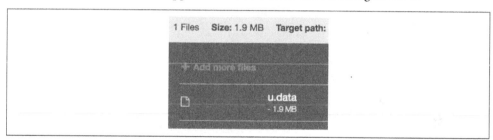

Figure 11-9. A file uploaded to an S3 bucket

The data is now available in S3. However, attempts to look at it from Hadoop at this point will fail, because public access to the S3 bucket contents is not established. Additional configuration is necessary for Hadoop to be able to authenticate to AWS using an account with permissions to look into S3.

Configuring S3 Authentication

The s3a filesystem implementation can retrieve credentials for S3 from many different locations, including environment variables, properties in *core-site.xml*, Hadoop's own credential providers, and the instance profile[6] associated with the EC2 instances where Hadoop runs. Here, properties in *core-site.xml* are used.

The *core-site.xml* properties themselves support a few different means of authentication, but the simplest is to use a typical AWS access key and secret key pair. The keys associate Hadoop with a user under your AWS account, and when that user has permissions to work with S3, Hadoop is able to work with S3.

A user is needed for AWS keys, so make one using the Identity and Access Management (IAM) service, which is available from the AWS console. Select Users from the menu on the left side of the page, and click the Add User button above the empty user list. In the form that appears, shown in Figure 11-10, provide your choice of username and select the Programmatic access checkbox, which triggers the creation of keys. Click the Next: Permissions button to pick what the new user can do.

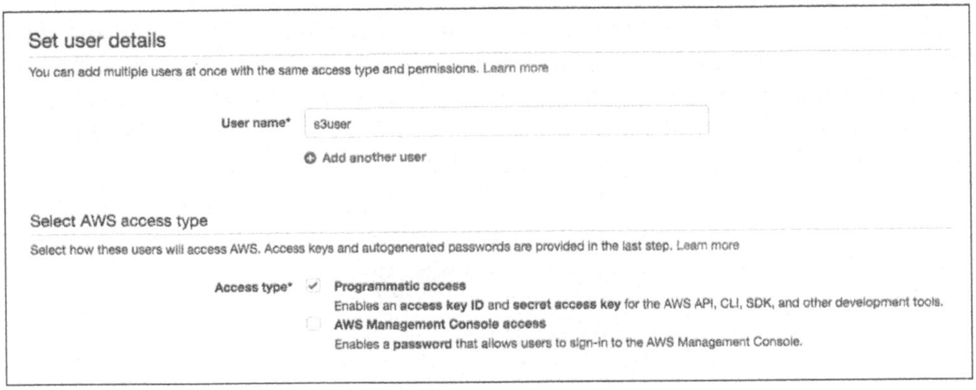

Set user details

You can add multiple users at once with the same access type and permissions. Learn more

User name*   s3user

⊕ Add another user

Select AWS access type

Select how these users will access AWS. Access keys and autogenerated passwords are provided in the last step. Learn more

Access type*   ✓   **Programmatic access**
Enables an **access key ID** and **secret access key** for the AWS API, CLI, SDK, and other development tools.
☐   **AWS Management Console access**
Enables a **password** that allows users to sign-in to the AWS Management Console.

Figure 11-10. Creating a new user in IAM

From the choices in the next form, as shown in Figure 11-11, select "Attach existing policies directly," since there are no groups or users existing yet.

---

6 An instance profile for an EC2 instance links to a role in AWS. Processes running on the instance automatically gain the permissions associated with the role.

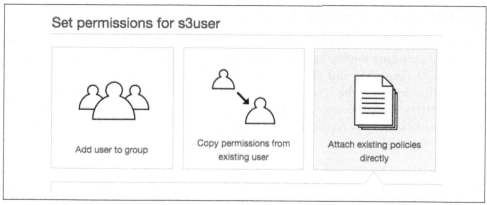

Figure 11-11. Permission choices for a new IAM user

Below these choices, a list of security policies appears. Each policy can grant a set of permissions to the new user. Look for the policy named "AmazonS3FullAccess," as shown in Figure 11-12, and check its checkbox.[7] Click the Next: Review button to check over the settings for the new user, and then "Create user" to create it.

Figure 11-12. An S3 policy selected for a new IAM user

The next page should display a success message along with a table containing the keys for the new user. Record both key values and then click the Close button. This is the only time that AWS will tell you the secret access key, so do not miss the opportunity to save it; if you do, then you must delete the user and start again.

Keys in hand, edit */etc/hadoop/core-site.xml* on each cluster instance and add the `fs.s3a.access.key` and `fs.s3a.secret.key` properties. (Obviously, the keys in the following XML have been masked out.)

```
<property>
  <name>fs.s3a.access.key</name>
  <value>AKIAXXXXXXXXXXXXXXXX</value>
</property>
<property>
  <name>fs.s3a.secret.key</name>
  <value>XXXXXXXXXXXXXXXXXXXXXXXXXXXXXXXXXXXXXXXXX</value>
</property>
```

---

7 For even more security, choose "AmazonS3ReadOnlyAccess." However, this will prohibit Hadoop writing to S3 in the future.

Configuring the S3 Endpoint

If your S3 bucket resides in a region that was added to AWS after January 30, 2014, then calls accessing the bucket must be authenticated with the AWS Signature Version 4 (V4) algorithm, and not with the older Signature Version 2 (V2) algorithm. Usually this detail can be ignored, since the AWS SDK handles the details for you, but it matters for S3 access. The default endpoint for S3 is *s3.amazonaws.com*; this endpoint works for any region under V2, but under V4 it only works for the default us-east-1 region.

So, if your bucket is in a V4-only region, edit */etc/hadoop/core-site.xml* on each cluster instance and add the `fs.s3a.endpoint` property with the unique S3 endpoint for the region. For example, if you are using the Frankfurt region eu-central-1, add the following:

```
<property>
  <name>fs.s3a.endpoint</name>
  <value>s3.eu-central-1.amazonaws.com</value>
</property>
```

Now that S3 authentication and the correct S3 endpoint are in place, go ahead and restart HDFS and YARN. This will activate the s3a filesystem implementation with authentication in place using the new user account. Once HDFS is ready, you can try to look into S3 using the HDFS client. Pass a URL that follows the s3a scheme, starting with the bucket and proceeding down through the folders:

```
$ hdfs dfs -ls s3a://myhivebucket/ml-100k
Found 1 items
-rw-rw-rw-   1    1979173 2017-01-01 12:34 s3a://myhivebucket/ml-100k/u.data
$ hdfs dfs -tail s3a://myhivebucket/ml-100k/u.data
# last 1K of file
```

If s3a listings do not work, make sure that the AWS keys were entered correctly, that the updated classpaths are correct, and that you have set the S3 endpoint if required for your region.

External Table in S3

All of the prerequisites are in place for Hive to work with data in S3. Return to the Beeline client and create a new table for the MovieLens data loaded into the new bucket. This table is an external table, indicating that the data should be left in its original location and not copied into HDFS:

```
CREATE EXTERNAL TABLE u_data_s3 (
    userid INT,
    movieid INT,
    rating INT,
    unixtime STRING)
ROW FORMAT DELIMITED
```

```
FIELDS TERMINATED BY '\t'
LOCATION 's3a://myhivebucket/ml-100k/';
```

Notice that the s3a URL for the folder containing the data is provided as the location for the table. You should now be able to work with the data just as when it was available in HDFS:

```
SELECT COUNT(*) FROM u_data;
...
OK
+----------+--+
|   c0    |
+----------+--+
| 100000  |
+----------+--+
```

What About Google Cloud Platform and Azure?

If you are using Google Cloud Platform, you can use the Google Cloud Storage Connector to link up Hadoop and Google Cloud Storage. Like the s3a filesystem implementation, the connector establishes a filesystem, usually named "gs", that is backed by Google Cloud Storage. It is implemented by a JAR that must be placed into the necessary classpaths, and it authenticates via the service account associated with the cluster's GCE instances. Consult Google Cloud Platform documentation for details on installation and configuration.

Hadoop ships with an implementation for a "wasb" filesystem backed by Azure Blob Storage. It is activated in a similar fashion to the s3a filesystem, by including it in the necessary classpaths and configuring authentication using an access key. The implementation supports both block blobs and page blobs. Consult the Hadoop documentation for the hadoop-azure module for more information.

An even better option for Azure is to use the "adl" Azure Data Lake Store (ADLS) Hadoop filesystem implementation. ADLS has stronger consistency guarantees than Azure Blob Storage or even S3, so it should better support scenarios where updates occur.

Once any of these provider-specific filesystems are in place and working, external Hive tables should work from locations containing their URLs.

A Step Toward Transient Clusters

It is certainly convenient to be able to work with relational data directly from cloud provider object storage services, but there is another, greater motivation for doing so. With data given a safe home on a storage service, you do not need to worry about the Hadoop cluster that works with it; it no longer needs to store the data for the long term. If the cluster should be lost, due to problems in the cloud provider or even a mistake made by administrators, the data remains. In this chapter, you've worked with reading data stored in S3, but of course data can be written to S3 too.

When you begin to think of cloud storage as the durable, available home for important cluster data, then you can understand how the clusters themselves do not need to live for a long time. To work with the data, you can spin up a cluster, query the data from S3, write final results back to S3, and then destroy the cluster. This has the potential to save money and make more efficient use of cloud provider resources. With the right automation, you can thereby support working with *transient* clusters.

"Long-Running or Transient?" on page 215 goes into greater detail about using transient clusters, but this chapter has given you initial exposure to the idea.

A Different Means of Computation

While working with Hive, you may have noticed some warnings like this:

```
WARNING: Hive-on-MR is deprecated in Hive 2 and may not be available in the
future versions. Consider using a different execution engine (i.e. tez, spark)
or using Hive 1.X releases.
```

So far, the steps in this book for setting up a Hadoop cluster have only covered setting up YARN, so that is all that is available for conducting MapReduce jobs to satisfy Hive queries. As the warnings suggest, different providers for Hive computation are supported.

The next chapter covers adding one of those providers, Spark, to your cloud cluster. Not only will Spark be configured as another execution engine for Hive, but it will also be used for processing streaming data, which is one of its more powerful capabilities.

## CHAPTER 12

Streaming in the Cloud with Apache Spark

The venerable MapReduce computation framework, part of Apache Hadoop from the beginning, is falling out of favor now that newer and more flexible solutions are available. The original MapReduce implementation of job trackers and task trackers is obsoleted by YARN, which scales better and can support distributed work beyond MapReduce jobs.

One of the most popular alternatives to MapReduce is Apache Spark, which supports a wide variety of algorithms including mapping and reducing, and also manages the chaining of the distributed computations together. Much like Hive caters to users who are familiar with relational data, Spark caters to developers who can focus more on the algorithmic features of the jobs they write, so they need not try to hammer them into the MapReduce mold.

The content in this chapter starts off with installing Spark in a cloud cluster. The instructions assume that you have a cluster set up in the configuration developed in Chapter 9 but, as usual, you should be able to adapt the instructions to your specific situation. Later on, the instructions cover running Hive on Spark, and it's expected that your cluster is set up for Hive as described in Chapter 11.

Planning for Spark in the Cloud

Spark running in a cluster can use any of several execution engines, including its own "standalone" manager and worker processes that can run in an integrated fashion with a Hadoop cluster. However, Spark can use YARN for running jobs, which is already available in your cluster. By configuring *Spark on YARN*, you can get running more quickly and take advantage of the resiliency already present in the YARN framework.

Installing and Configuring Spark

These instructions are based on the standard Spark download (*http://spark.apache.org/downloads.html*) and configuration (*http://spark.apache.org/docs/latest/running-on-yarn.html*) instructions and use the standard binary distribution from Apache. If you already have a tried-and-true set of steps for Spark installation, or if you prefer to use a customized or bundled distribution from a Hadoop vendor, you may be able to adapt these instructions.

Prepare for installing Spark by creating a dedicated account for it,[1] just like those for HDFS and YARN (see Chapter 9). These instructions will assume that the username for the account is "spark" and that the account belongs to the "hadoop" group. SSH key pairs are used for logging in. Since Spark will run jobs on YARN, which is already installed in the cluster, it's not necessary to establish a "spark" account on workers or to have passwordless SSH established across the cluster for the account:

```
$ sudo useradd -G hadoop -m -s /bin/bash spark
$ sudo mkdir /home/spark/.ssh
$ sudo cp ~/.ssh/authorized_keys /home/spark/.ssh
$ sudo chmod 700 /home/spark/.ssh
$ sudo chown -R spark /home/spark/.ssh
```

Download a binary Spark distribution from *spark.apache.org* to your manager instance, under the standard login account. You can choose a prebuilt package that matches your specific Hadoop version, or a package that needs to be configured for a "user-provided" Hadoop; these instructions use the latter to be more widely applicable. In keeping with the use of */opt/hadoop* as the installation location for Hadoop, install Spark to */opt/spark*:

```
$ curl -O http://mirrorhost/path/to/spark-x.y.z-bin-without-hadoop.tar.gz
$ sudo tar xzfC spark-x.y.z-bin-without-hadoop.tar.gz /opt
$ sudo ln -s /opt/spark-x.y.z-bin-without-hadoop /opt/spark
```

If you plan to run Hive on Spark and are using a version of Hive before 2.2.0, then you will need to install a 1.x version of Spark. You may also install a 2.x version of Spark in a separate directory to benefit from its improvements elsewhere, but it is not compatible with Hive before version 2.2.0.

---

1 A dedicated account is not truly needed for Spark on YARN, but it provides better separation of Spark jobs from other cluster work.

Example commands in this chapter will use the version number x.y.z to stand in for the real Spark version numbers. Unless you have a specific need otherwise, you should simply use the latest stable releases.

Now that Spark is installed, it can be configured. The instructions here are simple ones, just to get Spark going. Again, if you are used to configuring Spark clusters, go ahead and adapt what you normally do.

Create the file */opt/spark/conf/spark-env.sh*; the easiest way is to copy the empty template file for it:

```
$ sudo cp /opt/spark/conf/spark-env.sh.template /opt/spark/conf/spark-env.sh
```

Then, define the `HADOOP_CONF_DIR` environment variable, pointing to */etc/hadoop*, so that Spark can find the cluster's configuration files. If you installed the Spark package for user-provided Hadoop, then also define the `SPARK_DIST_CLASSPATH` environment variable so that Spark can locate Hadoop binaries:

```
export HADOOP_CONF_DIR=/etc/hadoop
export SPARK_DIST_CLASSPATH=$(/opt/hadoop/bin/hadoop classpath)
```

This is a good checkpoint to make sure that Spark is configured correctly, before continuing to connect it to YARN. Try running the "SparkPi" example job locally:

```
# as spark
$ cd /opt/spark
$ ./bin/run-example SparkPi 10
```

In the midst of a lot of informative logging, you should see a result like this:

```
Pi is roughly 3.1421711421711422
```

It is not much more work to get Spark jobs running on YARN; Spark is already configured with Hadoop's configuration directory. To make it easier to find the output from Spark jobs, enable log aggregation in YARN; this causes logs from each node manager involved in a job to be gathered and stored in HDFS for later retrieval. To enable log aggregation, edit */etc/hadoop/yarn-site.xml* on each cluster instance and add the `yarn.log-aggregation-enable` configuration property, set to true:

```
<property>
  <name>yarn.log-aggregation-enable</name>
  <value>true</value>
</property>
```

Startup

Since Spark is set up to run on YARN, there are no Spark components to start. Do ensure that HDFS and YARN are running, though. If YARN had been running before enabling log aggregation, restart it.

Running Some Test Jobs

You can run Spark jobs under any account, and so for the account you choose, create a home directory in HDFS, using the hdfs account. These instructions assume that the new "spark" user account is used for running Spark jobs:

```
# as hdfs
$ hdfs dfs -mkdir -p /user/spark
$ hdfs dfs -chown spark /user/spark
```

The example job can now be run again, this time using YARN instead of local execution. The command for running the example differs based on the Spark version:

```
# as spark
$ cd /opt/spark
# for Spark 2.x
$ ./bin/spark-submit --class org.apache.spark.examples.SparkPi --master yarn \
> --deploy-mode cluster examples/jars/spark-examples_2.11-x.y.z.jar 10
# for Spark 1.x
$ ./bin/spark-submit --class org.apache.spark.examples.SparkPi --master yarn \
> --deploy-mode cluster lib/spark-examples-x.y.z-hadoop2.2.0.jar 10
```

You should see the Spark job submitted to YARN and visible in the resource manager web interface. After a short runtime and a good amount of local output describing the progress of the job, you should see a report that the job was successful. The application master IP address and hostname in the tracking URL will use the private IP address of the YARN resource manager, and the timestamps and application IDs will reflect the time that the job was executed:

```
16/12/27 13:59:13 INFO yarn.Client: Application report for application_
1482846864508_0002 (state: FINISHED)
16/12/27 13:59:13 INFO yarn.Client:
    client token: N/A
    diagnostics: N/A
    ApplicationMaster host: 203.0.113.101
    ApplicationMaster RPC port: 0
    queue: default
    start time: 1482847140363
    final status: SUCCEEDED
    tracking URL
    : http://ip-203-0-113-101.ec2.internal:8088/proxy/application_
    1482846864508_0002/
    user: spark
```

There is no indication of the job output, because that is echoed to standard output by one of the Spark containers that executed the job. The result can be found in the aggregated log results for the job, which can be viewed using the yarn logs command. Find the application ID for the Spark job in the output from running it, or consult the resource manager web UI:

```
# as spark
$ $HADOOP_PREFIX/bin/yarn logs -applicationId application_1482846864508_0002 | \
> less
```

The standard error and standard output logs for each container are listed, and one of those standard output logs should contain the result:

```
Pi is roughly 3.1417631417631418
```

Congratulations, your Hadoop cluster running in the cloud now supports Spark jobs! You should feel free to try running more example Spark jobs or other analyses through it.

Configuring Hive on Spark

Hive queries are converted under the hood into jobs to be run on the underlying cluster, and by default those are ordinary MapReduce jobs. You can configure a different "execution engine" if one is available, and now that Spark is installed in your cluster, you can use it instead of MapReduce jobs on YARN for satisfying Hive queries.

There is documentation (*https://cwiki.apache.org/confluence/display/Hive/Hive+on +Spark%3A+Getting+Started*) on this subject, but as usual, the steps here attempt to represent the minimum needed to get to a working state.

Add Spark Libraries to Hive

Hive ships with the ability to run a Spark driver, but it does not ship with the necessary Spark code. That must be installed by you. For Spark versions before 2.0, a single "assembly" JAR is all that is required:

```
$ sudo cp /opt/spark/lib/spark-assembly-*.jar /opt/hive/lib/
```

Starting with Spark version 2.0, there is no longer an assembly JAR, but several smaller JARs take its place:

```
$ sudo cp /opt/spark/jars/scala-library-*.jar /opt/hive/lib/
$ sudo cp /opt/spark/jars/spark-core_*.jar /opt/hive/lib/
$ sudo cp /opt/spark/jars/spark-network-common_*.jar /opt/hive/lib/
```

Be sure to use a version of Spark that is compatible with the version of Hive.

Configure Hive for Spark

Edit */opt/hive/conf/hive-site.xml* and make the following changes:

- Configure the `spark.master` property with the value "yarn". This indicates that Spark should itself rely on YARN for compute capability, as opposed to its own standalone implementation, for example.

- Configure the `spark.home` property to point to the Spark installation that is compatible with Hive; for example, */opt/spark*.

- Optionally, configure the `hive.spark.job.monitor.timeout` property with a custom timeout, in seconds, larger than the default of 60. When using a small, untuned test cluster, it may take longer than 60 seconds for some Hive queries to be serviced by Spark, in particular, the first query in each session. You may leave this property out and add it later if you find that jobs submitted by Hive are timing out after just over a minute:

```
<property>
  <name>spark.master</name>
  <value>yarn</value>
</property>
<property>
  <name>spark.home</name>
  <value>/opt/spark</value>
</property>
<property>
  <name>hive.spark.job.monitor.timeout</name>
  <value>120</value>
</property>
```

Switch YARN to the Fair Scheduler

To configure YARN to use the fair scheduler, as recommended by Hive documentation, edit */etc/hadoop/yarn-site.xml* and configure the `yarn.resourcemanager` `.scheduler.class` property with the class name for the fair scheduler. (The following XML is edited for fit.)

```
<property>
  <name>yarn.resourcemanager.scheduler.class</name>
  <value>org.apache.hadoop.yarn.server.resourcemanager.scheduler.fair.
       FairScheduler</value>
</property>
```

Try Out Hive on Spark on YARN

Restart the Hive metastore server and the Hive server to pick up the new Hive configuration. If you have multiple Spark installations, specify the SPARK_HOME environment

---

variable with the same value as the `spark.home` configuration property in *hive-site.xml*. Without the environment variable, the startup scripts for Hive may guess incorrectly as to the location of the Spark installation:

```
# as hive
# export usual environment variables, but then add:
$ export SPARK_HOME=/opt/spark
$ $HIVE_HOME/bin/hive --service metastore -p 9083 > /var/log/hive/metastore.log &
# wait for the metastore server to come up
$ $HIVE_HOME/bin/hiveserver2 &
```

Also restart YARN to switch it to use the fair scheduler.

Finally, run the Beeline client as usual, but before running your first query, tell it to use Spark for query executions:

```
set hive.execution.engine=spark;
```

Now when you run a query, instead of seeing information about MapReduce being used, you will see details about how Hive submitted work to Spark, and how Spark is itself running on YARN. (The following output is edited for fit.)

```
0: jdbc:hive2://localhost:10000> SELECT COUNT(*) FROM u_data;
Query ID = hive_20161228174515_9bfd160e-6c6b-413f-9f7e-5eff85d04124
Total jobs = 1
Launching Job 1 out of 1
In order to change the average load for a reducer (in bytes):
  set hive.exec.reducers.bytes.per.reducer=<number>
In order to limit the maximum number of reducers:
  set hive.exec.reducers.max=<number>
In order to set a constant number of reducers:
  set mapreduce.job.reduces=<number>
Starting Spark Job = 72d7b61d-9f19-4a31-ae87-385ac80676c7
Running with YARN Application = application_1482938585635_0013
Kill Command = /opt/hadoop/bin/yarn application -kill
  application_1482938585635_0013

Query Hive on Spark job[1] stages:
2
3

Status: Running (Hive on Spark job[1])
Job Progress Format
CurrentTime StageId_StageAttemptId:
SucceededTasksCount(+RunningTasksCount-FailedTasksCount)/TotalTasksCount
  [StageCost]
2016-12-28 17:45:16,760 Stage-2_0: 0(+1)/1  Stage-3_0: 0/1
2016-12-28 17:45:19,775 Stage-2_0: 1/1 Finished Stage-3_0: 1/1 Finished
Status: Finished successfully in 4.02 seconds
OK
+---------+--+
|   c0    |  |
+---------+--+
```

```
|  100000  |
+----------+--+
1 row selected (4.285 seconds)
```

Spark Streaming from AWS Kinesis

Besides being able to perform complex analytics on data stored at rest, whether in HDFS or elsewhere, Spark can also work on data that is streamed into it. Spark Streaming lets you process large amounts of incoming live data in much the same way as typical *resilient distributed datasets* (RDDs). Batches of data generated through *discretized streams* or "DStreams" can be operated upon similarly to RDDs, and the results can be saved to persistent storage for further analytics.

Spark supports several sources for DStreams, including Apache Flume and Apache Kafka. It also ships with support for streaming data from Amazon Kinesis, a component of AWS that supports the establishment and management of data streams within AWS.

This section describes how to set up a Spark Streaming job that reads from a Kinesis stream, performs some simple processing on it, and saves the results to HDFS.

The streaming pipeline developed in this section operates on Apache access logs. In a real-life scenario, Apache web servers would be configured to forward their access logs to the Kinesis stream, but to make the work here simpler, access log data is faked using a basic generator. The basic architecture of the streaming pipeline is shown in Figure 12-1.

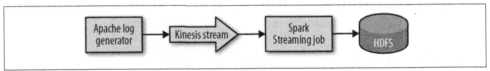

Figure 12-1. Data flow for a Spark Streaming job through AWS Kinesis

Creating a Kinesis Stream

To create a Kinesis stream, use the AWS console to select the Kinesis service. Be sure to select the region where you want the stream to be created. On the Kinesis home page, click Go to Streams. Click the "Create stream" button on the next page to reveal the form—shown in Figure 12-2—for creating a new stream.

Provide a name for the stream, such as "apache-access-logs". For the simple stream used in this section, use just one shard. The form automatically calculates the read and write throughput for the stream, which is more than enough for exploration purposes. Click the "Create stream" button to begin the process of stream creation.

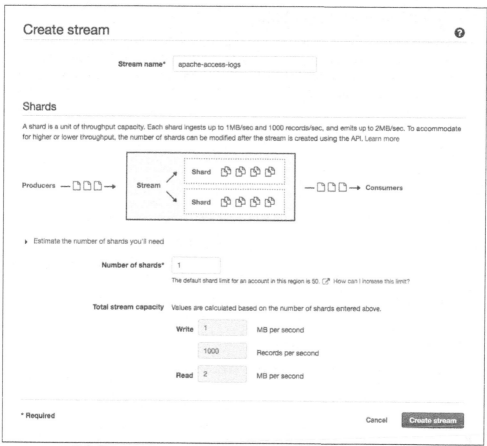

Figure 12-2. Creating a Kinesis stream

The stream eventually appears in the list of streams. Soon, the stream should be reported as ACTIVE, as shown in Figure 12-3, meaning it is ready to accept and provide data.

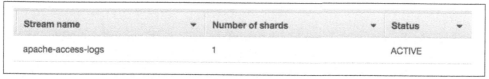

Figure 12-3. An active Kinesis stream

Once the generator begins to send data into the stream and the stream job reads data from the stream, the Monitoring tab for the stream will provide graphs summarizing the data flow.

Populating the Stream with Data

The simplest way to populate the new Kinesis stream is to use a simple standalone generator program. The Kinesis client available in the AWS SDK can be used to send one generated log line at a time, as bytes, to the stream. The main body of a generator program is listed in Example 12-1.[2]

As in the rest of this book, code in this chapter is written in Java.

Example 12-1. Loop for sending log lines to a Kinesis stream

```java
AmazonKinesisClient client = new AmazonKinesisClient();

int numPasses = (numRecords + recsPerSecond - 1) / recsPerSecond;
int recordsLeft = numRecords;
for (int i = 0; i < numPasses; i++) {
  int numToGenerate = Math.min(recordsLeft, recsPerSecond);
  for (int j = 0; j < numToGenerate; j++) {
    String logLine = generateLogLine();

    PutRecordRequest request = new PutRecordRequest()
      .withStreamName(streamName)
      .withPartitionKey(PARTITION_KEY)
      .withData(ByteBuffer.wrap(logLine.getBytes(StandardCharsets.UTF_8)));
    PutRecordResult result = client.putRecord(request);
    System.out.println(String.format("Wrote to shard %s as %s", result.getShardId(),
                                    result.getSequenceNumber()));
  }

  recordsLeft -= numToGenerate;
  if (recordsLeft > 0) {
    Thread.sleep(1000L);
  }
}
```

The loop in Example 12-1 sends a batch of records each second (roughly) to the Kinesis stream and reports the sequence number assigned by Kinesis to each record as a sign that the transfer was successful.

The work of creating a fake Apache access log line is done by the `generateLogLine()` method. There are many ways to implement the method; the code in Example 12-2

---

2 Find the complete source at: *https://github.com/bhavanki/moving-hadoop-to-the-cloud*.

uses a combination of `java.util.Random`, weighted distributions supported by Apache Commons Math 3, and the Java Faker library (*https://github.com/DiUS/java-faker*) to create realistic-looking log lines. (The example here is edited down for clarity.)

Example 12-2. Generation of a random Apache access log line

```java
private static final String FORMAT =
  "%s - - [%s] \"%s %s HTTP/1.0\" %s %d \"%s\" \"%s\"";

private Random random = new Random();
private Faker faker = new Faker();
private static final DateTimeFormatter TIMESTAMP_FORMATTER =
  DateTimeFormatter.ofPattern("dd/MMM/yyyy:HH:mm:ss Z");
private static final EnumeratedDistribution<String> METHODS = makeDistribution(
  Pair.create("GET", 6.0), Pair.create("POST", 2.0)
);
private static final EnumeratedDistribution<String> RESOURCES = makeDistribution(
  Pair.create("/page1", 10.0), Pair.create("/page2", 9.0)
);
private static final EnumeratedDistribution<String> RESPONSES = makeDistribution(
  Pair.create("200", 8.0), Pair.create("404", 2.0)
);
private static final EnumeratedDistribution<String> USER_AGENTS = makeDistribution(
  Pair.create("user agent string 1", 4.7), Pair.create("user agent string 2", 3.8)
);

@SafeVarargs
private static EnumeratedDistribution<String> makeDistribution(Pair<String,
                                               Double>... items) {
  return new EnumeratedDistribution<String>(Arrays.asList(items));
}

private String generateLogLine() {
  String ipAddress = faker.internet().privateIpV4Address();
  String dateTime = TIMESTAMP_FORMATTER.format(ZonedDateTime.now());
  String method = METHODS.sample();
  String resource = RESOURCES.sample();
  String status = RESPONSES.sample();
  int bytes = random.nextInt(10000);
  String referer = faker.internet().url();
  String userAgent = USER_AGENTS.sample();

  return String.format(FORMAT, ipAddress, dateTime, method, resource, status,
                  bytes, referer, userAgent);
}
```

A Kinesis stream can hang on to data for a while, but the processing job will read from the leading edge of the stream. So, in order to see the job in action, the generator must run simultaneously.

The generator program can run anywhere that has access to the Kinesis stream. AWS credentials are necessary for putting records in the stream, and one way that they can be supplied to the program is through an AWS access key ID and secret access key assigned to an IAM user with the necessary permissions. See "Configuring S3 Authentication" on page 161 for instructions on how to add a new IAM user with the permissions you choose. The policies required are:

- "AmazonKinesisFullAccess" for reading from and writing to Kinesis streams
- "AmazonDynamoDBFullAccess" for checkpointing progress in reading Kinesis streams
- "CloudWatchFullAccess" for reporting stream metrics to AWS CloudWatch

The keys may be passed to the program in a few different ways. The most straightforward is to set the `AWS_ACCESS_KEY_ID` and `AWS_SECRET_ACCESS_KEY` environment variables before running.[3]

Streaming Kinesis Data into Spark

A streaming job that processes records from a Kinesis stream starts by creating a DStream from it. All the usual stream manipulation capabilities of Spark are available to perform processing on the data, and the end result may be saved to any of several locations. The job in Example 12-3 alters each log record to have an anonymized IP address and a generic user agent, and then maps each line to a pair with a unique identifier so that it can be saved to Hadoop.

Example 12-3. Processing of Apache log lines in Spark Streaming

```
public void process(String streamName, String region, int batchInterval,
                    String hadoopDir)
  throws InterruptedException {

  String kinesisEndpoint = String.format("https://kinesis.%s.amazonaws.com/",
                                         region);

  AmazonKinesisClient client = new AmazonKinesisClient();
  client.setEndpoint(kinesisEndpoint);

  int numShards =
    client.describeStream(streamName).getStreamDescription().getShards().size();
  SparkConf conf = new SparkConf().setAppName(APP_NAME);
```

---

3 This exposes the key values in the command line reported by utilities like ps. Other ways of passing the keys are described in the AWS SDK documentation for managing credentials (*http://docs.aws.amazon.com/sdk-for-java/v1/developer-guide/credentials.html*).

```
JavaStreamingContext ctx = new JavaStreamingContext(conf,
                                      new Duration(batchInterval));

JavaDStream<byte[]> kinesisStream =
  KinesisUtils.createStream(ctx, APP_NAME, streamName, kinesisEndpoint, region,
                    InitialPositionInStream.LATEST,
                    new Duration(batchInterval),
                    StorageLevel.MEMORY_AND_DISK_2());

// Make more DStreams
JavaDStream<ApacheLogRecord> processedRecords = kinesisStream
  .map(line -> new ApacheLogRecord(new String(line, StandardCharsets.UTF_8)))
  .map(record -> record.withIpAddress(anonymizeIpAddress(record.getIpAddress())))
  .map(record ->
      record.withUserAgent(categorizeUserAgent(record.getUserAgent())))
;

// Only pair streams can be written as Hadoop files
JavaPairDStream<String, ApacheLogRecord> markedRecords = processedRecords
  .transformToPair(recordRdd ->
                recordRdd.mapToPair(
                  record -> new Tuple2<>(UUID.randomUUID().toString(), record)
                ));

// Write out to Hadoop
markedRecords.print();
markedRecords.saveAsHadoopFiles(hadoopDir, "txt", Text.class, Text.class,
                        TextOutputFormat.class);

ctx.start();
try {
  ctx.awaitTermination();
} catch (InterruptedException e) {
  System.out.println("Streaming stopped");
  return;
  }
}
```

The processing code in Example 12-3 uses lambdas, introduced in Java 8, to be more readable. This requires that the Hadoop cluster, or at least YARN, run under Java 8 as well.

The ApacheLogRecord class referenced in Example 12-3 is a basic implementation of an object that can manage the fields in a log record.

When the streaming job is run, each batch delimited by the batch interval is processed, and its results are saved into a separate directory in Hadoop. To avoid an explosion of directories, make the batch interval somewhat large, on the order of at least a minute.

Packaging the streaming job

As with any Spark job, the streaming job should be packaged into an all-in-one JAR that can be uploaded to the cluster for execution. The Spark Streaming library does not need to be included, since the job runs within Spark. This will dramatically reduce the size of the JAR.

With complex systems like Spark, the AWS SDK, and Hadoop all being used at once, it is likely that dependency conflicts will arise when running the streaming job. Here are some conflicts to watch out for, and how to resolve them:

- The Amazon Kinesis Client Library (KCL) available through Spark uses a specific version of the AWS Java SDK. If you use a different version for your job, classes in the SDK may be reported missing or incompatible. Try using the same version of the AWS SDK for your job that the KCL packaged with Spark uses.
- Spark and the AWS SDK may rely on different versions of the Jackson JSON library, leading to class-loading problems. Override the versions of Jackson so that the latest ones are bundled.
- The Amazon KCL also uses a specific version of Apache Commons HTTPClient, which may be newer than the version embedded in the Hadoop cluster. Use Apache Maven's package relocation capability to move the HTTPClient code used by the job to a different "shaded" package to avoid the conflict altogether.

Example 12-4 illustrates how to use Apache Maven to implement the workarounds that resolve dependency conflicts among Spark, the AWS SDK, and Hadoop.

Example 12-4. Maven settings resolving dependency conflicts among Spark, AWS SDK, and Hadoop

```
<dependencyManagement>
  <dependencies>
    <dependency>
      <groupId>com.amazonaws</groupId>
      <artifactId>aws-java-sdk-bom</artifactId>
      <version>1.10.20</version><!-- KCL in Spark 2.1.0 uses 1.10.20 -->
      <type>pom</type>
      <scope>import</scope>
    </dependency>
    <!-- Jackson libs in AWS 1.10 are too old for Spark 2 -->
    <dependency>
      <groupId>com.fasterxml.jackson.core</groupId>
      <artifactId>jackson-databind</artifactId>
      <version>2.6.5</version>
```

```
        </dependency>
        <dependency>
          <groupId>com.fasterxml.jackson.dataformat</groupId>
          <artifactId>jackson-dataformat-cbor</artifactId>
          <version>2.6.5</version>
        </dependency>
      </dependencies>
    </dependencyManagement>

    <build>
      <plugins>
        <plugin>
          <groupId>org.apache.maven.plugins</groupId>
          <artifactId>maven-shade-plugin</artifactId>
          <version>2.4.3</version>
          <executions>
            <execution>
              <phase>package</phase>
              <goals>
                <goal>shade</goal>
              </goals>
              <configuration>
                <relocations>
                  <!-- Apache Commons HTTPClient in Hadoop may conflict -->
                  <relocation>
                    <pattern>org.apache.http</pattern>
                    <shadedPattern>com.mh2c.shaded.org.apache.http</shadedPattern>
                  </relocation>
                </relocations>
              </configuration>
            </execution>
          </executions>
        </plugin>
      </plugins>
    </build>
```

Running the streaming job

To run the streaming job, upload its JAR to the Hadoop cluster and run it in a
Hadoop user account like "spark". Use the spark-submit utility to start the job driver
in YARN and to pass essential Spark configuration properties and command-line
arguments:

```
# as spark
$ ./bin/spark-submit --class com.mh2c.LogProcessor --master yarn \
> --deploy-mode cluster \
> --conf spark.yarn.appMasterEnv.AWS_ACCESS_KEY_ID=AKIAXXXXXXXXXXXXXXXX \
> --conf spark.yarn.appMasterEnv.AWS_SECRET_ACCESS_KEY=XXXX....XXXX \
> --conf spark.executorEnv.AWS_ACCESS_KEY_ID=AKIAXXXXXXXXXXXXXXXX \
> --conf spark.executorEnv.AWS_SECRET_ACCESS_KEY=XXXX....XXXX \
> /home/spark/apache-access-log-processing-1.0.0.jar \
```

```
> apache-access-logs us-east-1 60000
> hdfs://203.0.113.101:8020/user/spark/access-logs/stream
```

Notice that the AWS keys are passed to both the application master and the Spark executors. Failing to do both leads to authentication failures working with Kinesis or DynamoDB.

The arguments in this command line, which correspond to the arguments of the process method in Example 12-3, are:

- The name of the Kinesis stream
- The region of the Kinesis stream, which is used to determine the Kinesis endpoint URL
- The batch interval for Spark Streaming, in milliseconds
- The "prefix" for Hadoop files written by the job

The Hadoop file prefix is the start of the URL for where files should be written. An hdfs:// URL directs Spark to write the files into HDFS. If the s3a filesystem implementation is installed and available in the Hadoop cluster, then the job can write files directly to S3, provided that the IAM user associated with the AWS keys also has write access to S3. That is how you can create a Spark Streaming job that not only reads from a cloud service, but also writes to one as well, leaving no critical data resident in the cluster itself. See "Configuring the S3 Filesystem" on page 158 for instructions on setting up the s3a filesystem.

Stopping the streaming job

The spark-submit command is merely reporting on the status of the YARN application hosting the Spark Streaming job, so it can be stopped at any time using Control-C. This leaves the YARN application itself running, and it continues to run until you kill it through YARN. Find the application ID for the job, as reported by spark-submit, and then kill the application. (The following output has been edited for fit.)

```
# as spark
$ /opt/hadoop/bin/yarn application -kill application_1484496337475_0014
17/01/15 20:58:47 INFO client.RMProxy: Connecting to ResourceManager at
    /203.0.113.101:8032
Killing application application_1484496337475_0014
17/01/15 20:58:47 INFO impl.YarnClientImpl: Killed application
    application_1484496337475_0014
```

With YARN log aggregation enabled, you can find the output from the job as usual, using yarn logs. The logs contain output from Spark itself, including the output from print() calls on DStreams:

```
# as spark
$ $HADOOP_PREFIX/bin/yarn logs -applicationId application_1484496337475_0014 | \
> less
```

The actual output files can be found in Hadoop at the location specified to the job as the "prefix." For example, a prefix of "hdfs://203.0.113.101:8020/user/spark/access-logs/stream" leads to a set of directories in HDFS starting with "stream" and time-stamped at each batch. Each directory houses "part" files with the text records from the processor. (The following output is edited for fit.)

```
# as spark
$ hdfs dfs -ls /user/spark/access-logs/
Found 5 items
drwxr-xr-x   /user/spark/access-logs/stream-1484513640000.txt
drwxr-xr-x   /user/spark/access-logs/stream-1484513700000.txt
drwxr-xr-x   /user/spark/access-logs/stream-1484513760000.txt
drwxr-xr-x   /user/spark/access-logs/stream-1484513820000.txt
drwxr-xr-x   /user/spark/access-logs/stream-1484513880000.txt
```

With the streaming results in place, other analysis jobs using Spark, MapReduce, or other frameworks that can read the files can be run later to drill further into the data.

What About Google Cloud Platform and Azure?

If you are using Google Cloud Platform, Google Cloud Pub/Sub is the analogous service for AWS Kinesis. There is a Java library for the service, although it is still very new. Spark does not ship with built-in support for working with Cloud Pub/Sub, but connecting should be possible with the Pub/Sub Java library or the grpc library. Another tack is to use Apache Kafka as the source for the streaming job, and use the CloudPubSubConnector (*https://github.com/GoogleCloudPlatform/pubsub/tree/master/kafka-connector*) to move data from Cloud Pub/Sub through Kafka to the job.

If you are using Azure, Azure Event Hubs is the analogous service for AWS Kinesis. Microsoft's HDInsight team maintains a Spark connector for Azure Event Hubs (*https://github.com/hdinsight/spark-eventhubs*) that can take the place of the AWS KCL in Spark Streaming jobs.

Apache Kafka alone is a viable alternative for any of the stream services offered by the cloud providers. Choosing Kafka gives you more control over how your streams are managed, at the cost of having to maintain Kafka itself and the instances Kafka runs on.

Building Clusters Versus Building Clusters Well

Configuring Spark, including Hive on Spark and Spark Streaming, on a cluster is a complex affair. If you also installed Hive as described in Chapter 11 and enabled high availability as described in Chapter 10, you did a lot of work and ended up with a powerful, capable cluster in the cloud.

It is time now to take a step back and think about other issues with deploying cloud clusters beyond the mechanics of installation and configuration, which has been the focus of this book up until now. Part V begins by exploring the pricing decisions to be made when designating resources for clusters, weighing them against performance requirements. After all, while a cloud cluster is powerful and useful, it is even better if it is also cost-effective and fast.

Care and Feeding of Hadoop in the Cloud

By now you have created a simple Hadoop cluster running on a cloud provider, run some jobs on it, and possibly enhanced it to be highly available or tried out some other Hadoop components on it. The goals so far have been centered on getting things working and exploring, but now that you have some experience with clusters running in the cloud, it's time to focus on getting things to work well. That entails understanding how the features offered by cloud providers, as well as their trade-offs and limitations, can influence the choices you make in architecting clusters.

## CHAPTER 13

Pricing and Performance

As the saying goes, you get what you pay for. When it comes to cloud providers, in general, the more you are willing to pay, the more resources you can have at your command. For a small price, you can provision some modest instances with a small amount of storage and use them for proof-of-concept work, small websites, or simple server hosting. On the other hand, if you have money to spend, you can employ the full range of compute and storage offerings from your cloud provider, which enable you to field entire enterprise-scale infrastructures—for a corresponding enterprise-scale price.

Fortunately, Hadoop was designed from the start not to require enterprise hardware, and it can run on a small handful of instances, at least to start with. Even in cloud deployments, it is not necessary to deploy the most powerful resources in order to architect a powerful cluster. You can build a decent cluster at a decent price.

Regardless of the scale of your clusters, there's no need to waste money. By taking a careful look at the menu of selections for instances and storage, and building your network out well, you can be sure that you are getting the most bang for your buck.

Picking Instance Types

One of the first decisions to confront when designing a cluster running in the cloud is which instance type or types to use. Some instance types are too underpowered for most cluster roles, while some are overpowered except for very large-scale deployments. Even though there is a lengthy list of instance types to choose from, it's enough to focus on a few characteristics common to all of them to find a good fit.

The Criteria

The primary criteria to consider when choosing instance types for a cluster are:

- Number of vCPUs or cores
- Memory
- Associated block storage or disk space

In general, and as you probably expect, an instance type is priced higher when it has more vCPUs, more memory, or more block storage. However, the ratios between these criteria do not stay constant across the set of available instance types. Some instance types go heavy on memory, while others have a tremendous amount of block storage.

Instance types can usually be categorized by what their expected role is, and the role for a type derives from what criteria are emphasized in its makeup. Role classifications can apply to Hadoop cluster architectures as well as other uses. Here are some common roles for instance types:

- *General-purpose* instance types provide a balanced amount of vCPUs, memory, and block storage. These are analogous to general-purpose physical computers, which are configured to perform most tasks well, but without any specializations.
- *Compute* instance types provide more vCPUs and a lot more memory, while reducing available block storage. These instance types excel at number-crunching and analysis tasks that can eat up a lot of memory, but which don't require large amounts of block storage.
- *Storage* instance types are light on vCPUs and memory but deliver large amounts of block storage. While these instance types can still perform nontrivial compute tasks, they serve best as data repositories.

Cloud providers do offer other instance types aimed at different roles, such as very high memory or GPU availability. If you are just getting started with Hadoop in the cloud, those more specialized instance types are not usually necessary, but as your expertise grows and the needs of your clusters become apparent, they can become useful.

General Cluster Instance Roles

As a Hadoop cluster architect, you have complete freedom to choose the instance types you want to use for your cluster (provided you have the budget). A common-sense starting point is to define some basic cluster instance roles, where each role maps to some set of Hadoop daemons. The needs of those daemons then influence the proper instance type for the role.

Here is a good starter set of instance roles:

manager
> An instance that hosts the "master" or "manager" daemons for each cluster service, such as the HDFS namenode and the YARN resource manager

worker
> An instance that hosts the more numerous daemons for each cluster service, such as an HDFS datanode or a YARN node manager

gateway
> An instance that hosts daemons that interface with the world outside the cluster, like Flume agents, and/or host clients for cluster services

If you built out a cluster in Part II, you will recognize the manager and worker roles.

In a cluster that follows these roles, there are usually only one or two manager instances, a large number of workers, and a handful of gateways. More sophisticated architectures would evolve to include different worker roles optimized for specific cluster services, or even different manager instances.

Given these roles, it's straightforward to map them to appropriate instance types:

Table 13-1. Some cluster roles and their matching instance types

Role	Instance type
manager	more powerful general purpose
worker	compute and/or storage
gateway	less powerful general purpose

Because manager instances host the most crucial daemons in the cluster, they need to have the best and broadest resources available. They themselves do not store much data or execute cluster jobs, so general purpose-hardware is suitable. For larger clusters, an instance type with somewhat more memory can help keep things running smoothly.

Since cluster work is spread out across workers, they can be less powerful compared to a manager instance, but they make up for it in numbers. Workers that run jobs can take advantage of the extra vCPUs and memory of a compute instance, while HDFS datanodes can take up the additional storage associated with storage instances. In larger clusters, you may choose to run storage daemons and compute daemons on separate instances with optimized instance types, but on smaller clusters all of the worker daemons will host both kinds of daemons, in which case compute instances tend to be the better choice. If you need additional storage on a compute instance, you can always attach more volumes, but you can't as easily add vCPUs or memory to a storage instance, if it's possible at all.

Gateway instances are used lightly and mostly serve to feed the cluster or to host interactive applications for people to use, so they typically do not require a lot of horsepower.

As always, there are exceptions, depending on what the cluster needs, but these are good guidelines to start with.

Persistent Versus Ephemeral Block Storage

Each instance you launch comes with at least one persistent root volume[1] for data storage. Some instance types provide additional ephemeral volumes, where data survives as long as the instance is not stopped or terminated. After an instance is launched, you can attach new persistent volumes and may be able to add more ephemeral volumes, at least up to a limit. So, with all these block storage options, what should you use for a Hadoop cluster?

One option is to use persistent volumes for all block storage. Cloud providers take measures to ensure that they are available and can survive outages. However, persistent storage has two primary drawbacks over ephemeral storage:

- *They are slower.* Persistent volumes are not necessarily attached to the same hardware, or even nearby in the same network, as an instance. In contrast, ephemeral storage is either directly connected to the same physical hardware or extremely close to it, so data access is fast.

- *They cost more.* While the cost of persistent volumes is not generally considered *expensive*, it is more than that of ephemeral storage. Once your clusters scale up to storing huge amounts of data, the cost of maintaining that data, triple-replicated in the case of HDFS, may start to add up.

While ephemeral storage is relatively fast and cheap, its primary drawback is that it's ephemeral. Whenever a cluster instance stops, its ephemeral storage is wiped out. Therefore, it's likely unsafe to use it for data that needs to be stored long-term only within the Hadoop cluster.

The primary issue is using ephemeral storage as the backing disks for HDFS. Because HDFS replicates data across datanodes, a cluster can automatically recover from the loss of a single datanode and the corresponding loss of its share of data. As usual, a

---

1 Well, not always. Cloud providers like AWS allow you to start an instance with an ephemeral root volume, but for most uses, including Hadoop clusters, this is not recommended.

cluster can safely lose as many datanodes as the value of its replication factor, less one. Losing more than that risks data loss, unless the data is saved off elsewhere.

In some cases, you may not be able to use ephemeral storage for HDFS at all. Perhaps information-handling policies require that cluster data be stored on more robust forms of storage, or perhaps there is concern that the cluster will lose too many datanodes while jobs are running. If so, persistent storage is the better option.

The dichotomy between persistent and ephemeral storage is not as simple to discern as perhaps one would like. Other factors blur the lines.

As one example, some cloud providers offer different types of persistent block storage with faster or slower access times and throughput, with corresponding differences in cost. You could choose faster, more expensive types of persistent storage for commonly used clusters or instances, and choose slower ones for less busy corners of your architecture. With different options for persistent storage, you may not need to consider ephemeral storage at all.

If you architect data flows such that data you cannot afford to lose is kept safely outside of Hadoop clusters, perhaps in object storage, then in-flight data is no longer as critical to preserve, and it becomes more feasible to use ephemeral storage for cluster data. The trade-off is that it can take time to retrieve data from storage and send final results back to it; is that extra time and data transfer cost offset by increased cluster performance?

Finally, it is important not to forget that you can, and should, back up your cluster data periodically (see Chapter 18). With reliable backups in places, the risk of using ephemeral storage is reduced, but now there is a need to restore data once in a while, which can slow things down and incur data transfer costs.

In summary, then, here are two overarching strategies for block storage use in a Hadoop cluster:

- Use persistent storage for all data. Optionally, go with slower and cheaper storage types where performance is not an issue.
- Use ephemeral storage for HDFS, and persistent storage for the rest. Save critical data to object storage, and restart processing from there if too many datanodes are lost.

Current trends are to go with the first strategy and use persistent storage for everything. The cost savings and performance boost of ephemeral storage are often not enough to make up for the increased criticality of data backups and the lack of intrinsic reliability compared to persistent storage. It is also more akin to running on-prem, which organizations are today still more comfortable with.

Exclusive use of persistent storage also makes it easier to start and stop clusters.

Stopping and Starting Entire Clusters

Running clusters on a cloud provider opens up new usage patterns and operations practices. There is added flexibility, due to the fact that instances are not actual physical pieces of hardware, but abstract collections of resources.

One practice that becomes viable in a cloud provider is shutting down clusters when they are not needed. In a typical on-premises architecture, it does not usually make sense to shut down entire machines when they are not needed, except to save on power and cooling costs; instead, you might try to have those machines serve multiple purposes, so that they are in use as much as possible. Of course, this makes administration of those instances more complex and can lead to conflicts among the software packages installed.

This pursuit of machine-level efficiency isn't as necessary in the cloud, because it is easy to stop and start instances as often as you wish. There is no need for a human to physically visit hardware and push buttons and rewire network connections; everything is controlled through the cloud provider's consoles and APIs.

This practice can save money. However, it's also a way to effectively field a larger set of clusters than with a more static operational stance. For example, instead of running ten general-purpose clusters all the time, you could run six general-purpose clusters, but then use the remaining capacity for a shifting set of eight other clusters for specialized needs. At any moment, only some of those specialized clusters would be running, but they can be swapped in and out in response to business needs. There is still the cost of maintaining the block storage associated with all of the instances, but this costs less than it would with all of the instances running with their storage attached. This scheme is shown graphically in Figure 13-1. On the left, all of the resources are constantly used by ten running clusters. On the right, six clusters always run, but other clusters are defined that can be started and stopped to use the rest of the resources.

There are important caveats with this practice. Perhaps the most important is that all data residing on ephemeral block storage is destroyed when instances are stopped. The process of stopping specialized clusters must involve backing up any important data that ends up on ephemeral storage, and likewise the process for starting them must involve putting it back. For this reason, it's usually recommended to use persistent storage exclusively for clusters that are stopped and started.

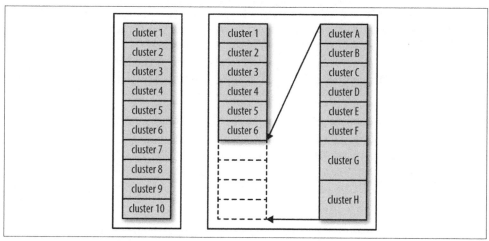

Figure 13-1. Ways to manage clusters with limited resources

Another important caveat is that providers may grant a restarted instance a different IP address from when it was last running. Cluster configurations that rely on those IP addresses must be updated in order to bring the cluster back up to fully operational status. For example, a GCE instance that is stopped and restarted will receive a new ephemeral public IP address by default, unless a static IP address has already been established for it. Generally, private IP addresses do remain assigned to instances as they are stopped and started, which is a good reason to configure clusters using them.

Finally, not all cloud providers meter instance usage at a fine level, but instead at larger time units, such as whole hours for EC2. As a result, it is not always economical to bring up clusters frequently but for short periods of time; the provider will round up charges to the next time unit anyway. For example, if a cluster is brought up and shut down three times in a single hour, and billing is done in units of hours, then the cloud provider will charge for three hours of usage for each instance. So, bring up clusters at times when there is a batch of jobs to be run; this will maximize their time used within the billing unit. In general, trying to game cloud provider billing practices to save a few dollars is tricky and prone to creating higher charges.

Automation is extremely helpful for managing the starting and stopping of clusters, which is covered in Chapter 17.

Using Temporary Instances

Another attractive way to save money on clusters besides stopping them when not in use is to use temporary instances. As explained in "Temporary Instances" on page 25, a temporary instance works just as well as a standard instance and costs much less, but can or will be terminated without warning after some time.

Some roles in a cluster are naturally suited for temporary instances. In the set of basic instance roles defined previously, the worker role is the most appropriate to host on temporary instances, because a cluster has so many of them. As temporary instances are reclaimed, new ones can be provisioned to take their place. Hadoop automatically copes with the disappearance and appearance of worker daemons like datanodes and node managers, so operating in this fashion is practical.

It's important to maintain a minimum number of nontemporary instances for some cluster roles. The HDFS datanode role is a prime example. If all of the datanodes are running on temporary instances and are reclaimed by the host provider, then all of your HDFS data is lost. Even if only some datanodes disappear, if those hosted all of the replicas of some HDFS data and they disappeared too quickly for the replicas to be copied to remaining datanodes, then that data is lost.

Automation of the maintenance of temporary cluster instances is required to work with them for a significant period of time. It's wasteful and slow to have someone manually allocating new temporary instances as older ones are reclaimed. Scripts, tools, or cloud provider features should be employed to notice when the pool of temporary instances in your clusters falls below a certain level, provision new temporary instances to take their place, and configure them into your clusters. Chapter 17 covers ways that you can get started with monitoring your clusters.

One common tactic is to use temporary instances for YARN node managers, expanding a cluster's compute capacity. If there is, say, a surge of end-of-month jobs to run, or a busy shopping day coming up, and the additional load on the cluster is certain to abate after some time, then expanding a cluster with temporary compute instances is a cost-effective and easy way to cope. Even as some node managers drop away when the cloud provider pulls back its instances, YARN can automatically push the work to the remaining node managers without intervention.

It isn't too difficult to "manually" expand a cluster, but with the right combination of monitoring and automation, you can arrange for clusters to grow in response to increased demand as it is sensed. See "Elastic Compute Using a Custom Metric" on page 260 for pointers on how to implement *autoscaling* of compute capacity, which works with both temporary and ordinary instances.

Always keep in mind that you cannot rely on temporary instances to last for any amount of time. Even if historically you find that they survive for a long time, there are no guarantees that history will continue to repeat itself. AWS spot instances, for example, can theoretically last for weeks if the initial bid is high enough and the market price stays low, and this can lull you into a false sense of security. In contrast, Google Cloud Platform preemptible instances are guaranteed to be terminated within 24 hours, specifically to avoid that, but that makes them less reliable for some cluster operations.

Geographic Considerations

The cost of running clusters in a cloud doesn't depend just on *what* you run with, but *where* it runs.

Regions

The price for an instance type, or gateway, or other element of cloud infrastructure can vary from region to region. The hardware and connectivity in each of a cloud provider's regions is roughly the same, so you can realize significant cost savings by running in a region that has lower rates.

There are reasons to run in a more expensive region. The most important one is network performance between instances running in the region and their users; this is even more important when the users are customers outside of your organization. You may find that your clusters need to run closer to their users to meet your needs. For example, clusters running in Asian regions will tend to exhibit higher latencies for users in Europe than users also in Asia. If the performance is bad enough, you may consider replicating your clusters in a European region.

You should never construct a cluster that spans regions. Not only are network speeds much slower than even between availability zones in the same region, but there is additional cost associated with data flowing into or out of regions, which are significant given the amount of network traffic within Hadoop clusters.

Availability Zones

Resources are not priced differently depending on the availability zone within which they run, so that need not influence your cluster design. However, some cloud providers do charge for network traffic between availability zones. A cluster that spans availability zones will cost more, although not nearly as much as one spanning regions.

Network speeds between availability zones are slower than within availability zones, although again not as slow as between regions. Still, larger clusters and more extensive workloads benefit from being contained within a single zone, since they will run faster.

You may wish to build clusters that span availability zones as part of a high-availability strategy (see Chapter 10), but heavier workloads may have trouble running and costs may shoot up, and you may be driven to stay within a single zone. Keeping cluster data backed up or safe in a cloud provider storage service (see Chapter 5) can enable moving work from a cluster lost in one availability zone to another running in a separate zone, as an alternative to a single HA cluster.

Performance and Networking

The performance of Hadoop clusters in the cloud is determined by more than the sort of instances they run on and the kinds of storage they use; how the instances are networked also has a major effect. The geographic considerations of regions and availability zones covered here only touch on the topic of networking Hadoop clusters. Chapter 14 goes further, developing and comparing network topologies while keeping in mind performance as well as security.

Network Topologies

Cloud providers let you design almost any network architecture you could imagine to support your instances. You have options for where in the world the instances are running, their IP addresses and DNS names, and all of the rules for how they can talk to each other and the outside world. All of that freedom can be overwhelming.

Cloud providers start you off with a default network that gets you up and running quickly. However, even establishing a single Hadoop cluster leads you to outgrow that initial state, and compels you to confront many questions about how your instances should be arranged, and the rules that they should play by. Your organization may also have its own requirements for where data can live and the protections for it both at rest and in transit, including access rules and redundancy requirements.

The collective layout for a network of computing resources can be called its *topology*. This chapter defines some common concepts behind cloud network topologies and shows how Hadoop clusters can work within them.

Public and Private Subnets

When it comes to networking and security, perhaps the most fundamental question to ask about a single instance, or an entire cluster's worth of them for that matter, is: Who can see it?

It's essential that all of the instances within a single Hadoop cluster be able to see each other. In the typical, basic case, all of the instances run in the same subnet in the same availability zone, so that they have the fastest network connectivity to each other. Security rules also allow for unrestricted communication between them, so there is no internal obstacle to the cluster's functionality.

It is possible to set up security rules so that only the ports relevant to Hadoop clusters are reachable, even from instances in the same cluster. In practice, this is very difficult, as there are so many of them to cover. The better model is to assume that cluster instances can completely trust each other with no obstacles blocking their way. If instances within a single cluster cannot trust each other, there are deeper architectural problems!

If the cluster instances in a subnet are also reachable, in some way, from the internet, then the subnet is called a *public subnet*. If there is no network routing between the instances and the internet, or security rules completely prevent communications, then the subnet is called a *private subnet*.

A cloud provider generally starts you off with public subnets, by automatically allowing at least SSH access from either the internet or from your apparent IP address to instances residing in it. After all, without any other way to reach your instances, they are not of much use. You can manipulate the security rules to allow wider access, or eliminate all outside access and turn the subnet private.

A good rule of thumb for securing any system is to minimize the attack surface. So, in general, using private subnets for your clusters is more secure than using public subnets. The trade-off is in convenience, as it takes extra steps to reach a private subnet. The rest of this chapter explores the trade-offs.

If you use a public subnet to host clusters, then access from the internet should be tightly restricted:

- Prefer allowing only SSH access, using tunneling or proxies (see "SOCKS Proxy" on page 201) for any other form of communication.
- Prefer key-based authentication over password-based authentication. For SSH access in particular, there is no reason to use passwords.
- Prefer secure, encrypted communication protocols or layers, such as HTTPS instead of HTTP.
- Use security rules that restrict outside access to known IP address ranges instead of allowing in the entire internet (CIDR 0.0.0.0/0).

Imagine an HDFS namenode running in a public subnet, and suppose cluster users want to check on it through its web interface. The worst configuration for it would be to allow access from anywhere on the internet to its unencrypted HTTP port. While this is undoubtedly *convenient*, it is completely exposed to attack from anywhere. Moreover, anyone who stumbles upon it can learn about your internal cluster architecture, including IP addresses of your instances. Just enabling HTTPS for the namenode's web interface is not enough; authentication is also required, which involves setting up Kerberos and configuring the namenode appropriately. Fortunately, in the cloud, there are alternatives to doing all of that work for securing the namenode.

SSH Tunneling

One alternative is to prohibit direct access to the namenode's HTTP port from outside the subnet. As described in "SSH Tunneling" on page 112, you can establish an SSH tunnel from outside the subnet to the HTTP port of the namenode. This is less convenient than direct access, but it carries the benefits of key-based authentication and encryption, and reduces the exposure of the subnet's instances; it's one less port that's exposed.

To create a tunnel, make an SSH connection to an instance inside the public subnet, and request that it establish a tunnel to the desired instance and port within the subnet. Here is an example of creating a tunnel for reaching a namenode:

```
$ ssh -i /path/to/cloud_provider_key.pem -n -N \
> -L 50070:localhost:50070 userid@bastion.cloud-provider.example &
```

In this example, the SSH command is purely for creating a tunnel, and so it runs in the background with the -n option. A different pattern is to create the tunnel along with a normal, active SSH connection to the instance where you will be issuing commands. The -N option instructs the SSH client not to run a command on the instance hosting the tunnel, since it is running only to maintain a tunnel.

An important concept to understand for tunneling is that the instance on the other end of the tunnel does not need to be the same as the desired destination. In the preceding example, the SSH connection is made to an instance "bastion.cloud-provider.example", and then the tunnel's remote end is directed to port 50070 on "localhost". The tunnel is illustrated in Figure 14-1.

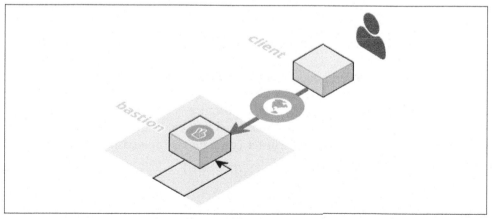

Figure 14-1. An SSH tunnel to a bastion host that forwards to a port on the bastion host

The network diagrams in this chapter were generated using Cloud-craft (*https://cloudcraft.co*).

The address for the remote end of the tunnel is specified *relative to the serving instance.* So, "localhost" here means *bastion.cloud-provider.example*, because the namenode is running on that same instance. If the namenode were running else-where, and the routes and security rules allowed connecting from the instance, the tunnel could direct requests there. This arrangement is shown in Figure 14-2, created by a command like the following:

```
$ ssh -i /path/to/cloud_provider_key.pem -n -N \
> -L 50070:nn1.cloud-provider.internal:50070 \
> userid@bastion.cloud-provider.example &
```

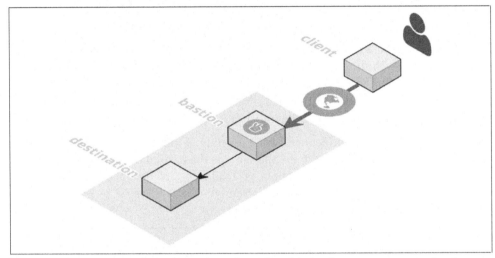

Figure 14-2. An SSH tunnel to a bastion host that forwards to a port on another host

The single instance *bastion.cloud-provider.example* can be used for SSH tunneling to lots of other instances, and serves as a kind of communications center on behalf of all the instances in the public subnet. Such an instance is called a *bastion*, because it is like a fortified part of the subnet that is exposed to the internet, protecting the rest of the instances. You should not run cluster components on a bastion, but use it as a dedicated communications hub.

Since the desired destination is resolved on the bastion, you are free to use the private IP address or private hostname of the destination when describing the tunnel. They do not mean anything to your local computer hosting the local end of the tunnel, but the bastion runs in the cloud provider and can interpret them. So, with the right network and security configuration, this allows a bastion to reach private subnets as well.

Once an SSH tunnel is established, you use it by pointing your browser to the local port on your own computer, e.g., *http://localhost:50070/*. The SSH client is listening on that port locally, and forwards the request through the tunnel to the bastion, which sends it to the remote destination and port. Response data flows back through the same path. So, communication is enabled by only having the SSH port of the bastion exposed.

SOCKS Proxy

Another method for reaching into a public subnet in a more secure way is to establish a SOCKS proxy server, again on a bastion host. A SOCKS proxy listens on a single port and forwards requests to it on to the desired destination.

There are many SOCKS proxy server implementations available. As it turns out, the OpenSSH client process can act as a SOCKS proxy:

```
$ ssh -i /path/to/cloud_provider_key.pem -n -N \
> -D 8157 userid@bastion.cloud-provider.example &
```

This command connects to the bastion host, as when performing SSH tunneling, but it also starts a SOCKS proxy server listening locally on port 8157. Any TCP requests that are sent to that local port are forwarded through the encrypted SSH connection and then issued from the bastion host to the desired destination. This method adds an additional layer on top of the basic SSH tunnel.

To use a SOCKS proxy, a client program like your web browser needs to be configured to send requests through it instead of directly to the destination. Using an SSH tunnel requires you to explicitly send requests to the local end of the tunnel, but using a SOCKS proxy does not, as the client program automatically knows that it needs to communicate via the proxy. So, a SOCKS proxy is less intrusive once configured, but requires support from the client.

A SOCKS proxy connecting through an SSH tunnel is illustrated in Figure 14-3. The client application is configured to work with the SOCKS proxy, which forwards requests through SSH to a bastion host, and onward from there to the desired destination.

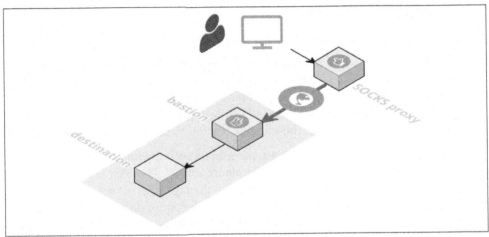

Figure 14-3. A SOCKS proxy with an SSH connection

To connect to the example namenode, you would point your configured browser to port 50070 of its instance's *private* IP address or *private* DNS hostname. The browser will send the request to the SOCKS proxy running on your local computer, which forwards it through the SSH tunnel to the bastion, and the SSH daemon on the bastion will be able to resolve either private identifier and send the request to the namenode instance.

It is possible, depending on your network configuration, that you can use the *public* IP address or hostname, which is more natural when you are operating outside the cloud provider. However, if the cloud provider routes requests to those public identifiers outside the subnet, as it would for any other external address, then the connection can fail. The route for the request will exit the subnet and attempt to re-enter, but the subnet may be locked down. This situation is illustrated in Figure 14-4.

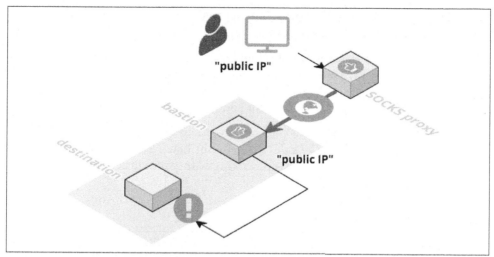

Figure 14-4. A SOCKS proxy with an SSH connection with a bad destination address: because the bastion host resolves the public IP address to a route that leaves the secure network, the connection fails

An advantage of using a SOCKS proxy is that once one is established, you are free to send requests to any reachable host and port within the subnet. With SSH tunneling, you must establish one tunnel per host and port. A disadvantage is that you must configure applications on the client side to use the proxy; SSH tunneling does not require that, although you must then target the tunnels explicitly.

Instead of relying on SSH, you can set up a standalone SOCKS proxy server on the bastion host. The server would listen on its own port, which is available outside its subnet, and client programs would be configured to use it as their proxy. When using such a server, it's important to establish strong authentication and not run it as an "open proxy" that the whole world can use. Restricting access to only IP addresses in the range used by you or your organization is also prudent, whether for a SOCKS server or SSH in general.

VPN Access

An organization that uses a cloud provider heavily may establish access directly from the organization's VPN. Conceptually, this is like extending private access to virtual networks to clients that are connected to the VPN; at a minimum, clients are able to reach instances using their private IP addresses. It may also be possible for clients to resolve the cloud provider's internal hostnames, which are normally only resolvable inside the cloud provider, if DNS is included in the arrangement. Sometimes, cloud instances can even connect out of their subnets and into clients running on the VPN, making the connection truly two-way. In practice this is uncommon, since it complicates the security posture of the organization's own network.

With VPN access, it is as if your local computer connected to the VPN is also present in the subnet; in a way, your computer is itself a bastion. SSH tunnels or SOCKS proxies are not necessary to gain access to instances because of the hard work that your network administrators have done for you.

VPNs do have outages, though, so your only access to critical clusters should not be through a VPN. Having security rules defined, but inactive, that allow access when the VPN link is down will let you keep working with your clusters. It's just another part of keeping clusters available.

Access from Other Subnets

In a large enough cluster architecture, multiple subnets will be in use. Cloud providers allow you to establish routes between subnets and to set security rules for how instances in different subnets can connect to each other. Each subnet may be either private or public. Most importantly, instances in a public subnet can connect to instances in a private subnet. This opens up different possibilities for where clusters live and how they are accessed and used.

Cluster Topologies

A cluster topology describes what runs on instances in a cluster as well as how they are connected to each other and to cluster users. Now that concepts for public and private access have been laid out, some cluster topologies can be built with them.

The Public Cluster

This topology is the least secure and arguably the worst choice of them all, but serves well as a basis for comparison with better topologies. In a public cluster, all of the instances run in a public subnet,[1] and all of the ports involved in cluster operations are open to the internet. In the least secure case, all ports on all instances are reachable from any IP address, either inside or outside the cloud provider. A public cluster is illustrated in Figure 14-5.

---

[1] Topologies for clusters running in multiple subnets are not considered here, since they have cost and performance problems.

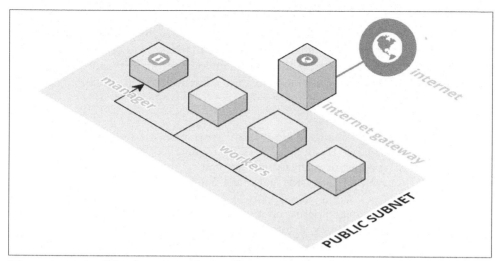

Figure 14-5. A public cluster, in which access is completely open to the internet

Considering a basic cluster that is running HDFS and YARN services, this means that all of the ports for the namenode, datanodes, resource manager, and node managers are accessible from outside the subnet. This includes the standard ports used by the daemons to communicate with each other (e.g., port 8020 for the namenode, port 50010 for a datanode) and those used by users and other clients (e.g., HTTP port 50070 for the namenode).

This topology puts up no roadblocks to accessing it, which is convenient. Anyone can use the cluster from any location. However, it is terrible for security. Anyone can configure a Hadoop client to connect to the cluster and peruse data stored in it, and use it to run jobs. Even if steps are taken to secure the Hadoop services, such as enabling Kerberos and requiring TLS, the cluster components are still exposed to the public and vulnerable to attacks. The convenience is not worth the risk.

The Secured Public Cluster

An important step in securing a public cluster is to restrict the ports that are accessible outside the subnet. A cluster with many services running can make use of a large number of standard ports, but most of them are not pertinent to people or processes outside the cluster. For example, port 50010 is the standard port that a datanode listens on for cluster operations, but cluster clients do not need to reach that port to do their work. So, that port does not need to be exposed outside the subnet hosting the cluster. Port for daemons like the HDFS journalnodes and the ZooKeeper servers, which are purely for internal cluster functioning, need not have any ports exposed at all.

So which ports are necessary? It depends on what clients need to do with the cluster. For people checking on cluster health, it's enough to expose the HTTP ports—or better yet, HTTPS ports—for the namenode, resource manager, and other key daemons. Client processes that run jobs on the cluster or look through its stored data need access to the primary ports of daemons like the namenode (8020), resource manager (8032), and the Hive server (10000).

You could configure nonstandard ports as a means of obscuring the fact that Hadoop daemons are running on your instances. A naïve port scan might assume that a process listening on port 8020 is an HDFS namenode, but might not assume that for the same process listening on, say, port 23456. However, port scanners can perform fingerprinting on responses that they receive, which give away the nature of listening processes. Also, the use of nonstandard ports makes cluster and client configuration much more difficult. So, the practice is pointless.

Source address restrictions are also important to secure a public cluster. Just because the cluster is reachable from the internet does not mean it has to be reachable from the entire internet. Security rules placed on the subnet can easily limit access to IP ranges that are known to be safe.

A secured public cluster is illustrated in Figure 14-6.

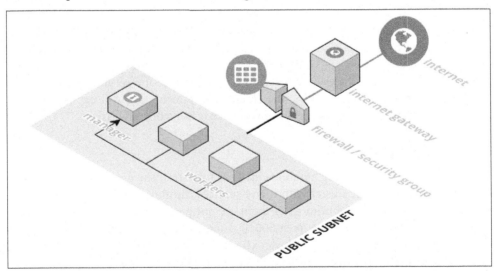

Figure 14-6. A secured public cluster; security rules control what outside sources can access the cluster and which ports are available

The cluster can be configured with authentication and authorization, using Kerberos for example, as an additional layer of protection. This is not a topological choice, but is very effective in further locking down a cluster. *Hadoop Security* by Ben Spivey and Joey Echeverria (O'Reilly) covers "Kerberizing" clusters and many other security topics in great detail.

Gateway Instances

To make a secured public cluster even more secure, you can limit its availability to clients. For example, the HTTP port for the namenode does not need to be directly accessible from outside the cluster; you can use SSH tunneling or a SOCKS proxy to reach it indirectly. It is harder to reach it, but the attack surface of the cluster is reduced, since communications are now encrypted and authenticated with SSH.

It's one thing to want to reach an HTTP port on a cluster with a browser, but another to run a MapReduce job. Client applications do need direct access to work effectively. The strategy here is to only allow client applications to run on designated resources that are specifically configured to have direct access to the cluster. The resources might not even run any cluster daemons, but are there purely for using the cluster. Such a resource running in the cloud provider is called a *gateway instance*, because it provides a gateway for accessing the cluster. Figure 14-7 shows the addition of a gateway instance to a secured public cluster. Access from the internet to the cluster is normally only through the gateway instance, although it still may be possible to reach the cluster directly.

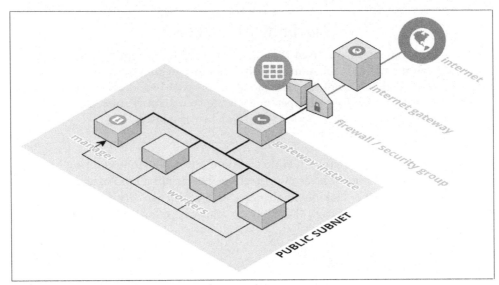

Figure 14-7. A secured public cluster with a gateway instance

Use of gateway instances is less convenient.[2] No longer do users simply run jobs from their local computer or their favorite nearby server; they must connect to a gateway instance, potentially copying their application over, and work from there. Server applications that use a backing Hadoop cluster must be installed out in the cloud provider on gateway instances, instead of on on-premises hardware. They, in turn, must enforce their own security using TLS, passwords, and/or other measures.

The Private Cluster

A gateway instance can be viewed as a kind of bastion, a fortified and controlled entry point for working with a cluster. With gateway instances in place, cluster instances running Hadoop daemons no longer need to be accessible at all from the internet.

A private cluster topology places all of the instances that constitute the cluster in one private subnet. The only way to access the instances is through other subnets. Some of those may in turn be private, but at least one of them, somewhere down the line, is public and hosts gateway instances. Cluster users only ever directly connect to the gateway instances which, ensconced in the cloud provider and locked down, safely access the cluster. A private cluster is illustrated in Figure 14-8. Access to the cluster is only possible through the gateway instance, and access from the internet is routed only to the gateway instance.

---

2 Establishing VPN access to the cluster is an alternative that preserves convenience.

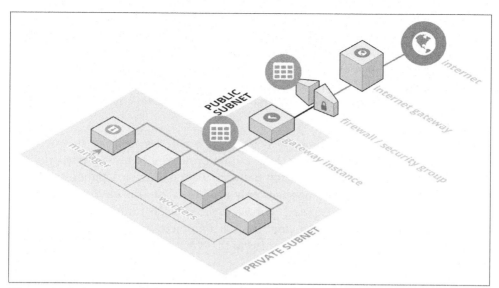

Figure 14-8. A private cluster

A private cluster does not strictly require additional security measures to be implemented, such as TLS or Kerberos, because all communications are either contained within its subnet or on controlled paths to client applications. The cloud provider shields the "soft underbelly" of the cluster from the outside. You may still need to, or want to, implement those measures, depending on the nature of the data that the cluster manages and the number and skill of the users of the cluster.

Administrators can still access cluster instances by tunneling or proxying through gateway instances to the relevant ports.

Cluster Access to the Internet and Cloud Provider Services

The preceding topologies assume that the cluster doesn't initiate interactions with the outside world, but this assumption does not hold true in many real-world deployments. For example, a job executing on a cluster may reach out to a website or to a database running outside the cloud provider to pull down data for analysis. A different job could rely on another cloud provider service, such as object storage, and calls to those service endpoints might be routed outside of the private subnet.

Fortunately, it isn't necessary to open the cluster all the way back up to the internet to satisfy these situations. If a cluster is running in a public subnet, the security rules for outbound traffic can be fashioned to allow exactly the connections that jobs in the cluster need. If there's confidence that the cluster will not be used maliciously, all outbound traffic can be permitted.

A fully locked down private subnet permits no outbound traffic, though, except to gateway instances in order to deliver results. Those gateway instances run in a public subnet, with access to the outside world, so they can be used in routes the cluster uses to reach out. Sometimes, client applications that make use of the cluster can arbitrate that access themselves, so there is no additional work to be done; otherwise, a gateway instance needs to be set up, this time to serve the cluster's needs, and not just users' needs.

One general solution to this problem is to set up a gateway instance as a network address translation (NAT) instance. Like a home router, a NAT instance provides controlled access outside of an isolated network. It must run in a public subnet in order to do its job, but cluster instances only need to talk to the NAT instance, and are not themselves directly exposed. For example, if a job running on the cluster needs to save a data blob to the cloud provider's object storage service, then the request sent to the storage service is routed to the NAT instance, which then handles sending it on to the service.

A proxy instance is a similar solution. Instead of performing NAT, a proxy instance runs a proxy server, such as a SOCKS server, which forwards any requests from the cluster out and returns the results. This could be considered more heavyweight than a NAT instance.

Cloud providers support NAT and proxying in different ways:

- EC2 provides both *NAT instances* and newer *NAT gateways*. A NAT instance is an EC2 instance that launches from a special AMI containing network configuration scripts that, on launch, set up the instance to perform NAT. A NAT gateway is a more abstract element that EC2 automatically manages; it is the newer and usually the better choice.

- GCE does not have first-class support for NAT instances, but supports creating either a NAT instance that uses iptables or a proxy instance that uses Squid to enable access from a private subnet to the internet.

- Azure automatically uses Source Network Address Translation (SNAT) to support outbound connections. If the virtual machine is under a load balancer with a public IP address, the connection is made through the load balancer's IP address; otherwise, a temporary, unconfigurable public IP address is associated with the connection.

Sometimes a NAT or proxy instance is not necessary, because it is possible to run part of a cluster service on a gateway instance directly. A good example of this is Flume, which uses agent processes to accept incoming data and save it to HDFS. Flume agents can run on gateway instances in a public subnet, thereby allowing external sources to deliver data to them directly, but also having a controlled outbound path into the cluster on the private subnet to save that data (or to other agents, depending on the flow architecture).

Geographic Considerations

The topologies developed in this chapter are all logically defined, without concern for where the availability zones in a cluster's subnet exist in the real world. It is not possible to completely ignore this aspect of cluster topology, but fortunately it does not have a large impact on it.

Regions

The guidance for cluster topologies across regions is simple: each cluster should reside in just one region. As described in "Regions" on page 195, network speeds are too slow and data transfer costs are too high to make cross-region topologies practical. Moreover, it is essentially impossible to construct a single working cluster in separate regions where the instances all reside in private subnets, as heavy amounts of NAT or proxying would be necessary for the large volume of traffic between cluster daemons.

Availability Zones

Most clusters will exist in a single availability zone. A cluster that spans multiple availability zones should be set up for high availability (see Chapter 9) in order to cope with the loss of a zone hosting the namenode or resource manager. Under high availability, it is possible to have the two namenodes and two resource managers in separate availability zones.

 See "Planning HA in the Cloud" on page 126 and "Availability Zones" on page 195 for discussions on the price and performance trade-offs of running a cluster that spans availability zones. The higher costs and lower performance that come with such a cluster may drive you to avoid it altogether, making network topology choices moot.

In any of these cases, clusters can reside in private subnets and rely on gateway instances for working with them. The important question becomes: where should gateway instances reside?

A rule of thumb to follow is: *For the highest availability for use of the cluster, gateway instances should run in the same availability zones as the namenodes and resource managers.*

Consider the case of a non-HA cluster running in a single availability zone. Its gateway instances could run in the same zone or in a separate zone. When they run in the same zone, and that zone drops out, then the gateway instances are unavailable, but so is the cluster, so the client applications would not work anyway. When they run in a separate zone, there are two ways to lose functionality:

1. The cluster's availability zone drops out but the gateway instances remain available. The client applications are only usable for the few features, if any, that do not require the cluster.

2. The gateway instances' availability zone drops out but the cluster remains available. However, without any gateway instances, the cluster is effectively unavailable, if it is running in a private subnet.

There is limited advantage to running gateway instances separately from the cluster, so it is generally better to host them in the same availability zone for speed and ease of administration. However, if the client applications are still useful without the cluster, or if some basic "emergency use" gateway instances are running in the same zone as the cluster, then running the client applications separately could still be a good option.

The possibilities for an HA cluster are a little more complex. Here, usually there are one or two key availability zones hosting namenodes and resource managers.[3] If the namenodes and resource managers are all running in a single availability zone, then the calculus does not change compared to the non-HA case. If they are split across two availability zones, things become more interesting, because even if one zone drops out, the daemons in the other zone take over and the cluster remains available.

One option for gateway instances for an HA cluster is to host them in a third availability zone. This way, no matter which of the two cluster's zones drops out, the cluster and its client applications remain available. There is only one set of client applications in existence, so managing them is straightforward. One downside, as in the non-HA case, is that if the third zone drops out, the cluster is still available yet unusable without gateway instances. Also, network speeds between the gateway instances and the cluster are worse, no matter the state of the availability zones.

Another option is to include gateway instances in both of the key availability zones for the cluster. If one of the zones drops out, the client applications are still available and the cluster, configured for HA, still works, so there is no loss of functionality. Including instances in just one zone creates a new single point of failure for using the cluster, so it is better to use both.

---

3 It is theoretically possible to spread out the active and standby daemons across up to four availability zones, but those scenarios are exceedingly rare and not explored here.

However, this complicates management of the gateway instances and client applications since there are two copies of them. Load balancing, application data replication, and other measures are necessary to create a seamless user experience. Still, this option ensures that the cluster is usable whenever it is available.

Starting Topologies

For your first few clusters, it's reasonable to use a secured public cluster topology where only SSH access is required to a small number of bastion hosts. This topology is nearly as secure as a private cluster topology and takes less work to establish and maintain. Gateway instances can be deployed for hosting server applications, and those instances can be protected just like bastions.

As you gain more experience deploying clusters in the cloud, you should think about moving to the private cluster topology for critical clusters. They are more difficult to administer, but experience gained along the way in configuring virtual networks and subnets and defining security rules will lessen the burden. Structurally, they are similar to public secured clusters, except that the gateway instances reside in a separate subnet from the cluster.

You may come up with your own topologies. After all, the practice of deploying Hadoop in the cloud is still evolving, so there is yet room for new ideas. Good topologies will always follow the guiding principles that have been covered in this chapter: minimize outside access, use controlled access points, prefer stronger modes of authentication, and ensure adequate performance.

Higher-Level Planning

The chapters so far in Part V of this book have focused on understanding low-level concepts for designing clusters and making the right choices for cost, performance, and security on a cluster-by-cluster basis. There are concepts at a higher level to consider as well, which come to the forefront once you have become somewhat adept at creating clusters and have resolved many of those low-level questions. Chapter 15 takes a wider view and considers options for how all of your cloud clusters can be managed.

Patterns for Cluster Usage

Eventually you, or your organization, will be at the point where the use of clusters running in your cloud provider is no longer just for research or proof-of-concept work. The important questions now change from whether it is a good idea at all to how best to take advantage of the clusters:

- When should clusters be created and how long should they last?
- Who should be able to use them?
- How should they be created?
- How much work should be sent to the cloud?

Every organization has different answers to these questions, but knowing that there are choices to be made helps you formulate the plan to get from experimentation to regular use of cloud clusters.

Long-Running or Transient?

Of all the questions, the one that tends to come up the earliest and has the most effect on the answers for others is the question of when. When do you create clusters running in your cloud provider, and relatedly, how long should those clusters be available?

There are two dominant answers to the question. The first, which is most like the way that on-prem clusters are used, is that clusters should be set up in advance and tended so that they are always available for anyone to use. Administrators monitor them and resolve problems as they arise, perhaps even increasing or decreasing their sizes or adjusting the mix of service components in response to demand. Meanwhile, users coordinate to work on them, each sharing the storage and computation facilities with everyone else. This arrangement can be called *long-running clusters*.

The second, opposing answer is that clusters should be set up when they are needed and destroyed when they are done with their work or there is no longer demand for them. Each cluster encompasses the storage, compute power, and Hadoop components necessary for the jobs at hand, as laid out by the (usually automated) systems that built it. If the cluster experiences problems, it is destroyed and replaced by a working one. If it is not powerful enough, a new and larger one replaces it. Users can share clusters or have their own, but overall cloud resource usage is managed across all users. This arrangement can be called *transient clusters*.[1]

Most organizations start out in the cloud thinking mostly about long-running clusters, because they are most like on-prem clusters in how they are managed. An existing Hadoop administration team can apply most of their expertise right away; it's as if the instances are simply in a server room they cannot physically access, but otherwise much like any other resources to manage. Users who are already familiar with the standard practices for on-prem clusters can easily transition to cloud clusters that run in the same way.

It's not long before it becomes obvious that long-running clusters can be a waste of money. For example, why run a 20-node cluster all day, every day, when it's only used for 8 hours each work day? Instead, the cluster should be shut down somehow, so that charges aren't incurred every night while the cluster is idle. So, the next stage in the evolution of cloud cluster usage is to have clusters reserved for long spans of time, but running only during certain time periods when demand is anticipated.

"Stopping and Starting Entire Clusters" on page 192 explains more about this mode of operation, including some caveats that come along with it such as the disappearance of ephemeral storage and shifting IP addresses. Beyond those issues lies another problem: What do users do when they want to use a cluster that is stopped? Perhaps they are working outside the normal work day, to finish work during some crunch time. The problem is exacerbated for teams spread across time zones, in which case there may not be a lot of common downtime. How can these users get working, or do they have to wait until the morning in your time zone?

There's also the issue of dealing with workloads that are still in progress on a cluster when it's time to stop it. Even if it is somehow feasible to "freeze" these workloads, the users waiting for the results are out of luck and have to wait even longer for the cluster to restart.

---

1 Sometimes these are instead called *ephemeral clusters*, but to avoid confusion the term *ephemeral* in this book is applied only to ephemeral storage (see "Block Storage" on page 47).

A less severe tactic, similar to wholesale stopping and starting, is to reduce the size of clusters during off-peak hours. A Hadoop cluster can cope with the loss of YARN node managers and, to a certain extent based on replication, HDFS datanodes, while continuing to function. Clusters can therefore be shrunk and grown at certain times of the day or in response to demand, which naturally reduces at off-peak times. *Elastic* clusters like these do a good job of balancing efficiency with availability, but require the help of automation to trigger size adjustments, to reduce or eliminate the burden of performing the work, and to ensure data is managed safely.[2] After all, there is more to adding and removing cluster instances than just allocating or terminating them in the cloud provider.

Instead of focusing on the clusters, and trying to figure out how to run them so that users can get their work done, it can be a good idea to focus on the users, and figure out how to run clusters that cater to them. This change in perspective seeds the idea of creating entire clusters on demand. Why stop and start the same old clusters over and over, when fresh ones can be created and terminated whenever you like? Why struggle to get just the right sizes and components in place, when each cluster can be tailor-made from the start with exactly what users want? Why try to guess when clusters are needed, when they can be made at will?

The idea of transient clusters isn't necessarily obvious at first, because it is not practical with expensive, slow-changing on-prem hardware. It also requires even more automation than elastic clusters, since it involves creating and destroying entire clusters, each with potentially different characteristics; this is much more drastic than just adding or removing instances.

Finally, it creates a new requirement to store critical data somewhere outside the clusters. Fortunately, as described in Chapter 5, there are plenty of options for cloud data storage, and ways to connect to it, like the AWS s3a connector used in "Hive on S3" on page 158, that merge well with workloads. Users do have to adjust their workloads, and their thinking, to have data flow from storage to transient clusters and back again.

However, transient clusters solve many of the problems with long-running clusters. They help to minimize expenses, virtually eliminate ongoing maintenance with the help of robust automation, and avoid struggling with unpredictable times of peak demand.

Both long-running clusters and transient clusters can work well in the cloud, and each mode of operation has its benefits and costs. However, of the two, the benefits to

---

2 For example, simply dropping HDFS datanodes out of a cluster can lead to data loss if blocks are under-replicated or if the dropped datanodes house all of a block's replicas. Shrinking must be done in a controlled fashion to preserve data.

using transient clusters can move you and your organization to a higher level of efficiency and performance.

Single-User or Multitenant?

A cluster for each user? That concept doesn't seem like it could be efficient at all, at first. Yet, once an organization becomes proficient at using transient clusters, it's a possibility worth considering.

Imagine a system where every data scientist and every analyst can have their own bespoke cluster, or even clusters. Since each cluster is made according to the user's specifications, it's much more likely that workloads will succeed for everyone. Since they do not have to share local storage, there is no danger of data being mixed inappropriately or accidentally overwritten. If a cluster starts failing, due to hardware problems or data corruption, it can be torn down and recreated, because it's transient anyway, and only the cluster's single user is affected.

Single-user clusters shift the problem of resource sharing out of each cluster and into the system that allots clusters to users. Because users are no longer sharing cluster instances and disk storage, overall resource requirements can slightly increase. However, because each user doesn't need clusters at all most of the time, resource requirements can decrease, if the clusters are managed effectively (see "Self-Service or Managed?" on page 219).

Confining users to their own clusters leads to effective isolation of their workloads, taking advantage of the strong network and security capabilities of the cloud provider. The problem of preventing users on a shared cluster from accidentally accessing each other's data goes away. This can help to satisfy security requirements for that data.

If single-user clusters are too extreme of an idea, then you could consider per-team clusters, where only a few users have access to a cluster, instead of just one user. It is easier for a small team of users to coordinate among themselves to share cluster resources than for an entire organization. If they all have the necessary authorizations to access cluster data, security requirements within the cluster are relaxed.

The fewer users that have access to a cluster, the more desirable it is for the cluster to be transient. A cluster for a single user should be limited to his or her immediate needs, so that its resources can be returned in good time to the pool for others to use. On the other hand, a multitenant cluster should be long-running, since more people rely on it, and collectively use it more often.

Self-Service or Managed?

Suppose that you are thinking about taking advantage of the flexibility of your cloud provider to create many clusters, some of which are transient, and some of which are for only one or a few users. Whose job is it, exactly, to create and destroy all of these clusters, and how do they know what to do?

In keeping with the questions considered so far, here are two possible answers. The more traditional one is that cluster management is performed by a single controlling entity, perhaps a cloud team, on behalf of the entire organization. A user requests a cluster, describing exactly how big it should be, what Hadoop components must be installed, and who needs access. The cloud team weighs the request against others based on its priority, the clusters that have already been allocated, and other factors. Finally, it creates the cluster and provides its addresses and credentials back to the requester. The cluster is assigned a lifetime and is destroyed when it elapses or when the user indicates that the cluster can be terminated.

The function of managing cluster allocations is certainly one that can be automated, even beyond the core process of creating and destroying clusters. Monitoring systems can track how many instances of what types are being used, and other factors, in order to keep the overall cloud usage within budget. Watchdog processes can clean up clusters automatically after their lifetimes or once they are idle for a while. After automating business processes like these, there might not be much left for a human to do.

If that's so, then why not take humans out of the loop completely, and make the entire process user-driven? A self-service system parallels the consoles and APIs of the cloud providers, working on the level of entire clusters instead of instances and networks and Hadoop components. As is the case with transient clusters, there is a cost to create such a system, but it can lead to increased user satisfaction and greater efficiency in cloud resource usage.

Even with maximized automation around cluster creation, careful monitoring is still vital. It's a boon to users to be granted the power to create their own clusters, but users can forget about them and leave them idle and costing money, reserve too many resources, or misuse what they've been given. At least a light touch of oversight is still necessary to ensure the health of all clusters and to ward off unexpectedly high cloud provider bills.

No matter which choice you pick, it's a reasonable idea to offer only predefined cluster types for users to select. The assumption is that the grand majority of users can make do with a typical, say, "Hive cluster" or "Spark cluster." They needn't be concerned with the details of which network the cluster resides in, or what the security rules are, or even which instance types to use; those can be determined at an organizational level, taking into account the cloud budget, the infrastructure that's already been established, and technical recommendations. Users should be free instead to devote their attention to their workloads and the jobs that they want to get done.

Cloud-Only or Hybrid?

Despite all of the benefits cluster users can reap from using cloud clusters, some may be stuck on-prem. A common reason is data security: it may be necessary by law, regulation, or contract to keep data within local data centers with the approved geographic location, physical security, and network defenses. Another reason is that your organization may not have enough money to afford sending everyone to the cloud. Another is that licenses for essential software used in clusters may require it to be installed only within your own facilities.

The question that is relevant here is: How much of your Hadoop work should be shipped off to cloud clusters? Two simple answers, of course, are "all of it" and "none of it." A third is "some of it," but this answer goes beyond just running some clusters in the cloud provider and others on-prem.

Data analysts prefer to think in terms of their workloads, and not in terms of the clusters they run on. It's why single-user, on-demand clusters are so appealing to them, and it is also key to seeing that a single workload could be arranged to be performed partially on-prem and partially in the cloud. An architecture that works in this way is called a *hybrid cloud*.[3]

A workload running in a hybrid cloud is not a single, enclosed entity. It would usually have a primary segment running on-prem, and secondary segments running in cloud clusters. The idea is to offload processing to the cloud where it makes sense to do so, so that the local demand for resources is lessened. At dividing points in the overall workload, data and logic are transferred up to the cloud, and then results are pulled back.

A hybrid cloud certainly uses less cloud resources than running everything in the cloud, but it does incur data transfer costs, since providers charge for data being sent to and from instances and storage services. Rates are usually quite modest, but it is still wise to design hybrid workloads so that they minimize data transfer. Of course, excessive data transfer stages also extend processing time.

---

3 Some may use the term "hybrid" to refer to elastic clusters that have some instances that exist for the life of the cluster and others that come and go to adjust capacity.

Here are some examples of workloads that could benefit from a hybrid cloud architecture:

- Regulators have determined that data being processed must remain on machines within a locked server room. Processing unrelated to the sensitive data has already been migrated elsewhere, but things are still running too slowly. Some of the work that is peripheral to the sensitive data and that doesn't use it directly is relocated to ancillary jobs in the cloud, which eases the load on the server room. To send even more work to the cloud, identifiers in the data are replaced with anonymizing tokens locally; the scrubbed data is deemed safe to process in the cloud, and other local processes de-anonymize the resulting data once it returns. While overall the amount of work has increased, large portions have been offloaded to the cloud, where it is easier and cheaper to expand.

- There already exists a large on-prem data processing system, perhaps using Hadoop clusters, which works well. In order to expand its capacity for running new analyses, rather than adding more on-prem hardware, Hadoop clusters can be created in the cloud. Data needed for the analyses is copied up to the Hadoop clusters where it is analyzed, and the results are sent back on-prem. The cloud clusters can be brought up and torn down in response to demand, which helps to keep costs lower.

- Vast amounts of data are streaming in, and it all needs to be centralized and processed. To avoid having one single choke point where all of the raw data is sent, a set of cloud clusters can share the load, perhaps each in a geographic location convenient to where the data is generated. These clusters can perform preprocessing of the data, such as cleaning and summarization, thereby spreading the work out. The preprocessed data is finally sent on the final centralized system to be merged.

Notice that the last two examples are not situations where some portion of the workload *must* remain on-prem. You could imagine alternative layouts where all of the processing occurs in the cloud, and only final results are returned, if ever. Just because you can move completely into the cloud does not mean you need to, and a hybrid cloud architecture is one way to take a measured approach that balances the benefits of the cloud with your budget and the time you have to invest.

Watching Cost

A key factor for selecting a cluster usage pattern for your organization is cost. No pattern has a guaranteed cost advantage over another, because so much depends on when and how clusters are used. It takes research and experimentation to find the patterns that give you the most value for what you are paying your cloud provider.

Table 15-1 compares the patterns explained in this chapter through highlighting how they can either save you money or cost you money.

Table 15-1. Comparing cluster usage patterns by cost

Pattern	Possible savings	Possible extra cost
Long-running clusters	Less time waiting for clusters to start and stop, lower resource demand	Wasted idle time, maintenance burden, growing size over time
Transient clusters	Minimal maintenance, high efficiency	Spin-up time, higher resource demand, data transfer to permanent storage
Single-user clusters	Simpler security, smaller size	Higher overall resource demand
Multitenant clusters	Efficient use of resources per user	Complex management, security risks
Self-service clusters	Efficiency of on-demand creation	Need to maintain tooling, waste through overuse
Managed clusters	Easy alignment with budget constraints	Waiting time for usage, administrative effort
Cloud-only clusters	Data transfers stay within the cloud, minimal on-prem costs, integration with provider	Security risks, higher cloud expenditure
Hybrid clusters	Lower cloud expenditure, simpler security	Complex workflows, on-prem maintenance, data transfer costs

While cost is indeed a critical factor for settling on the best way to use the cloud, it is not the only one; fundamentally clusters need to be up and ready when needed. Focusing only on spending on the cloud provider may lead to the implementation of inefficient patterns whose wastefulness outweigh the savings, either in time or money.

The Rising Need for Automation

Running clusters on a cloud provider opens up new options for how to architect your clusters, while making it easier to exercise other options that are already available on-prem. The best choices for your organization can depend on outside factors and on your budget, but cloud providers can support you no matter which paths you choose.

Some of the answers to the questions examined in this chapter drive the need for automation. Even if you have been performing some of the practices described here manually so far, having a cloud provider at your disposal tends to increase cluster usage, simply because of the lower barrier for setting up new clusters. It would quickly grow tiresome to manually create clusters in the face of increased user demand and adjudicate who gets which clusters when. Chapter 16 kicks off the discussion of ways to manage clusters using scripts, tools, services, and cloud provider features. The first technique, that of using images, is a straightforward and highly effective initial way to get more efficient at building more clusters.

Using Images for Cluster Management

It is worthwhile to go through the exercise of building out a Hadoop cluster "by hand," as laid out in Part III, in order to understand how instance allocation, networking, and security rules all play their parts. Once you are building clusters over and over again, though, you'll want to be much more efficient.

You don't usually need to establish virtual networks, routing, and security rules for every new cluster. They can all happily coexist within one or a few networks and abide by the same rules. Each cluster needs its own instances, but starting those up is also straightforward, either by using a provider console or by a single API call. It's Hadoop installation and configuration that takes most of the time.

One method to speed things up is to create images for cluster instances with most of the installation and configuration work baked in. Instances based on those images can already have Hadoop components almost ready to go, requiring only a minimum of additional configuration to become fully functional.

Stamping out cluster instances like this is not only faster, but results in fewer mistakes or unintentional variations. It also lends itself to automation; you could imagine it as part of a complete automatic process for building Hadoop clusters.

Images can be shared. That means that a valuable base image for creating Hadoop cluster instances can benefit not just who built it, but their friends, coworkers, and even their customers.

This chapter starts out by describing the structure of an image, and then covers creating and maintaining them directly and through the use of Packer. At the end, tooling options for creating and managing clusters are described, along with their relationships to images.

The Structure of an Image

The concept of images was introduced in "Images" on page 27.

What makes up an image varies from cloud provider to cloud provider. Fundamentally, though, an image is a set of one or more disk snapshots along with metadata that makes the snapshots available for launching new instances. The snapshot of the root disk, which houses the operating system, is the essential ingredient in an image. Images can include snapshots of additional data disks that are always to be associated with instances launched from the image. The metadata about an image holds its name, describes its features and limitations, links to the snapshots for the image's disks, and may include permissions or other guidance on using it.

Each cloud provider offers a starter set of images for many different operating systems. The operating systems are preconfigured to work within the provider infrastructure, primarily so that they can be seamlessly integrated into virtual networks. Usually, the cloud provider's own client utilities are preinstalled as well, but for all practical purposes they are uncustomized, vanilla installations of the operating systems.

Because base images are so minimal in content, they frequently serve as the basis for new, custom images. For example, a software vendor may start with an instance created from a standard Ubuntu image, install its own software on it and configure it properly, and then create a new image. You can imagine a custom image, then, that already has Hadoop components installed and mostly ready to run.

EC2 Images

An EC2 image, called an *Amazon Machine Image* or *AMI*, consists of the snapshot for a root volume, permissions for who can use the image, and a block device mapping laying out additional EBS or instance store volumes to attach, based on their own snapshots.

The root volume for an image can be hosted on either EBS, making it persistent, or the instance store, making it ephemeral. You should always use EBS-backed instances for Hadoop clusters. They are created faster, have larger root volume capacity, can be stopped and started without losing data, and are stored more efficiently and thus more cheaply within AWS.

Permissions are applied to each AMI to determine who can use them. By default, those you create yourself are private, but you can grant permission to specific users or to the public. You are not charged for others' use of your AMI, only for storing it.

GCE Images

A GCE image consists of a boot loader and templates for the operating system and root filesystem as a single persistent disk. Images can be grouped into *image families* as a framework for versioning them; this way, it is easy to figure out, for example, the latest image available for a specific purpose.

GCE images can be shared in one of two ways. The simpler way is to grant other Google Cloud Platform users the necessary permission to use images in the image's project. While this is straightforward, the permission allows access to all images in the project. The more complex but fine-grained way is to save images to Google Cloud Storage as compressed "raw disk" images. Access controls in Google Cloud Storage govern the saved image files and therefore dictate who may use them.

Azure Images

An Azure image is comprised of the snapshot for a root volume, optional snapshots for additional volumes, and a Resource Manager template defining metadata for the image. Each disk snapshot is formatted as a virtual hard disk (VHD) file, which means that it is possible to supply your own VHD files created outside Azure as the basis for new images. While images available in the Azure Marketplace are treated as single units, your own images are managed as the component VHD files and accompanying template.

The VHD files underlying an Azure image are kept in Azure Storage, and so they may be shared by applying the appropriate permissions to those files, along with distributing the associated template. Users of the image may update the template, which is written in JSON, for their own needs before creating new virtual machines from it and the disk snapshots.

Image Preparation

Suppose that you have an instance running that is just how you like it, and you want to be able to create new instances from the same pattern. If you worked your way through Part III, then you have a cluster's worth of these instances. It's a lot of work, and almost all of it would need to be done again for your next cluster. Even just building the first cluster, there were a lot of steps that had to be repeated on every instance. To save time and effort, then, you'll want to make an image of one of the cluster instances.[1]

---

1 It is possible to create a new image "from scratch," but it is a much more complex effort. Consult your cloud provider's documentation for information.

For easy management later, it's good to work with a single image for any cluster instance. They all have the same software installed, and most Hadoop configuration files are identical, or nearly so, across all of the instances.

A useful variation for complex clusters is to have one image per role, to cover any special infrastructure choices you make. For example, an image for a worker node may call for extra volumes to be attached to be used for HDFS storage, something manager or gateway nodes don't usually need.

Images do not mandate the size of the instance types that may be used for them. The same image can be used for a small gateway node and a heavy manager node, since images focus on the disk storage used for an instance. There may be instance types that are incompatible with an image, but normally many of them apply.

So, decide which cluster instance or instances you'd like to image. You'll want to make changes to it to make it generic, but there's plenty to leave just the way it is, including these items:

- The JDK installation
- The Hadoop user accounts, such as "hdfs" and "yarn"
- The installed Hadoop software
- The Hadoop configuration files and most of the properties in them (read on for exceptions)
- Directories created for Hadoop

There are some files and configurations you can keep, but you might wish to change for improved security:

SSH keys for the Hadoop user accounts
The keys are necessary to control Hadoop services from the manager instance or instances, but there is no reason that every future cluster has to use the same set of keys. Leaving the keys in place would let a manager instance in one cluster connect via SSH to instances in another cluster, which may be a security issue for you. The SSH key used to connect to the instances from your own local computer, however, needs to remain, or else you will be unable to reach your cluster.

The file $HOME/.ssh/authorized_keys in each Hadoop user account
This keeps track of which SSH keys are trusted for logging in. If you dispose of the SSH keys for the user accounts, then this file should be cleaned out to no longer include them. It does need to retain the SSH key used for outside connections from your local computer.

Finally, there are some things that should be changed, as they are specific to the cluster:

IP addresses in the Hadoop configuration files
> A new cluster built from the image will have different IP addresses, so replace those in *core-site.xml*, *yarn-site.xml*, and the others with tokens indicating what they should be. If someone uses the image and forgets to fill in the token, it will be obvious in error messages. For example, you should change the "fs.defaultFS" property in *core-site.xml* to something like "hdfs://${manager.ip}:8020/".

ZooKeeper configuration files
> The file *zoo.cfg* contains the IP addresses for each quorum server, so those should be replaced with tokens like other IP addresses. The content of *myid*, which unfortunately must be unique per server, should be replaced as well, or else the file should just be removed.

Local data and code
> If you uploaded files to the cluster for import into HDFS, uploaded job code to run, or extracted files from the cluster to look at or save, they should be wiped away so that new clusters do not waste space carrying them forward. In addition, any data still resident in cluster data stores such as HDFS should be deleted and/or purged. Each image should provide a clean starting state for new clusters.

The file $HOME/.ssh/known_hosts in each Hadoop user account
> Because IP addresses will be different in new clusters, the mapping between hosts and IP addresses in this file will be obsolete or, if some IP address does happen to get reused, incorrect, causing SSH connections to fail. The file should be deleted.

It's easy to miss a change or two when preparing an instance. Fortunately, the process can be performed iteratively, where each image is better than its predecessor. As time goes on, the needs for the image will evolve anyway, perhaps to include more Hadoop components or third-party applications.

Wait, I'm Using That!

Obviously, preparing an instance to be imaged as just described will break it as a cluster instance. If you cannot spare the instance, there are other ways to proceed.

The simplest alternative is to image the instance as it is, and then create a separate instance from the image to do the preparation work. You will need to stop the original instance in order to create the image, so that it is guaranteed that there are no ongoing writes to the disk that could cause a disk snapshot to be corrupted. So, this doesn't require breaking a cluster, but does require degrading it. A worker node is a good candidate here, since Hadoop can recover when one drops out.

Another alternative is to create a new instance from the original image used for the cluster and work through the Hadoop installation and configuration steps from the beginning, modifying them here and there so that the end result is correct for imaging. This method is attractive since it eliminates the possibility that anything will be left over from the real cluster, but it takes more time, and it's easy to miss some steps.

Eventually you will want to automate this manual, error-prone work. See "Automated Image Creation with Packer" on page 234 for how to get started with using Packer for image creation; for now, imaging an existing instance yields quick results.

Image Creation

Once the instance is prepared, it can be imaged. The procedure for doing so varies depending on your cloud provider.

Image Creation in AWS

Creating an AMI from an EBS-backed instance is straightforward.[2] First, stop the instance to be sure that there is no changing disk state. Then, locate your instance in the list of EC2 instances and select it. Click the Actions button and select Image, then Create Image from the drop-down menu.

In the Create Image dialog, as shown in Figure 16-1, give the new image a name and description. The table of instance volumes lists each attached volume that will be snapshotted as part of the image creation process. You can add more volumes, either as EBS snapshots or as ephemeral instance store volumes. Finally, click Create Image to create a new AMI.

A snapshot is taken of the root volume and any other attached EBS volumes, and AMI metadata is generated and registered with AWS. The process can take some time, mostly due to the snapshot work. Eventually, the AMI will appear in the list of images shown when you select AMIs from the EC2 menu.

---

2 Because you should not use instance store-backed AMIs for Hadoop clusters, the differing procedure for creating those is not described here.

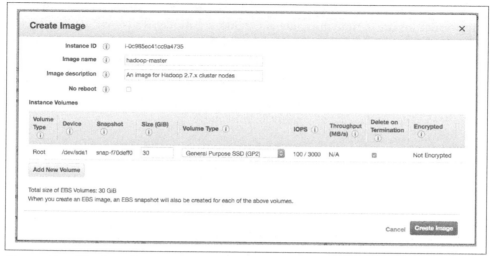

Figure 16-1. The form for creating a new AMI

Image Creation in Google Cloud Platform

An image can only be created from an unattached root disk. The first step in creating an image from an instance is to ensure that the root disk for the instance is not automatically deleted when the instance itself is terminated. In the Google Cloud Platform console, select VM instances from the Google Cloud Platform menu. Follow the hyperlink for the name of the instance to image, so that a page with its details is displayed. Look for the "Boot disk and local disks" table, as shown in Figure 16-2; below it is a checkbox labeled "Delete boot disk when instance is deleted." If the checkbox is checked, then select Edit from the menu at the top of the page, clear the checkbox, and click the Save button.

Figure 16-2. The disk attached to an image and the cleared deletion checkbox

Now it is safe to delete the instance by using the Delete option in the top menu. If the confirmation dialog includes a checkbox for deleting the boot disk, be sure it is not checked.

Select Disks from the Google Cloud Platform menu. The table of disks should include the former root disk for the instance. Eventually the "In use by" column for the disk will be empty, as shown in Figure 16-3, indicating that the disk is no longer attached to its former instance. Note the name of the disk.

Figure 16-3. The unattached disk ready for imaging

Select Images from the Google Cloud Platform menu. The many public images available from Google are listed, but you will be making your own private image. Select the Create Image option from the menu at the top of the page. Fill in the form for the new image, as shown in Figure 16-4, including its name, family, and description. Select Disk for the source of the image, and pick the disk from the recently deleted instance as the "Source disk." Click Create to create the new image.

Figure 16-4. The form for creating a new image in GCE

Return to the Images page. Eventually, the new image appears in the table of available images. At this point, if you wish, you can return to the list of disks and delete the snapshot used as the foundation for the image.

Image Creation in Azure

Creating an image in Azure is a largely manual process that does not involve the Azure portal. The first step, for a Linux virtual machine, is to "deprovision" the instance to be imaged by running a command on it. This eliminates data on disk that would be problematic for new instances created from the image:

```
$ sudo waagent -deprovision+user -force
```

The remaining steps require use of the Azure CLI, properly configured to work with your account. The three steps to execute, after ensuring that the CLI is in Resource Manager mode, are to deallocate (stop) the virtual machine, then "generalize" it, and finally capture it as VHD snapshots and a JSON template. The snapshots are saved in Azure Blob Storage and named with the prefix you provide:

```
# switch to Resource Manager mode
$ azure config mode arm
# stop the virtual machine
$ azure vm deallocate -g my_first_cluster -n manager
# generalize the virtual machine
$ azure vm generalize -g my_first_cluster -n manager
# capture its disks and generate a template
$ azure vm capture -g my_first_cluster -n manager -p snap -t manager.json
```

Image Use

It's simple to use your new image in AWS and Google Cloud Platform. When launching an instance, instead of selecting a standard base image for your instances, select your own. Other than that, the procedure for launching instances does not change.

In Azure, use the JSON template generated by the image creation process to launch a new virtual machine. This can be done from the Azure CLI. It is up to you to define additional resources needed for the virtual machine that otherwise can be automatically created by the Azure portal when creating virtual machines. You can target an existing virtual network and subnet for the new virtual machine, but you must allocate a NIC and, if you wish, a public IP address. These resources can be created in the Azure portal or through the Azure CLI. After creating the NIC, find its ID, a path-like string, which you then must supply to the interactive virtual instance creation process:

```
# create a public IP address
$ azure network public-ip create my_first_cluster manager3_ip -l "eastus"
# create a NIC that uses the public IP address
$ azure network nic create my_first_cluster manager3_nic \
> -m cluster_net -k default -p manager3_ip -l "eastus"
# find the ID of the new NIC
$ azure network nic show my_first_cluster manager3_nic
```

```
# create the new virtual machine from the template
$ azure group deployment create my_first_cluster my_image_deployment \
> -t manager.json
info:    Executing command group deployment create
info:    Supply values for the following parameters
vmName: manager_3
adminUserName: root
adminPassword: password
networkInterfaceId: /subscriptions/.../networkInterfaces/myNic
```

Once your instances are ready, connect to them via SSH using the same key used to access the original instance. Reconfiguring instances launched from a Hadoop image takes much less work than starting from scratch:

- If necessary, generate new SSH keys for the Hadoop user accounts and add them to the necessary *authorized_keys* files. Then, use them to connect from the manager instance to each worker instance in order to populate the *known_hosts* files.

- Edit the Hadoop configuration files with the private IP addresses for the new cluster instances, replacing the placeholder tokens.

- Edit or recreate the *myid* files for the ZooKeeper servers.

- Edit the database server hostname for the remote Hive metastore.

Scripting Hadoop Configuration

The preceding steps should only take a few moments, but since they are well-defined and only depend on a few pieces of information, they are ripe for scripting. Appendix B provides example scripts for automating the work.

Image Maintenance

A custom image remains available until you decide to deregister or delete it. Your cloud provider charges for the storage used by the snapshots backing the image, and some also charge a small amount for the image definition itself, but instances launched from an image are charged for separately. In fact, even after an image is no longer available, instances launched from it keep running.

It's common to want to improve an image, to address problems with it, or to add new stock configurations or installed software. Because snapshots are immutable, you cannot update the image itself. Instead, launch an instance based on the image, make the desired changes to it, and then create a new image from the instance.

Under GCE, successive images can be placed in the same image family. This mechanism gives you the option to launch the most recent (and likely "best") image in a family.

It may not be long before you have made a lot of images, and you will want to consider ways to track them and to enable users to understand what they contain and which ones to use. Cloud providers do not provide services to help with these tasks, so here are some ideas to get you started:

- Use image names and tags in well-defined ways to describe image contents and purposes.
- Maintain an image registry, using a spreadsheet, wiki, or simple web page.
- Wrap tools that automate image creation in calls to databases holding image information.

Image Deletion

Over time, then, images tend to pile up. To save money and make tracking images easier, you'll want to get rid of older images that should no longer be in use. As with image creation, the image deletion process varies across cloud providers.

Image Deletion in AWS

Select Images from the EC2 menu, and highlight the image to delete in the list of images. Look at its details and note the IDs of the snapshots for the root EBS volume and any other attached EBS volumes listed as "Block Devices"; each ID begins with "snap-". Then, click the Actions button and select Deregister from the drop-down menu.

A deregistered AMI is no longer available for use in launching new instances, but deregistration does not destroy the snapshots backing the former image. Select Snapshots from the EC2 menu to see the list of snapshots, select the snapshots used for the deregistered AMI, and select Delete from the Actions button drop-down menu.

Image Deletion in Google Cloud Platform

GCE lets you either *deprecate* or *delete* an image. A deprecated image can still be used, but does not appear by default in the list of available images. When an image is deprecated, an image must be named as its replacement. A deleted image, in contrast, is simply no longer available.

To either deprecate or delete an image, select Images from the Google Cloud Platform menu. Select the image to work with, and select either Deprecate or Delete from the options in the menu at the top of the page. After confirming, the image will disappear from the list of images. To see a deprecated image once again, use the "Show deprecated images" link at the bottom of the list.

Image Deletion in Azure

To delete an image in Azure, simply discard the JSON template and delete the VHD files from storage.

Automated Image Creation with Packer

Creating images manually is fine for small-scale or exploratory work, but a production environment requires speed, predictability, and robustness. Packer (*https://www.packer.io/intro/index.html*) from HashiCorp is a leading tool for this purpose. It takes as input a JSON template describing how to build an image, runs through the steps as prescribed, and then creates a new image in the cloud provider. The template serves as one form of documentation for what the image contains, and it can be placed in version control for safekeeping and to track changes over time.

Example 16-1 shows a simple Packer template that creates an AMI.

Example 16-1. Example Packer template

```
{
  "variables": {
    "ami_name": null,
    "region": null,
    "source_ami": null,
    "ssh_username": null
  },
  "builders": [{
    "type": "amazon-ebs",
    "ami_name": "{{user `ami_name`}}",
    "instance_type": "m3.large",
    "region": "{{user `region`}}",
    "source_ami": "{{user `source_ami`}}",
    "ssh_pty": "true",
    "ssh_username": "{{user `ssh_username`}}"
  }],
  "provisioners": [{
    "type": "shell",
    "inline": "sudo yum install --assumeyes wget"
  }]
}
```

A Packer template uses one or more *builders* to build images for different platforms and tools that can use images. There are builders for creating images for EC2 and GCE and VHDs for Azure. Each builder requires information about the source image to work from. In the template in Example 16-1, the source AMI is specified as a variable passed to the template, along with other variables.

Provisioners in the template can run processes on the instances being used by the builders to perform installation and configuration tasks. Some provisioners use shell scripts, run either on the instances or locally, while others use common infrastructure automation tools like Ansible, Chef, and Puppet. The provisioner in Example 16-1 performs an installation of the wget utility on the build instance, so the final image will have it already installed.

Packer can run on your local computer, remotely connecting to the cloud provider using credentials that you supply. Each builder accepts credentials differently; the EC2 builders look in a variety of typical locations for the access key ID and secret access key, including the environment:[3]

```
$ export AWS_ACCESS_KEY_ID=...
$ export AWS_SECRET_ACCESS_KEY=...
```

Assuming those keys have been set, the following command line works to build an image from the example template. It works in us-east-1 and selects a specific CentOS AMI as the source:

```
$ packer build -var 'region=us-east-1' -var 'source_ami=ami-6d1c2007' \
> -var 'ami_name=PackerTest1' -var 'ssh_username=centos' packer.json
```

Packer outputs progress as it builds and provisions, and then finally reports the ID of the new AMI. (Yours will be unique.)

```
==> Builds finished. The artifacts of successful builds are:
--> amazon-ebs: AMIs were created:

us-east-1: ami-5c29154b
```

Packer has just done the work of creating an instance from a source image, installing software on it, and using it to create a new image. Along the way it handled deciding the choice of network and security rules for the temporary instance, generating an SSH key pair to use, and cleaning up after itself. Even for making simple images, automation has compelling advantages.

The example template can be augmented to perform all of the work needed to create a base image for a Hadoop cluster; it's a matter of encoding the steps performed in Chapter 9 and elsewhere. Shell provisioners can perform software downloads and

---

3 This is one of the less secure methods. See the builder documentation for all of the options.

installations, file provisioners can copy up templates for configuration files, and other shell provisioners can use hands-off editing tools from sed up to Perl and Python to add and change configuration information.

Unfortunately, Packer cannot do all of the work. Specifically, the information listed in "Image Use" on page 231 still is not available until an actual cluster is being constructed. So, there is still room for automation outside of Packer to get to a complete, working Hadoop cluster in the cloud.

Automated Cloud Cluster Creation

Cloud providers have their own services for automatically creating Hadoop clusters, some of which are described in "Hadoop Solutions from Cloud Providers" on page 8. They present a more hands-off approach to cluster management, focusing instead on what you want to do with the clusters. If you are looking for a tool that builds cloud clusters that are more under your direct control, you have some choices.

Cloudera Director

Cloudera Director[4] supports creating clusters in AWS, Google Cloud Platform, and Azure. It can be run as a server process or through a standalone client, both of which are installed and run directly. Director handles creating instances and then installing Cloudera Manager, Cloudera's own cluster management tool, and the company's CDH distribution of Hadoop components. Once a cluster is created, Director can manage adding and removing instances from it, and terminate it when you are done with it.

Director can manage many clusters at once, and leaves it up to the user to select the components and define the topology for each cluster. The Director client works with configuration files defining all aspects of the Cloudera Manager and cluster installations and configurations. The server supports a RESTful API that enables scripting, and Cloudera distributes Java and Python client libraries.

Hortonworks Data Cloud

Hortonworks Data Cloud (HDCloud) is an AWS Marketplace application that runs inside EC2. Its web console lets you create clusters running the company's HDP distribution of Hadoop components, managed by Apache Ambari. Cluster templates can be defined and reused to create new similar clusters, and the application allows

---

4 Disclaimer: At the time of this writing, the author is an employee of Cloudera who works on Director. As such, the descriptions of Director and competing products in this section may be unavoidably uneven. Please interpret the descriptions as informative and avoiding advocacy.

for resizing, cloning, and termination on demand. The user interface includes links to the web interfaces for Ambari and other Hadoop components.

HDCloud offers a curated set of cluster types, some including Spark or Hive, and supports options that cover the instance types for master (manager) and worker instances, whether to use an existing or new VPC, and whether to use a shared remote Hive metastore database.

Each cluster template can be represented in JSON, and a CLI tool downloadable from HDCloud can use such templates to perform cluster operations.

Qubole Data Service

The Qubole Data Service (QDS), available online, includes a cluster management solution for creating and configuring clusters in AWS, Google Cloud Platform, and Azure. The service starts you off with definitions for a few default clusters to get you started, but you can create your own definitions, selecting from a set of predefined types. The core Hadoop components, as well as others including Spark and HBase, are compatible with the Apache distributions. QDS monitors cluster usage and terminates them when they are idle in order to manage costs.

QDS has topology options that include instance types for master (manager) and slave (worker) instances, parameters for AWS spot instance proportion and pricing limits, and virtual network and subnet placement. There is also access to Hadoop configuration property overrides, along with suggestions.

General System Management Tools

The tools just described are created and supported by third-party vendors, and some of them may cost money to use. For those reasons, or others, you may decide to create your own homegrown cluster creation tool. The cloud providers each have powerful APIs that can be used to perform the work otherwise done manually through their web consoles, and a general management tool like Ansible, Chef, or Puppet can be employed to direct any configuration tasks that need to be performed beyond what is already baked into images.

If it is not obvious yet, however, then it is important to understand before setting out that such an effort, while feasible, can be time-consuming. Creating your own tool may appear easy at first. However, it requires deep understanding of your cloud provider's API, including any quirks and known issues, and staying up-to-date with it as it changes. The tool must be able to reach out to new instances to issue necessary, nontrivial commands, all while coping with network configurations and security rules imposed on the instances. A cluster creation tool may eventually be called upon not just to create clusters but to destroy them as well, or change their size, or reconfigure them, all of which makes development and maintenance more expensive.

On the other hand, with your own tooling you have full control and can address any unique needs that vendor tools do not support. You are also free to use any Hadoop distribution you choose, including the "vanilla" versions offered directly by Apache. A custom tool may integrate more easily into your existing systems than an off-the-shelf, general-purpose product.

Images or Tools?

When it comes to choosing between managing clusters using either images or tools, you are strongly encouraged to use a tool that you can adapt to your desired processes. Images are excellent for preserving the static needs of cluster instances, but they do not apply well to the inescapable dynamic tasks that must be performed to fully create clusters. Besides built-in automation for cluster creation, tools can modify and destroy clusters and perform monitoring. They also abstract away the complexity of working with a cloud provider.

Some tools can themselves use images as a way to save work that they would otherwise need to do, like software installation or operating system updates. Clusters are then spun up more quickly, which saves money and reduces user-waiting times. Organizational requirements about the contents and configuration of all cloud instances are more easily enforced by creating and using "blessed" images for tools to consume.

When your organization is ready to consider automated cluster creation, first try some of the existing tools to see if they can meet your needs. Here are some reasons why, after trying what's already out there, you might decide to roll your own tooling:

- You have security requirements that cannot be satisfied by the tools already available.
- Your organization already has strong expertise in automation tools and in working with a cloud provider API.
- Lack of visibility into or precise control over existing tools' activity runs against organizational prerogatives.

If none of the existing tools are satisfactory, then at least trying them out will give you ideas for how your own tooling should work.

More Tooling

Image creation is just one area where scripting and tooling can make it easier to stand up Hadoop clusters in the cloud. Chapter 17 explores other areas, such as monitoring and automation, where tools and scripts shine.

Monitoring and Automation

As use of Hadoop clusters in the cloud grows in your organization, it becomes more important to be able to monitor them. Early on, monitoring focuses on ensuring that the clusters are fully up and not overloaded; this information can help guide your future choices for instance types, cluster size, storage size, and network configuration. As time goes on, monitoring data will become more important for keeping tabs on overall cloud expenditure. Of course, cloud clusters themselves will also become more crucial to the organization, so it becomes doubly important to be sure they are working properly.

The need for monitoring is somewhat less when clusters are transient (see "Long-Running or Transient?" on page 215). A transient cluster does not survive for long, so if it does have problems, it can be torn down and replaced using systems already established. Long-running clusters, on the other hand, need more monitoring, as it's necessary that they remain in good shape for continuous or on-demand use.

There are two facets to monitoring cloud clusters: monitoring the cloud provider resources themselves, and monitoring the Hadoop components running on them. As you may have noticed, the cloud provider's consoles already deliver health information, and so it's good to start by considering all the monitoring features they offer.

Monitoring Choices

When you're ready to start monitoring Hadoop clusters, you'll find that you have choices for which monitoring system to use. The major cloud providers each support monitoring infrastructures that you can tap into to get information about your instances, storage, and many other resources. You also have the option of using a system you create and maintain yourself.

Cloud Provider Monitoring Services

The information available in cloud providers' compute consoles is just the basics, what's necessary to give a useful overview of resource health; you can get much more information through their monitoring services.

Each provider's monitoring service has the advantage of being tightly integrated, delivering the most up-to-date metrics without extra effort on your part in terms of configuration. A downside for them is that they are generally agnostic of the software, like Hadoop, using the resources, so it is up to you to cover monitoring for them.[1] They can accept custom metrics, but you must install and run the code to generate each metric and upload it.

Besides watching numeric metrics, monitoring can entail saving and analyzing the contents of logs. Here again, cloud provider monitoring services can be configured to ingest logs, such as the HDFS namenode log and the YARN resource manager log, and perform basic analysis on them to look for signs of trouble. The logs are stored in the provider's own storage service, so you can look at them yourself as well.

Finally, monitoring services can issue alerts when metrics cross defined thresholds, or when logs indicate a problem. Email is always an option for receiving alerts, but integrations can enable alerting via pager, text message, or instant message. In some cases, you can also configure automatic actions that the provider should take on your behalf, such as creating new instances or restarting daemons.

Cloud provider monitoring is free for basic levels, but advanced features such as custom metrics can cost extra. Expense can be one reason why you might select your own monitoring solution instead of a cloud provider's, but the seamless integration and features that you get up front make them compelling and worth evaluating.

If you are using AWS, CloudWatch is the monitoring service to investigate. It supports a wide range of metrics for assessing the health of EC2 instances, RDS database servers, EBS volumes, and more, and its API can accept custom metrics that you send. Basic CloudWatch monitoring is automatically enabled under EC2. The service directly supports the submission of logs to its own storage and can be configured to scan them for patterns indicating trouble. Alarms raised from problem conditions can result in alerts sent to personnel or automated actions to be taken by AWS itself.

Google offers a monitoring service called Stackdriver, which can monitor both Google Cloud Platform resources as well as AWS resources.[2] Besides a large number of metrics for Google Cloud Platform, Stackdriver supports many metrics for AWS

---

1 A cloud provider's own Hadoop services, like Amazon EMR, will often integrate with its monitoring.

2 Stackdriver was originally an independent service, which Google acquired in 2014.

services as well as third-party applications running on either provider, including HBase, Kafka, and ZooKeeper. Beyond metrics, Stackdriver has a log ingestion and analysis capability called Stackdriver Logging as well as built-in support for uptime checks.

The monitoring capabilities in Azure are collected under the term Azure Monitor. By itself, Azure Monitor is a RESTful API for managing metrics and alerts, with SDKs available for several languages. However, it is possible to configure alerts for Azure's wide variety of metrics using the Azure portal, its CLI, or Powershell. The Log Analytics service, which is part of the Microsoft Operational Management Suite, is capable of receiving logs from applications running either on Azure or elsewhere and providing search and analysis on them. The Application Insights service, which runs within Azure, functions as a management portal for gathering application-specific metrics, gathered either through runtime or development-time integration.

Rolling Your Own

If you do not prefer using a cloud provider monitoring service, you can run a separate application that is capable of monitoring your clusters. Applications such as Apache Ambari and Cloudera Manager provide comprehensive monitoring capabilities[3] for Hadoop clusters, and they can be pointed to clusters running on a cloud provider, provided that network connectivity is established. Perhaps you already have a system established in your organization; it could similarly be extended to the cloud. Such applications are generally agnostic of whether clusters they monitor are in the cloud or on-prem, but for many monitoring needs that doesn't matter.

Appendix C contains tips for configuring Nagios, a popular open source monitoring system, to monitor a Hadoop cluster running on a cloud provider, beyond what normally would need to be done for an on-prem cluster. Before leaping into configuring it, or any other system, read on to learn about provider command-line interfaces, which are essential for building the foundational scripts to support your monitoring.

Cloud Provider Command-Line Interfaces

Thus far in this book, you've been pointed almost exclusively to cloud provider consoles to perform operations such as allocating and terminating instances, configuring networks, setting security rules, and checking on resource health. Becoming comfortable with your cloud provider's CLI is an important step to setting up efficient, automated monitoring and control capabilities.

---

3 As cloud usage for Hadoop clusters continues to increase, it is likely that the applications will become more aware of where clusters are running and provide new features to be more effective.

AWS CLI

The AWS CLI (*https://aws.amazon.com/cli/*) is a single Python-based application that can work with the gamut of services such as EC2, RDS, S3, and Kinesis. It can be installed using native operating system installers (like MSI for Microsoft Windows), or through pip, Python's package installation tool:

```
$ sudo pip install awscli
```

You must have an AWS access key and secret key to use the AWS CLI. The tool can locate the keys in any of several locations; a good option is to store them in the *.aws/credentials* file. After installing the CLI, you can configure it to use your keys in its default profile using the aws configure command:

```
$ aws configure
AWS Access Key ID [None]: AKIAXXXXXXXXXXXXXXXX
AWS Secret Access Key [None]: XXXXXXXXXXXXXXXXXXXXXXXXXXXXXXXXXXXXXXXX
Default region name [None]: us-east-1
Default output format [None]: json
```

The CLI can report results in JSON, as plain text, or in a tabular format. Interpretation of results by automated scripts is easiest with JSON, since it can be parsed in a straightforward fashion. The CLI itself can filter down its JSON results as well, using the JMESPath (*http://jmespath.org/*) query language.

To check if the CLI is working, try listing the available EC2 regions:

```
$ aws ec2 describe-regions
{
    "Regions": [
        {
            "Endpoint": "ec2.ap-south-1.amazonaws.com",
            "RegionName": "ap-south-1"
        },
        {
            "Endpoint": "ec2.eu-west-2.amazonaws.com",
            "RegionName": "eu-west-2"
        },
    ...
```

Google Cloud Platform CLI

The Google Cloud SDK (*https://cloud.google.com/sdk/*) houses the CLI for Google Cloud Platform, and is comprised of the tools gcloud, gsutil, and bq. Most operations are provided through the gcloud tool, while gsutil is used for working with Google Cloud Storage and bq with BigQuery. You install the SDK using native operating system installers.

After installation, the SDK must be configured using the gcloud init command. This establishes the default configuration for the CLI tools, including the account to authorize with and the default project. The authorization process includes the use of a browser window to confirm authorization of the local SDK installation for your account:

```
$ gcloud init
```

To check if the CLI is working, try listing your projects. The default output format is a general human-readable one, but many formats are available, including JSON, CSV, and YAML, through the --format option:

```
$ gcloud projects list
PROJECT_ID              NAME              PROJECT_NUMBER
my-first-cluster-1311   My First Cluster  123456789012
temporal-parser-127719  My First Project  372793013720
$ gcloud projects list --format=json
[
  {
    "createTime": "2016-05-14T17:05:48.748Z",
    "lifecycleState": "ACTIVE",
    "name": "My First Cluster",
    "projectId": "my-first-cluster-1311",
    "projectNumber": "123456789012"
  },
  {
    "createTime": "2016-04-10T19:52:51.350Z",
    "lifecycleState": "ACTIVE",
    "name": "My First Project",
    "projectId": "temporal-parser-127719",
    "projectNumber": "372793013720"
  }
]
```

Format-specific attributes and projections can be used to filter down and modify the output results as desired. For example, JSON output can be culled down using simple projections to pick out fields:

```
$ gcloud projects list '--format=json(name)'
[
  {
    "name": "My First Cluster"
  },
  {
    "name": "My First Project"
  }
]
```

Azure CLI

The Azure CLI (*https://azure.github.io/projects/clis/*) comes in two forms: a cross-platform CLI tool[4] and a set of PowerShell cmdlets. This section covers only the cross-platform CLI. It can be installed using native installers for macOS or Windows, or through the npm package management tool:

```
$ npm install -g azure-cli
```

Docker images hosting the tool are also available.

After installation, the CLI must be used to log in to Azure and become associated with your account. The authorization process includes the use of a browser window to confirm authorization of the local CLI for your account:

```
$ azure login
```

By default, the CLI operates in Azure Resource Manager mode, which is recommended for new Azure usage and is used throughout this book.

To check if the CLI is working, try listing your resource groups. The default output format is a general human-readable one, but you can request JSON by passing the --json option. The tool itself does not offer ways to filter down JSON output, but an external tool such as jq (*https://stedolan.github.io/jq/*) or JMESPath (*http://jmespath.org/*) can do that job for you. (The following command output is edited for fit.)

```
$ azure group list
info:    Executing command group list
+ Listing resource groups
data:    Name              Location  Provisioning State  Tags:
data:    ----------------  --------  ------------------  -----
data:    my_first_cluster  eastus    Succeeded           null
info:    group list command OK
$ azure group list --json
[
  {
    "id": "/subscriptions/12345678-.../resourceGroups/my_first_cluster",
    "name": "my_first_cluster",
    "properties": {
      "provisioningState": "Succeeded"
    },
    "location": "eastus"
  }
]
$ azure group list --json | jq '.[] | { name }'
{
  "name": "my_first_cluster"
}
```

---

4 At the time of writing, version 2 of the CLI is in development.

Data Formatting for CLI Results

Each cloud provider CLI is capable of generating output in human-readable formats, often with clarifying colors, indentation, and tabular markings. Each CLI also supports one or more machine-readable formats; notably, each CLI can produce JSON output. So, it's helpful to standardize on JSON as the output format of choice for scripting and automation, especially for systems that work across cloud provider boundaries. The rich ecosystem of applications that can consume and transform JSON also make it a great choice.

What to Monitor

Now that you have your cloud provider CLI ready to use, you can think about the questions you want to answer through monitoring. This section starts you off with some basic ones, to get you familiar with using the CLI or other ways to script checks.

Instance Existence

The first question to consider, one which is silly for on-prem clusters, is whether the instances a Hadoop cluster runs on exist at all. While you can be confident that in almost all cases an instance will not vanish without you knowing about it, things can get confusing in those rare cases when you assume an instance is there, but it's gone.

An instance existence check is not as useful for temporary instances (discussed in "Temporary Instances" on page 25), since those are expected to disappear after some amount of time. You will want to apply this check to ordinary, permanent instances, such as manager instances, nontemporary worker instances, or essential gateways.

Given the IP address of an instance,[5] how can you check that the instance exists in the cloud provider? The examples in Example 17-1 show how you can answer that question using the provider CLIs.

Example 17-1. Example existence checks using provider CLIs

```
# AWS
$ aws ec2 describe-instances --instance-id=i-12345678901234567
# Google Cloud Platform
$ gcloud compute instances describe instance-name
# Microsoft Azure
$ azure vm show resource-group-name vm-name
```

---

5 Should this be the private IP address or public IP address? See "Hadoop Daemon Status" on page 248 for discussion.

Instance Reachability

It's not enough for an instance to exist to know that it is fundamentally functional; an instance also needs to be reachable, so that you can work with it as necessary. The definition of reachability can vary. Here, an instance is considered reachable if an SSH connection can be established to it. There are other ways to reach instances such as through web interfaces, and those are important as well, but SSH reachability is fundamental for maintaining control of your clusters.

Reachability checks using a provider CLI

The AWS CLI supports a `describe-instance-status` EC2 command, which returns basic status information for instances. Including the `--include-all-instances` option permits the command to return status information for instances that aren't running:

```
$ aws ec2 describe-instance-status --instance-id=i-12345678901234567 \
> --include-all-instances
```

The JSON result describes not only the "state" of the instance, which indicates if the instance is running, stopped, or other values, but also overall system and instance status information. Consult the EC2 documentation (*http://docs.aws.amazon.com/AWSEC2/latest/UserGuide/monitoring-system-instance-status-check.html*) for full details on interpreting the command results. In general, if the instance status is "ok", AWS considers the instance reachable.

The Google Cloud Platform CLI does not include reachability checks for SSH, although you can configure a *health check* that monitors whether an instance is reachable over HTTP or HTTPS. For SSH, however, you have the option of using the CLI to connect, without needing to know what the IP address of the instance is. Combining that with a simple command to execute creates a good reachability check:

```
$ gcloud compute ssh --ssh-key-file /path/to/google_key.pem instance-name \
> --command "echo OK"
```

The Azure CLI does not include reachability checks over SSH. Here, your best course of action is to simply attempt an ordinary SSH connection. It is possible to retrieve the public IP address of a virtual machine through the CLI by using the name of its public IP address resource, and that can be embedded into a basic SSH command to form a basic reachability check:

```
$ ssh -i /path/to/azure_key.pem \
> userid@$(azure network public-ip show \
>           resource-group public-ip-address-resource --json | \
>           jq -r .ipAddress) \
> "echo OK"
```

If the name of the public IP address resource is not known ahead of time, it can be found dynamically by using the Azure CLI to first look up the virtual machine to locate its network interface, and then again to look up the network interface to find the public IP address. The private IP address is directly attached to the network interface:

```
# Find the network interface for a manager instance in a cluster
$ azure vm show my_first_cluster manager --json | \
> jq -r '.networkProfile.networkInterfaces[0].id' | sed 's/.*\///g'
manager516
# Find the private IP address for the instance
$ azure network nic show my_first_cluster manager516 --json | \
> jq -r '.ipConfigurations[0].privateIPAddress'
10.0.0.4
# Find the public IP address resource for the instance
$ azure network nic show my_first_cluster manager516 --json | \
> jq -r '.ipConfigurations[0].publicIPAddress.id' | sed 's/.*\///g'
manager-ip
# Find the public IP address for the resource
$ azure network public-ip show my_first_cluster manager-ip --json | \
> jq -r .ipAddress
203.0.113.101
```

Rolling your own reachability checks

There are many ways to perform straightforward checks of SSH connectivity using common utilities, and these work for on-prem hardware as well as cloud instances. One basic technique is to use the netcat utility to check if a daemon is listening on the SSH port (usually 22) of the instance. This does not check that it is the SSH daemon, nor does it ensure that an SSH connection can be established using the proper keys, but the check is quick and simple. If the command's exit code is 0, the check passes:

```
$ nc -w 10 -z 203.0.113.101 22
```

For a stronger check, just establish an SSH connection and issue a simple command. Include a connection timeout so that the command does not get stuck for long if the connection cannot be established. If the command's exit code is 0, or if the expected command output is emitted, then the check passes:

```
$ ssh -i /path/to/cloud_provider_key.pem -o ConnectTimeout=10 \
> userid@203.0.113.101 "echo OK"
OK
```

There are many other choices for implementing reachability checks. Be wary of using more powerful security scanning and troubleshooting tools, such as nmap. While they are effective, they could unintentionally trip defense mechanisms that cloud providers put in place to prevent abuse.

Hadoop Daemon Status

Once it's established that your instances exist and are reachable, a next logical step is to see if the expected Hadoop daemons are running on them.

Cloud provider custom metrics

The cloud provider monitoring services described in "Monitoring Choices" on page 239 support the definition of custom metrics, beyond the defaults pertaining to general system health that they automatically track. It is up to you to implement a script or application that determines the value of a desired custom metric and uploads it to the monitoring service. The core benefit of this approach is that you can rely on the provider monitoring service as a single location for tracking the health of your cloud resources and the Hadoop components running on them.

See "Custom Metrics in CloudWatch" on page 253 to learn how to establish a custom metric for AWS CloudWatch.

Rolling your own Hadoop daemon status checks

As is the case with reachability checks, status checks for Hadoop daemons that you create yourself work just as well for on-prem or hybrid clusters as for cloud clusters. If you already have monitoring systems in place for on-prem clusters, they can be easily extended to check cloud clusters.

Status check implementations for Hadoop focus on directly contacting the daemons at their expected ports, or else using client applications that connect for you. An important question is whether you should use the private IP addresses or public IP addresses for the daemons.

Using private IP addresses is a better choice, for three reasons. First, it is the more secure option, because communication to public IP addresses requires opening up security rules to permit traffic from outside the provider network or your organization's VPN. Second, it will have somewhat better performance, since network traffic remains within the cluster's virtual network or within VPNs that are reliably connected. Third, using private IP addresses allows you to use ephemeral public IP address assignments for cluster instances, which cost less, and are only necessary for gateway instances.

If you opt for using private IP addresses, you end up running the checks, or the monitoring application that houses them, either within the cloud provider or on your own VPN. This makes monitoring subject to the cloud provider's infrastructure functioning well. For example, if you monitor from a cloud instance that is coresident with your cluster and the availability zone for all of them goes down, you lose your monitoring capability. Another drawback is that it can be more difficult to integrate separate monitoring systems for cloud clusters with existing, perhaps global, monitoring systems already in place at your organization. Weigh the pros and cons of each possible home for your monitoring with these implications in mind.

The simple check for SSH reachability using netcat, suggested in "Instance Reachability" on page 246, can be applied to the well-known ports for Hadoop daemons. Table 17-1 is a quick reference for ports to check.

Table 17-1. Well-known TCP ports for Hadoop daemons

Daemon	Port
HDFS Namenode	8020
HDFS Datanode	50010
YARN Resource Manager	8032
YARN Node Manager	8040
ZooKeeper Server	2181

```
# check on the namenode
$ nc -v -z 203.0.113.101 8020
# check on the resource manager
$ nc -v -z 203.0.113.101 8032
```

For more detailed information, a scripted check can collect status information from the daemons by communicating with them. Consult the documentation for each Hadoop component to learn about what they offer.

The core HDFS and YARN daemons automatically provide monitoring information over HTTP that is managed internally using JMX. Table 17-2 provides example URLs for retrieving the information.

Table 17-2. Example URLs for retrieving JMX information from Hadoop

Daemon	Example URL
HDFS Namenode	http://203.0.113.101:50070/jmx
HDFS Datanode	http://203.0.113.101:50075/jmx
YARN Resource Manager	http://203.0.113.101:8088/jmx
YARN Node Manager	http://203.0.113.102:8042/jmx

The data returned is formatted in JSON, with one object for each MBean. You can pass the qry query parameter to request only the information from a single MBean:

```
$ curl http://203.1.113.101:50070/jmx?qry=beanName
```

With the returned JSON in hand, you can use parsing utilities like jq to whittle them down to what you want to monitor.

ZooKeeper servers do not use JMX, but you can retrieve textual status information from them by issuing the four-letter command `mntr` to them, and then use typical text processing utilities to narrow down what's returned:

```
$ echo mntr | nc 203.0.113.102 2181
```

The suggestions here just scratch the surface of monitoring Hadoop daemons. You can enable JMX on daemons that support it and then connect full-featured JMX console applications. You can design checks that use the standard client utilities for the Hadoop components to retrieve exactly the information you are interested in. There are many possibilities, and since they aren't specific to cloud clusters, they are not covered in this book. Consult texts such as *Hadoop Operations* by Eric Sammer (O'Reilly) to learn more.

System Load

Monitoring Hadoop daemons gives you a view into whether your cloud clusters are working *at all*, and also into whether they are working *well*, if you monitor metrics such as how full HDFS is or how long MapReduce jobs take to begin and then complete execution. Another view on whether clusters are working well is gained by monitoring the usual system-level metrics, like CPU load. Here again, as with general Hadoop monitoring, you can apply the same checks you normally would to on-prem hardware to cloud instances, and you have the option of using the cloud provider's own services.

AWS system monitoring

Once again, under AWS you can use CloudWatch to gather and report on metrics. CloudWatch automatically tracks some basic metrics for every EC2 instance, and you can opt to gather more by enabling detailed metrics, for additional cost.

To find out what metrics are available for an instance, use the CLI:

```
$ aws cloudwatch list-metrics --namespace AWS/EC2 \
> --dimensions Name=InstanceId,Value=i-12345678901234567
```

Fortunately, CPUUtilization is a basic metric, so it should be listed as available for any instance. Utilization can be retrieved by asking for metric statistics, specifying a start and end time for the metric and a period over which each reported value, such as an average or maximum, is to be calculated. This example reports on the maximum CPUUtilization over the course of a day, as seen on an hourly basis:

```
$ aws cloudwatch get-metric-statistics --namespace AWS/EC2 \
> --metric-name CPUUtilization \
> --dimensions Name=InstanceId,Value=i-12345678901234567 \
> --start-time 2017-02-04T00:00:00 --end-time 2017-02-05T00:00:00 \
> --period 3600 --statistics Maximum
```

Google Cloud Platform system monitoring

To work with anything beyond basic metrics in Google Cloud Platform, you need a Stackdriver account. Select Monitoring from the Stackdriver section of the Google Cloud Platform console menu, and log in with the account that you use. Create a new account and associate it with one of your projects, such as My First Cluster, as shown in Figure 17-1.

> ### Create your free Stackdriver account
>
> Start your 30 day free trial. No credit card required.
>
> Select or create a new Google Cloud Platform project to store your Stackdriver account settings and user permissions. The selection cannot be changed, but you can create other Stackdriver accounts later. Learn more
>
> **Google Cloud Platform project**
>
> My First Cluster ×
>
> Create Account Cancel

Figure 17-1. Creating a Stackdriver account

After associating your account with one project, add other projects as you like. It is not necessary to associate any AWS accounts during the account setup process, so that step may be skipped and performed later. Instructions are displayed for installing Stackdriver agents on your instances, as shown in Figure 17-2, so that you can gather more detailed monitoring data.

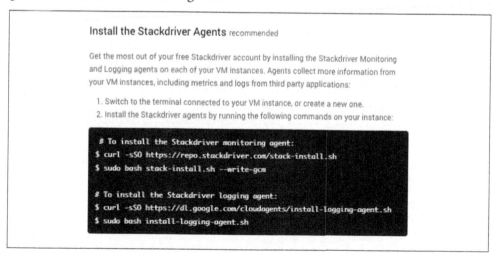

> ### Install the Stackdriver Agents recommended
>
> Get the most out of your free Stackdriver account by installing the Stackdriver Monitoring and Logging agents on each of your VM instances. Agents collect more information from your VM instances, including metrics and logs from third party applications:
>
> 1. Switch to the terminal connected to your VM instance, or create a new one.
> 2. Install the Stackdriver agents by running the following commands on your instance:

```
# To install the Stackdriver monitoring agent:
$ curl -sSO https://repo.stackdriver.com/stack-install.sh
$ sudo bash stack-install.sh --write-gcm

# To install the Stackdriver logging agent:
$ curl -sSO https://dl.google.com/cloudagents/install-logging-agent.sh
$ sudo bash install-logging-agent.sh
```

Figure 17-2. Instructions for installing Stackdriver agents

After working the rest of the way through account setup, click the Launch Monitoring button to go to the Stackdriver dashboard. You can use this dashboard to monitor many facets of your instances.

The `gcloud` CLI for Google Cloud Platform does not offer access to Stackdriver metrics. A good alternative for scripting is to use the Python API client library (*https://cloud.google.com/logging/docs/api/lib-api-python*) for Stackdriver. Consult its documentation to learn how to install the library and to use it with service accounts to query the Stackdriver metrics endpoints.

Azure system monitoring

Azure automatically tracks several metrics for virtual machines, including Percentage CPU. While the data is easy to access through the Azure portal, there is no easy way to get at the raw data using the Azure CLI.

The Azure REST API provides an endpoint for retrieving metrics under the Microsoft Insights banner. Consult the endpoint's documentation (*https://msdn.microsoft.com/library/mt743622.aspx*) to learn how to access it. Note that use of the API requires authentication using a JSON web token based on an approved principal in your account.

Rolling your own system checks

Use any system check that works for on-prem hardware for your cloud instances. For checks that require SSH connectivity, be sure to provide the necessary SSH key. It's good practice to establish a separate account with permissions for only what is required for the checks, so that the monitoring system cannot unintentionally perturb cluster operations.

A simple way to check CPUUtilization on any instance is to parse the results of the `uptime` command. For more detail, try the `mpstat` command, which you may need to install beforehand, depending on how minimal the base image for your cluster instances is. (The following `mpstat` output is edited for fit.)

```
# determine system load using uptime
$ ssh -i /path/to/cloud_provider_key.pem userid@203.0.113.101 uptime
 18:51:04 up  1:58,  0 users,  load average: 0.00, 0.01, 0.05
# determine system load using mpstat
$ ssh -i /path/to/cloud_provider_key.pem userid@203.0.113.101 mpstat -u
Linux 3.13.0-74-generic (ip-203-0-113-101)   02/20/2017   _x86_64_  (4 CPU)

06:51:20 PM  CPU    %usr   %nice   %sys ... %idle
06:51:20 PM  all    1.24    0.00   0.09 ... 98.56
```

Putting Scripting to Use

It's useful to spend some time with the provider CLIs to become comfortable with how they work and to understand what you can glean from them. Check out the built-in help that ships with the CLI for your provider, along with the online documentation; not only will you get more ideas for what you can monitor, but you can discover some convenient ways to work, beyond the confines of the provider web console.

The next section uses scripting to support defining a custom metric in AWS Cloud-Watch. A custom metric can be designed to map to a measurement pertinent to Hadoop, such as YARN job volume, or HDFS usage. This way, if you are using a cloud provider monitoring service, you can have your Hadoop monitoring in the same place as everything else.

Custom Metrics in CloudWatch

AWS CloudWatch automatically establishes custom metrics as soon as they are passed to it. Starting out, there are no custom metrics, but there are many basic metrics already tracked for several services. A brief look at working with those helps to get oriented for using custom metrics.

This section assumes that you have a cluster running in AWS like the one set up in Chapter 9.

Basic Metrics

Select the CloudWatch service from the service list in the AWS console to go to the CloudWatch console. Then, click the Browse Metrics button to begin looking at metrics.

The graph on the main portion of the page is empty because no metrics are selected for it. To add a metric, select EC2 from the "All metrics" tab, shown in Figure 17-3, which lists a few of the AWS services with basic metrics available. Each service maps to a *namespace* of metrics under CloudWatch.

Figure 17-3. Initial metrics namespaces in AWS CloudWatch

Then, drill further by selecting Per-Instance Metrics. All of the available EC2 metrics are listed, and checking any of them will have them begin to be plotted on the graph. As an example, select the CPUUtilization metric for the "manager" instance, as shown in Figure 17-4.

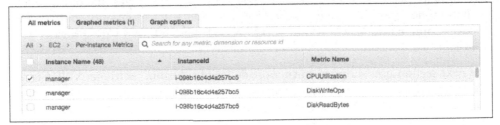

Figure 17-4. The CPUUtilization metric for the manager instance

Over time, the graph will fill up with the CPUUtilization metric for the manager instance, looking something like Figure 17-5. You can add the same metrics for the other cluster instances to make a single graph tracking CPUUtilization cluster-wide.

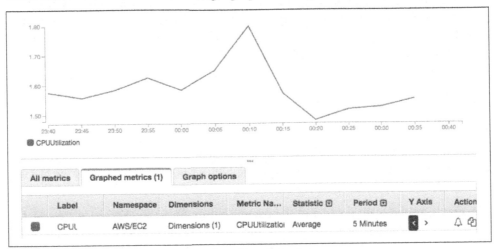

Figure 17-5. CPU utilization graphed in CloudWatch

Defining a Custom Metric

Working with a custom metric is similar to working with a basic metric, but first, the metric must be created. This section defines a new metric for how full HDFS is, expressed as a percentage (so, 0% is empty and 100% is full). Before defining the new custom metric in CloudWatch, a script or application must be available to determine it.

Fortunately, it is easy to get the figure needed for the metric using the `hdfs dfsadmin -report` command. This example command retrieves the first `DFS Used%` line from the DFS report, which covers the entire cluster, and extracts the field containing the percentage:

```
# as hdfs
$ hdfs dfsadmin -report | grep -m 1 "DFS Used%" | cut -d ' ' -f 3 | sed 's/%//g'
0.00
```

This command can form the basis for a script that finds the percentage and then submits it to CloudWatch. The latter task requires the AWS CLI, so install it on the manager instance, under the "hdfs" account, as described in "AWS CLI" on page 242. The CLI must be configured with credentials for an IAM user that can work with CloudWatch metrics. You can use your own, or you can create a new IAM user as described in "Configuring S3 Authentication" on page 161. If you create a new IAM user, be sure to request programmatic access and save the access key pair to use for CLI configuration. Applying the policy "CloudWatchFullAccess" will grant enough permissions to the user to work with CloudWatch.[6]

With the CLI installed and ready to run, it's time to think about how to name the new custom metric. CloudWatch will establish everything automatically as soon as the metric is first submitted, so no additional work is required in CloudWatch to get it ready:

- A custom metric in CloudWatch occupies a namespace, like any other metric, which groups similar metrics together. The namespace "HadoopClusters" works nicely for any metrics pertaining to Hadoop clusters.

- A metric needs a name describing what it measures. "DFSUsed" is a succinct and accurate name.

- A metric can have a unit associated with it, and for this custom metric "Percent" is perfect.

- Since there may be multiple Hadoop clusters running, each with their own usage, a *dimension* should be used to align the metric's datapoints. For example, the CPUUtilization metric has a dimension named "InstanceId"; this makes it possible to retrieve all of the datapoints for a single instance by its ID. The custom metric for DFS usage should be viewed per cluster, so a dimension named "Cluster" should be defined.

---

6 You can create custom policies for more security. See "Creating an IAM User for Log Streaming" on page 264 to learn about this process in the context of submitting logs to CloudWatch.

Feeding Custom Metric Data to CloudWatch

With the naming and dimensions worked out, a script for submitting usage information to CloudWatch can be written:

```
#!/usr/bin/env bash

dfs_used=$(/opt/hadoop/bin/hdfs dfsadmin -report | \
  grep -m 1 "DFS Used%" | cut -d ' ' -f 3 | sed 's/%//g')

/usr/local/bin/aws cloudwatch put-metric-data --metric-name DFSUsed \
  --namespace HadoopClusters --unit Percent --value "$dfs_used" \
  --dimensions Cluster=MyFirstCluster
```

Notice that the script uses full paths for the `hdfs` and `aws` commands. This is because this script will be called by the `cron` daemon, which passes a minimized set of environment variables to scripts that it runs. Use the correct path for `aws` for your instance, based on where `pip` installed it. You can test the script by calling it directly.

> The script could easily be adapted to become a Nagios service check, by removing the submission of the metric to CloudWatch and adding code to return different exit codes depending on the percentage value.

Add the script to the crontab for the hdfs user to have it run on a regular basis, sending the custom metric data to CloudWatch continually:

```
# as hdfs
$ crontab -e
# add a line for the script, as in the listing below
$ crontab -l
* * * * * /home/hdfs/dfs_used.sh > /home/hdfs/dfs_used.log 2>&1
```

Wait a couple of minutes after the job is added to the crontab for it to start feeding data to CloudWatch. Soon, in the "All metrics" tab of the CloudWatch metrics page, the new "HadoopClusters" custom namespace should appear, as shown in Figure 17-6.

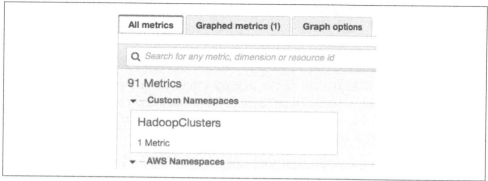

Figure 17-6. A custom namespace for Hadoop clusters in AWS CloudWatch

Selecting the HadoopClusters namespace reveals the single "Cluster" dimension, and selecting that dimension reveals the single custom metric, DFSUsed, for the dimension value "MyFirstCluster". It can now be selected, as demonstrated in Figure 17-7, and graphed like any other metric.

All metrics	Graphed metrics (2)	Graph options		
All > HadoopClusters > Cluster	Q *Search for any metric, dimension or resource id*			
✔	**Cluster (1)**			**Metric Name**
✔	MyFirstCluster			DFSUsed

Figure 17-7. A custom metric for DFS usage in CloudWatch

Also like any other metric, statistics are available for DFS usage:

```
$ aws cloudwatch get-metric-statistics --namespace HadoopClusters \
> --metric-name DFSUsage \
> --dimensions Name=Cluster,Value=MyFirstCluster \
> --start-time 2017-02-19T17:00:00 --end-time 2017-02-20T00:00:00 \
> --period 60 --statistics Average Maximum
{
    "Datapoints": [
        {
            "Timestamp": "2017-02-19T17:57:00Z",
            "Average": 0.0,
            "Maximum": 0.0,
            "Unit": "Percent"
        },
        ...
        {
            "Timestamp": "2017-02-19T17:55:00Z",
            "Average": 0.0,
            "Maximum": 0.0,
```

```
            "Unit": "Percent"
        }
    ],
    "Label": "DFSUsed"
}
```

If there is nothing in HDFS, all of the metrics values come back as zero, which is hardly exciting. An easy way to fill up the space is to run the `teragen` utility. The utility is normally used for running the Terasort benchmark, described in "Benchmarking HA" on page 139; it generates test data in HDFS in the amount that you request.

Run `teragen` under a user account that can run MapReduce jobs. See "Running a Test Job" on page 113 for steps to take for the account you choose. For the first run, try generating a small amount of data that fits easily in the available space in your cluster:

```
$ hadoop jar \
> /opt/hadoop/share/hadoop/mapreduce/hadoop-mapreduce-examples-x.y.z.jar \
> teragen 50000000 /user/userid/terasort-input
```

You can rerun `teragen` to add more and more data to HDFS, and watch the graph of DFS usage grow. An example graph showing increased DFS usage is shown in Figure 17-8. For each run, use a different HDFS directory as an argument.

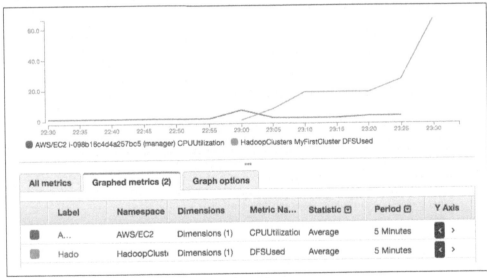

Figure 17-8. DFS usage graphed in CloudWatch

Setting an Alarm on a Custom Metric

CloudWatch is now tracking DFS usage for a cluster, but nothing is watching the metric to make sure usage doesn't go too high. Accordingly, you can set an alarm to trigger if usage exceeds a threshold. CloudWatch can take actions on your behalf if an alarm is triggered; a simple action would be to send an email, but a highly advanced action could add a datanode to the cluster to expand the available space. For now, only the basic alarm without actions is established.

An alarm needs a descriptive name, such as "DFS_Usage_Alarm" for alarming on excessive DFS usage. Various other parameters are needed as well:

- For an alarm that triggers at 80% usage, an alarm threshold of 80.0 should be used, along with a comparison operator representing the greater-than comparison. Thus, the alarm is triggered when the DFSUsed metric, already expressed as a percentage, crosses above 80.0.

- An alarm can be made more or less sensitive by defining the length of the period over which the metric is evaluated, and the number of periods to evaluate. To be quite sensitive, specifying a period of 60 (seconds) and only one evaluation period will narrow the alarm evaluation to each minute of time.

- Finally, an appropriate aggregated statistic for the metric should be chosen. Looking at the average usage is generally a good idea, but looking at the maximum over the evaluation period leads to a highly sensitive alarm.

These choices lead to a sensitive alarm, which in real-life usage would likely trip more often than necessary. Instead, you would have the alarm watch the DFS usage over a longer evaluation period, perhaps 10 or 20 minutes, and only look at the average usage, so that transient heavy use of HDFS would not trigger the alarm needlessly.

The AWS CLI can be used to create a new alarm:

```
$ aws cloudwatch put-metric-alarm --alarm-name "DFS_Usage_Alarm" \
> --no-actions-enabled --namespace HadoopClusters \
> --dimensions Name=Cluster,Value=MyFirstCluster --metric-name DFSUsed \
> --statistic Maximum --period 60 --evaluation-periods 1 \
> --threshold 80.0 --comparison-operator GreaterThanThreshold
```

After the new alarm is created, it appears in the Alarms page of the CloudWatch console. After a couple of minutes, depending on how full HDFS is, the alarm status will appear as either "OK", indicating that DFS usage is under 80%, or "ALARM", indicating that it is over 80%. Figure 17-9 shows the alarm in the "OK" state.

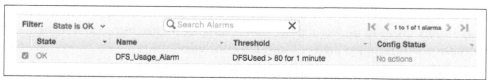

Figure 17-9. An alarm on DFS usage in CloudWatch

If usage is under 80%, run teragen again until HDFS usage crosses the 80% threshold (be careful not to fill up HDFS), and ensure the alarm is triggered, as in Figure 17-10.

Then, delete the HDFS directories holding the test data so that the usage drops again, until the alarm returns to the "OK" state.

State		Name	
☐ ALARM	▲	DFS_Usage_Alarm	▼

Figure 17-10. A triggered alarm on DFS usage in CloudWatch

You might notice that the CloudWatch interface calls out that there are no actions on the alarm. In the next section, an alarm on a different custom metric tracking the compute capacity of the cluster will trigger the addition of a new worker to the cluster.

Elastic Compute Using a Custom Metric

One of the best reasons to run clusters on a cloud provider is the flexibility to add and remove instances as your needs change. "Using Temporary Instances" on page 193 discussed using temporary instances as a cost-effective way to scale up clusters for short periods. Rather than scaling up "by hand," you can set up an automated process that detects when there is a need for more capacity and responds by *growing* your cluster. This process is called *autoscaling*.

Here again, a custom metric is introduced to AWS CloudWatch, but this time it tracks cluster compute capacity. When it gets too low, the action triggered by the metric's alarm adds a new worker to the cluster.

A Custom Metric for Compute Capacity

There are a few different ways to look at compute activity to determine if it is insufficient and needs more resources. A simple process could add compute instances at a fixed time in the workday, perhaps at the beginning, with the expectation that work will pick up as people arrive for work. A more targeted technique, though, is to look at how busy the compute system is, and if it crosses a threshold of activity, add more instances.

In practice, this technique may need to be governed; as more capacity is added, users may simply throw more work at the cluster, driving its size higher and higher. For simplicity here, no upper limit or throttling is included.

There are several ways to determine if YARN is "busy." Here, memory usage is used; low memory availability is taken to indicate that the system is running near its capacity. The yarn command can list the IDs of the compute nodes as well as each node's memory usage:

```
# as yarn
$ yarn node -list 2>/dev/null | grep -v Total | grep -v Node-Id | cut -d ' ' -f 1
ip-172-31-60-201.ec2.internal:57541
ip-172-31-60-202.ec2.internal:58543
ip-172-31-60-103.ec2.internal:43340
$ yarn node -status ip-172-31-60-201.ec2.internal:57541 2>/dev/null | \
> grep 'Memory-'
  Memory-Used : 0MB
  Memory-Capacity : 8192MB
```

With this information, a general memory usage figure can be determined, as the ratio of the memory used to the memory capacity across all nodes. A script can loop over the nodes to sum up their memory statistics and then report the final ratio:

```
#!/usr/bin/env bash

used_total=0
available_total=0

for n in $(yarn node -list 2>/dev/null | grep -v Total | grep -v Node-Id | \
  cut -d ' ' -f 1); do
  mem="$(yarn node -status "$n" 2>/dev/null | grep 'Memory-' \
    | cut -d ' ' -f 3 | sed 's/MB//g' | xargs)"
  used=${mem%% *}
  available=${mem##* }
  used_total=$(( used_total + used ))
  available_total=$(( available_total + available ))
done

if [[ $available_total == 0 ]]; then
  echo 0
else
  bc <<< "scale=4;($used_total/$available_total)*100"
fi
```

 This script is reaching the limits of what bash shell scripting can perform easily. Specifically, it uses techniques like xargs without a command to concatenate lines, bash arithmetic, and bc with a here string to perform a floating-point calculation. In practice, you may want to use a scripting language like Python to make a more maintainable script.

With a script available, a custom metric can be supplied to CloudWatch on a regular basis via a cron job:

```
#!/usr/bin/env bash

yarn_mem_used=$(/path/to/yarnmem.sh)

/usr/local/bin/aws cloudwatch put-metric-data --metric-name YarnMemUsage \
```

```
--namespace HadoopClusters --unit Percent --value "$yarn_mem_used" \
--dimensions Cluster=MyFirstCluster
```

Prerequisites for Autoscaling Compute

To make automatically adding a new compute instance fast and robust, you need an image at the ready for it. Chapter 16 lays out how much work can be saved by crafting an image with most of the Hadoop configuration already baked in. Without a custom image, the autoscaling work involves installing all of the Hadoop components and their dependencies, along with extensive configuration work. For speed and to reduce the chance of misconfiguration, an image should be used. You can certainly use the same image that you normally would for creating a new cluster.

Some configuration work must be done to a new instance before it can participate in a cluster. In "Image Preparation" on page 225, several items were called out as being necessary to modify for any new instance, including IP addresses. Most of the configuration in the image can remain as it is, so the scripting needed to finish off the configuration is minimal. A modified form of the cluster-wide configuration update script in Appendix B can do the trick. Some caveats:

- The script must have SSH access to the new instance, so establishing that must be part of the configuration process.

- Some components may require a restart in order to accept their new configurations. At a minimum, the daemons on the new instance must be started.

- To keep administration simple, add the private IP address of each new instance to the */etc/hadoop/slaves* file on each manager instance.

Triggering Autoscaling with an Alarm Action

YARN usage can be volatile. Under normal conditions, a cluster may experience spikes in activity followed by lulls of almost no activity. So, an alarm that can trigger adding a new instance should look for consistent heavy usage. In CloudWatch, this can be done by requiring the alarm condition to hold for more than just one consecutive evaluation period:

```
$ aws cloudwatch put-metric-alarm --alarm-name "YARN_Mem_Alarm" \
> --no-actions-enabled --namespace HadoopClusters \
> --dimensions Name=Cluster,Value=MyFirstCluster --metric-name YarnMemUsage \
> --statistic Maximum --period 60 --evaluation-periods 5 \
> --threshold 80.0 --comparison-operator GreaterThanThreshold
```

The preceding alarm has no actions, but one is needed to begin the process of adding an instance. With CloudWatch, there are choices as to how to architect this portion of the autoscaling flow:

- An *autoscaling action* can trigger the creation of an instance within an EC2 autoscaling group. An *autoscaling group* in EC2 is a grouping of instances that can be automatically grown and shrunk in size. Here, an autoscaling group can represent the additional workers that are added to a cluster. When you create an autoscaling group, you create a *launch configuration*, which includes the information needed to launch an instance, such as its AMI, subnet, and security group, and whether to request a spot instance. A tripped alarm can cause the addition of instances to the group, while an alarm subsiding can cause instances to be removed.

- A *notification* from an alarm can go to any of various listening or receiving entities, such as an HTTP server, an email address, or text message. Scripts triggered upon receipt of the message can use the AWS CLI to create a new instance as desired. The information normally in a launch configuration would be included in the scripts. This is a do-it-yourself form of autoscaling, which is more complex to set up but which relies less on AWS capabilities.

Whichever path you choose, you must provide a way to run the Hadoop configuration script for the new instance (and possibly the cluster at large). When performing your own autoscaling, you can use the information from the alarm to gain context about the cluster and thereby find its IP addresses, or simply have them hardcoded in the script; the script can be run anywhere that is convenient to your architecture. When using an autoscaling group, the script may be set up to run directly on the new instance, but it must be able to retrieve information necessary for the configuration work, such as the IP addresses of the managers in the cluster it is being added to. For that reason, if you are using AWS autoscaling, you may wish to also send a notification to a helper application that can make the necessary information available to the new instance when it has finished starting up.

Setting up autoscaling of Hadoop clusters is a challenging task. This section provides a plan and some starting materials for making it happen, relying on CloudWatch for metric tracking and alarming. Take the time to think about the conditions under which you'd want to scale up your clusters, and rely on automation for cluster creation you have already established to help with the similar task of adding new instances.

What About Shrinking?

Autoscaling also includes removing instances when they are no longer needed. The same metric can be used to determine when YARN memory usage (or your chosen metric) has gone back under some threshold for some length of time, and then terminate a worker that had been added (or any that are equivalent from the original cluster composition). The cluster should be configured again to no longer expect the destroyed instance to be around.

If you use temporary instances, then the need to shrink is not as strong, since they will disappear on their own after a time. However, you would still want to update the cluster configuration to account for their absence.

Other Things to Watch

The alarms and actions set up under CloudWatch so far have been based on numeric metrics that are sampled over time and analyzed. The next section looks at another source of information about a cluster, logs, and also shows how to send CloudWatch alarm notifications to an email list.

Ingesting Logs into CloudWatch

Aside from custom metrics that are tied to Hadoop components, logs are one of the best windows into seeing how your clusters are performing.

As part of their monitoring services, each of the cloud providers offers the ability to save off log content for later analysis, either to their standard storage services or dedicated storage, and perform automated scans and alerting based on their content. The basic procedure is to identify a logfile to track, specify how its content is organized in storage, and define alerts that are triggered by patterns in the logfile as it is incrementally saved off.

This section explores using AWS CloudWatch to monitor the log for an HDFS namenode and trigger alerts whenever an error appears. Before starting, determine the full path of the namenode log; the initial setup for CloudWatch logging includes configuration for the first logfile. It's assumed that the logfile exists and has some content in it already.

Creating an IAM User for Log Streaming

CloudWatch relies on an agent process running on your cloud instance to extract logfile content. The agent requires credentials to authorize itself with CloudWatch. If your instances already have IAM roles associated with them, then it's enough to add the necessary policies to a role. Otherwise, you can create a dedicated IAM user for the agent.

A tailored custom policy can grant the permissions necessary for the CloudWatch agent to work. Go to the IAM service in the AWS console, and select Policies from the menu on the left side. The list of predefined IAM policies is displayed. Click the Create Policy button, as shown in Figure 17-11, to create a new custom policy.

Figure 17-11. Starting to create a custom IAM policy for CloudWatch

Select the option to Create Your Own Policy. Then, in the form shown in Figure 17-12 for creating the policy:

- Provide a policy name, such as "CloudWatchLogSubmitter".

- Enter a description if desired.

- Fill in a policy document that matches the EC2 quick start documentation for AWS CloudWatch (*https://docs.aws.amazon.com/AmazonCloudWatch/latest/ logs/QuickStartEC2Instance.html*).

Click the Create Policy button to create the new custom policy.

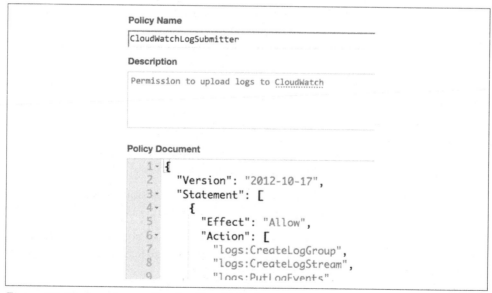

Figure 17-12. A custom policy for CloudWatch

Next, create a new IAM user with the custom policy applied. Instructions for creating a new IAM user are in "Configuring S3 Authentication" on page 161. Be sure to request programmatic access, and save the access key pair.

Installing the CloudWatch Agent

AWS provides a Python script for installing and configuring the CloudWatch agent on your instances. Download it to the desired instance (e.g., the manager node hosting the HDFS namenode) and run it, specifying the region where the instance runs:

```
$ sudo apt-get update # on Ubuntu instances only
$ curl -O \
> https://s3.amazonaws.com/aws-cloudwatch/downloads/latest/awslogs-agent-setup.py
$ sudo python awslogs-agent-setup.py --region us-east-1
```

The script installs `pip` and uses it to download and install the agent. Then it asks a series of questions to configure the agent and have it start streaming a log to Cloud-Watch. In the first set of questions, provide the access keys for the IAM user just created for submitting log data to CloudWatch, and the region. The output format response may be left empty.

The next set of questions establishes a log stream for the first logfile to monitor. You will need to determine the name of the *log stream* that represents the log contents as they arrive at CloudWatch, and the name of the *log group* where the log stream resides. The organization of log groups is up to you; one suggestion is to use a log group for each type of Hadoop daemon (HDFS namenode, ZooKeeper server, Hive server) and a log stream for each instance of a Hadoop daemon. For example:

- path of log: */var/log/hadoop/hadoop-hdfs-namenode-ip-203-0-113-101.log*
- log group name: mycluster/hdfs/nn
- log stream name: mycluster-hdfs-nn-manager

Finally, choose a timestamp format that you prefer, and pick the start of the file for the initial position to load, so that the log's entire contents are streamed.

After the agent is installed and configured, its configuration is written to */var/awslogs/etc/awslogs.conf*. More log streams can be defined there later.

If you proceed to the CloudWatch Logs service in the AWS console, you should see the new log group and log stream for the HDFS namenode log, as shown in Figures 17-13 and 17-14.

Figure 17-13. A CloudWatch log group for HDFS namenode logs

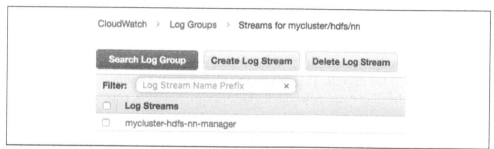

Figure 17-14. A CloudWatch log stream for the HDFS namenode log

Creating a Metric Filter

Now that namenode log data is being streamed to CloudWatch, the next step for monitoring it is to create a *metric filter* on the log stream. A metric filter generates a metric based on patterns occurring in the log contents. Here, a metric filter is created that looks for log messages containing the string "ERROR", which indicates an error logged by the namenode.

Start creating a metric filter by selecting the radio button for the new "mycluster/hdfs/nn" log group in the list of log groups, and then clicking the "Create Metric Filter" above the list, as shown in Figure 17-15.

Figure 17-15. Beginning to create a CloudWatch log metric filter

On the next page, define the filter pattern by entering "ERROR" (without quotes) in the Filter Pattern text field. Click the Assign Metric button to continue to the next step.

Fill in the remaining information for the filter on the last page, as shown in Figure 17-16:

- Choose a filter name, such as "Namenode Errors".
- Select a metric *namespace*, which is used to group similar metrics together in CloudWatch. The namespace "HadoopClusters", for example, could be used to group together all metrics pertaining to your Hadoop clusters.
- Select a name for the metric that is to be generated by the filter. Something simple like "NamenodeErrors" fits.
- Finally, open the "Advanced Options" if necessary and assign the Metric Value of "1", which is the default. This causes the filter to post a value of 1 to the metric whenever the filter pattern, which looks for error messages, encounters a match.

Click the Create Filter button to create the metric filter.

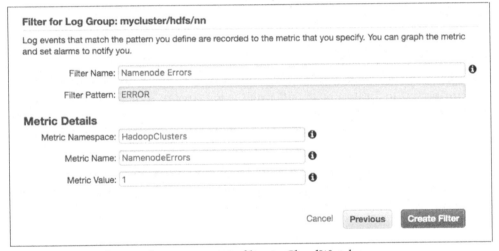

Figure 17-16. Definition for a new metric filter in CloudWatch

The new filter is shown as one of the metric filters associated with the namenode log group, as shown in Figure 17-17.

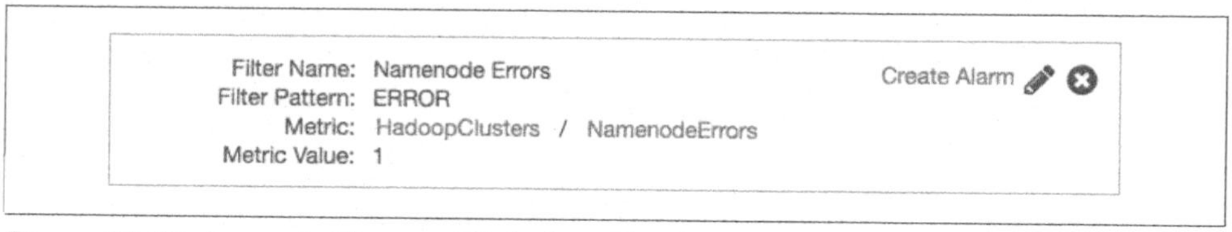

```
Filter Name:    Namenode Errors                              Create Alarm  ✏ ⊗
Filter Pattern: ERROR
        Metric: HadoopClusters  /  NamenodeErrors
Metric Value:   1
```

Figure 17-17. A metric filter established in CloudWatch

Creating an Alarm from a Metric Filter

There is now a metric representing the presence of errors in the namenode log, but without an alarm monitoring the metric, it is up to administrators to watch it. To create an alarm for the new metric, follow the "Create Alarm" link displayed for the metric filter. A dialog appears, with the second step in the alarm creation workflow, Define Alarm, already selected. The first step already refers to the metric associated with the filter.

Working in the Alarm Threshold section, first provide a name and description for the new alarm. The alarm is already focused on the "NamenodeErrors" metric; choose to have it move to an alarmed state whenever that metric is greater than or equal to 0 for one (consecutive) period. This will cause the alarm to trigger whenever an error appears in the log, because the metric filter will post a value of "1" at that time.

In the Actions section of the dialog, you can define notifications to send when the alarm changes state. Begin by selecting the default value of "State is ALARM" for the "Whenever this alarm:" menu, so that notifications are sent when the alarm is triggered, that is, when an error message appears in the namenode menu.

CloudWatch uses the AWS Simple Notification Service (SNS) to manage sending notifications. Rather than specifying email addresses directly for a notification, you create a named topic in SNS that includes your email address, and point to that in the alarm definition. Follow the "New List" link, and the form for the notification definition expands to allow you to enter a topic name and list of email addresses. Enter a topic name and email address of your choice. The final states of the Alarm Threshold and Actions sections of the dialog are shown in Figure 17-18.

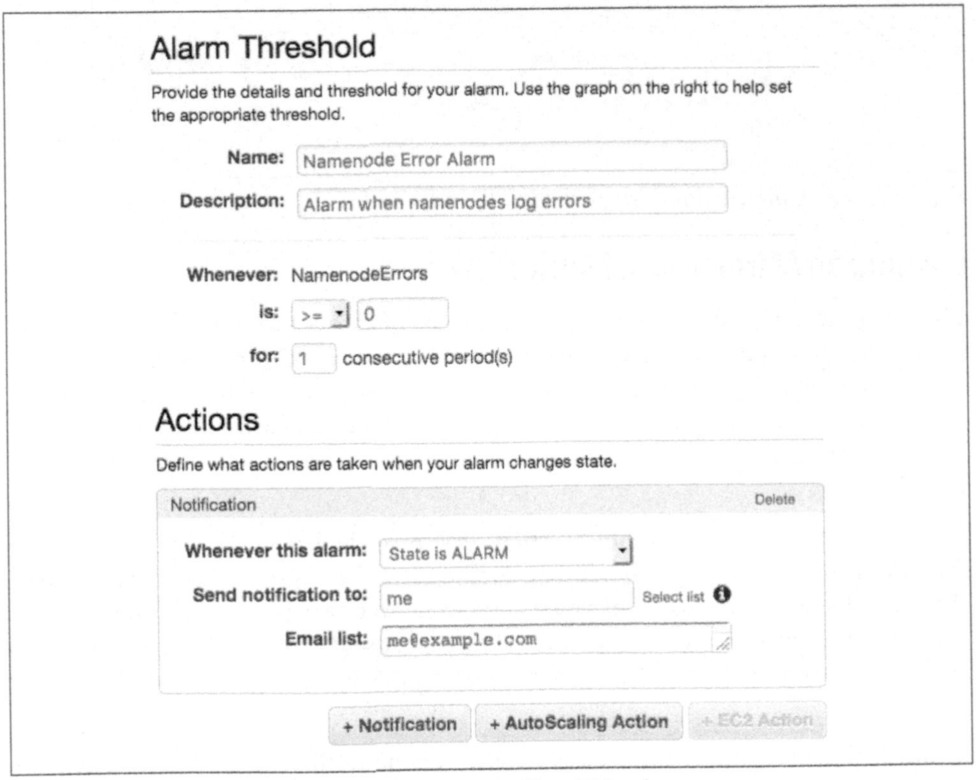

Figure 17-18. Alarm threshold and actions in CloudWatch

The period and statistic that the alarm uses to consider the metric is in the Alarm Preview section, shown in Figure 17-19. Together, they determine the calculation performed to decide if the alarm should be triggered. For this example, a period of 5 minutes and statistic of "Sum" states that the alarm should be tripped if the sum of the metric exceeds zero when evaluated over a 5-minute period. Since any error message will cause a value of "1" to be entered for the metric, these values will cause the alarm to be triggered within 5 minutes of an error appearing in the namenode log.

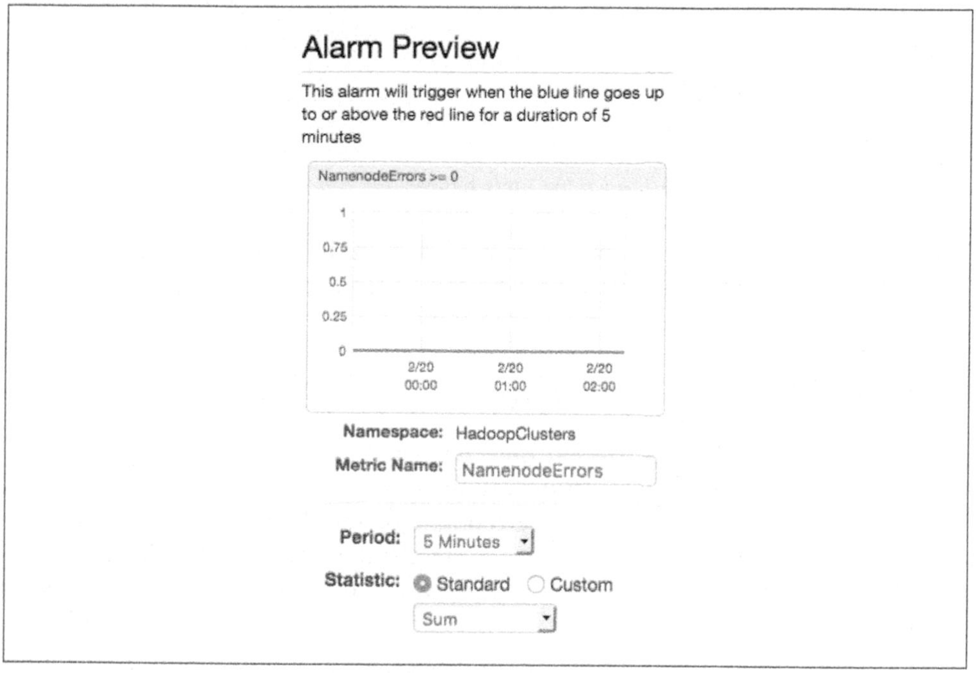

Alarm Preview

This alarm will trigger when the blue line goes up to or above the red line for a duration of 5 minutes

NamenodeErrors >= 0

```
1
0.75
0.5
0.25
0
        2/20        2/20        2/20
        00:00       01:00       02:00
```

Namespace: HadoopClusters

Metric Name: NamenodeErrors

Period: 5 Minutes

Statistic: ● Standard ○ Custom

Sum

Figure 17-19. Alarm preview in CloudWatch

Click the Create Alarm button to create the alarm. You may be presented with a dialog box asking you to confirm the email address you supplied for the notification list. You can do this now or later. Click the View Alarm button in the dialog to see the new alarm.

Select the Alarms section of CloudWatch from the menu on the left side of the console to see the new alarm listed. Its state of "INSUFFICIENT_DATA" notes that there are not enough datapoints for the metric to determine a state for the alarm; this is because the metric filter does not post anything at all for the metric unless there is an error message.

To get the alarm to trigger, induce an error message in the namenode log. An easy way to do that is simply to stop the namenode using the usual stop script:

```
# as hdfs
$ $HADOOP_PREFIX/sbin/stop-dfs.sh
```

An error message should appear in the namenode log indicating that it received a SIGTERM signal. Within 5 minutes, the state for the namenode error alarm should transition to ALARM, as shown in Figure 17-20, and you should receive an email from AWS notifying you of the problem.

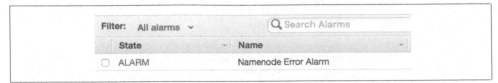

Figure 17-20. A tripped alarm for a log metric filter in CloudWatch

Receiving an email is very helpful, but you could expand on the notification capabilities in SNS to do more, such as ping a paging system, or even trigger a script that automatically restarts HDFS.

So Much More to See and Do

This chapter, despite its length, has only scratched the surface of the monitoring opportunities available for your clusters running in the cloud. There is much more you can learn about each cloud provider's offerings, and the reward is a much better view of the health and well-being of your clusters in the cloud. Having that assurance is both necessary to encourage moving more work to cloud providers and to keep tabs on what's already there.

Eventually, your monitoring will alarm you that one of your clusters is degraded. Perhaps HDFS has crashed, or all of the worker instances have vanished. When (not if) that happens, you will need to be able to restore the cluster and the data that it held. Chapter 18 briefs you on the options you have for cluster backup and restoration.

Backup and Restoration

Despite the reliability and availability benefits of running your clusters on a cloud provider, failures still can occur. It's essential to include disaster recovery procedures as part of your maintenance process, and that starts with safe backups of your cluster data. Even if you have faith in your cloud provider that your resources will remain operational as long as you need them, rules and regulations pertaining to your data can compel you to have a backup process in place.

There are many general techniques for performing backup and restoration for Hadoop clusters. This chapter focuses on aspects of those techniques that are relevant for cloud clusters.

Patterns to Supplement Backups

Besides explicit backup procedures, there are other measures you can, and should, employ to provide greater assurance that your cluster data, and clusters themselves, remain available in the face of problems.

"Long-Running or Transient?" on page 215 discusses the trade-offs between long-running clusters and transient clusters. By their nature, long-running clusters become more and more critical as they accumulate important data as well as unique configurations or software installations. Transient clusters, on the other hand, cannot become the permanent home of any data, and can be spun up easily with the proper automation. Adoption of transient clusters, therefore, can lead to an architecture that is more resilient to failure. When a transient cluster fails, a new similar one can be created with little trouble, and data is already stored off-cluster in robust cloud provider storage services.

Another measure that effectively preserves your work is the use of images, as covered in Chapter 16, to persist the required configurations of your cluster instances. Combined with the automation necessary to create new clusters, you are freed from concern that all of the effort put into configuring your clusters properly will be lost if those clusters become corrupted or disappear.

HDFS data can be similarly "imaged" by using HDFS snapshots. You can quickly create an HDFS snapshot to hold a read-only copy of a specified directory. If the directory contents become corrupted, you can restore the snapshot to return to a past, known good state. Note that HDFS snapshots, however, may be lost if a cluster loses enough datanodes.

Finally, Hadoop itself supports high availability (HA) clusters, covered in depth in Chapter 10, to eliminate single points of failure in your architecture such as the HDFS namenode and the YARN resource manager. The built-in resiliency of Hadoop to the loss of other daemons like HDFS datanodes, combined with an HA configuration that works with cloud provider features such as availability zones, can result in clusters that not only intrinsically back up data, but continue functioning in the face of failure.

In summary, the following architectural choices go a long way to ensuring that cluster data and configuration is backed up, before even performing direct data backup operations:

- Use images to bake in cluster configuration, with scripts to fill in what's needed at deployment time.
- Use transient clusters so that they do not accumulate essential configuration and data.
- Store data in cloud provider storage services, pulling them into a cluster when needed; likewise, save final results to storage services for safekeeping.
- Set up high availability.
- Use cloud provider features like availability zones and automatic failover.

After embracing some or all of these measures, you may still want an ordinary data backup. After all, a key tenet of data security, or information assurance in general, is *defense in depth*, which means setting up multiple layers of protection. In the end, your mind may be more at ease simply knowing that, if all else fails, there's always a copy of your data somewhere else, safe and sound.

Backup via Imaging

A cloud provider lets you create an image of any instance. So, why not just create images of each instance in a cluster as your backup?

This can work as a backup scheme, but it has a good number of drawbacks. Among them:

- The cluster components must be shut down, and often its instances stopped, in order to have a stable basis for imaging.

- An image must be made of every cluster instance, because they hold unique combinations of data and have unique configurations. Therefore, this technique does not scale well to large clusters.

- On restoration, all private and public IP addresses will most likely be different, so some reconfiguration work is still necessary. SSH access also needs to be updated.

- The images include files from the operating system and installed software, none of which is strictly necessary for backing up a cluster. So, a lot of space is wasted.

- Some of the data stored in the cluster may not need to be backed up, such as checkpoint data written in the middle of a larger workflow. So, even more space is wasted.

Few situations call for this form of cluster backup. Moving an entire cluster as is from, say, one region to another could be accomplished in this fashion, and that may be easier than using a selective backup scheme to manage what data needs to be copied over. A cluster that is highly critical, and whose configuration is fragile, may need to be backed up this way, because any other technique would be too risky.

However, it is much better not to get yourself into the position where backup via imaging is your only option. Instead, migrate to using base images plus automation to create clusters that can do the necessary work, and adopt transient clusters to prevent buildup of one-off configuration changes and vital data stored only in running clusters. Rely on whole-cluster imaging only for extenuating circumstances.

HDFS Replication

A common pattern for backing up a Hadoop cluster is to maintain a *disaster recovery* (DR) cluster, configured in much the same way as the original, primary cluster. The DR cluster could serve merely as a receptacle for the data that normally resides in the primary cluster, so that at recovery time the data must be copied back to a new operational cluster. Alternatively, the DR cluster could be fully capable of taking over workloads for the primary cluster, as a complete failover system.

The copying of HDFS data from one cluster to another is normally performed by the distcp tool, which ships with Hadoop itself, and cloud clusters are no different. You only need the IP addresses or hostnames of the namenodes in the source (primary) and destination (DR) cluster:

```
$ hadoop distcp hdfs://203.0.113.101:9820/datadir \
> hdfs://203.0.113.201:9820/datadir
```

Consult the `distcp` documentation (*https://hadoop.apache.org/docs/current/hadoop-distcp/DistCp.html*) for information on the available options, like `-update` and `-overwrite`, that affect where and how files are copied over.

Network connectivity is an important factor to consider when using `distcp`. `distcp` requires that the YARN node managers executing the copy be able to reach both the source and destination filesystems; so, network security rules that apply to the clusters must allow the communication. It's simplest for both clusters to reside in the same subnet, where unrestricted connectivity is the norm. However, since this is a backup scenario, you may wish to host the DR cluster in a separate network location, such as a separate region, so that it's less likely that it will experience an outage when the primary does. If so, check the security rules, and attempt a run or two of `distcp` to be sure that it works.

A related factor here is cost. Data transfer within an availability zone is generally free, but there can be costs associated with traversing availability zones and regions. Costs are especially important to consider if the DR cluster sits outside the cloud provider entirely. You must strike a balance between the costs incurred for performing HDFS replication, where the DR cluster resides, and how often replication runs. For example, you could replicate more often to a DR cluster hosted in a different availability zone, but replicate to another DR cluster in a separate region less often.

Cloud Storage Filesystems

`distcp` takes in Hadoop filesystem URLs as arguments, so it can work with filesystem implementations that are backed by cloud provider storage services: S3 for AWS, Google Cloud Storage for Google Cloud Platform, and Azure Blob Storage or Azure Data Lake Store for Azure. For example, once the s3a filesystem is installed as described in "Configuring the S3 Filesystem" on page 158, you can back up HDFS data to S3 directly:

```
$ hadoop distcp hdfs://203.0.113.101:9820/datadir s3a://mybackupbucket/datadir
```

This does not require a DR cluster running to work. Storage costs are significantly lower for object storage than for the block storage associated with cluster instances, and you also save on the cost of running the cluster instances themselves. The backup and replication guarantees for object storage may also be stronger than for block storage.

In the case of primary cluster failure, however, you will need to not only stand up a new cluster, but copy the data out of object storage to it. So recovery time may be affected. Once again, there is a balance to be achieved, based on your goals.

HDFS Snapshots

The distcp tool can take a long time to run. It needs to assemble a list of files to copy, as well as run the mappers that take time to perform the copies. During this time, changes can be written to HDFS, which causes inconsistency between the set of original files and the set of backed up files.

To avoid this problem, HDFS snapshots can be backed up instead of the live data. The distcp tool provides some performance optimizations based on analysis of the difference between snapshots. These can not just make the tool run faster, but also lead it to copy less data, an advantage that directly maps to lower cost for cloud data transfer:

```
# initial backup as snapshot
$ hdfs dfs -createSnapshot /datadir 101
$ hadoop distcp hdfs://203.0.113.101:9820/datadir/.snapshot/101 \
> hdfs://203.0.113.201:9820/datadir
# make snapshot 101 in other cluster
# next backup compares snapshots
$ hdfs dfs -createSnapshot /datadir 102
$ hadoop distcp -update -diff 101 102 hdfs://203.0.113.101:9820/datadir \
> hdfs://203.0.113.201:9820/datadir
```

The HDFS snapshot documentation (*https://hadoop.apache.org/docs/current/hadoop-project-dist/hadoop-hdfs/HdfsSnapshots.html*) explains how to enable, perform, and manage HDFS snapshots.

Hive Metastore Replication

HDFS data isn't the only important data to preserve in a cluster. The Hive metastore, which stores mapping information for tabular data accessed by Hive and other Hadoop components, also needs to be backed up, so that those components can be recovered without having to reconfigure them from scratch.

If you are using a local metastore, then its data is stored in HDFS, and HDFS replication is sufficient to back it up. Otherwise, if you are using a remote metastore, then some database server outside the cluster houses the metastore database, and it's that database that you must back up.

Fortunately, if you are using your cloud provider's cloud database service to host your remote metastore, there is not much that you need to do yourself. You don't need to directly manage the instance hosting the database server; in fact, it's hidden from you, cared for completely by the provider. Database backups, replication, and failover are all handled as well. For cost and speed reasons, the metastore should reside within the cloud provider anyway, so for all these reasons, you should use a cloud database to host a Hive metastore, and delegate the work of backups.

Logs

A complete backup regime for a cluster should include saving off logs for key daemons and for applications that run alongside the cluster. With logs backed up, it becomes easier to reconstruct whatever problems led to having to perform a restoration. Because cloud providers reclaim resources for other customers to use after you stop using them, deep forensic analysis of failures becomes impossible without your own log backups.

For easier analysis and reconstruction, you may also want to enable audit logging for those components that support it, such as HDFS and Hive.[1] Audit logs are more suited for analysis and reconstruction attempts than the usual daemon logs. Consult the documentation for each Hadoop component to learn about its auditing capability. Alternatively, you can deploy a separate application that supports auditing of Hadoop clusters, and use its capability to safely store audit logs.

Logs generally do not need to be restored into clusters, so there are more options for where they can be saved. A great choice is to use your cloud provider's monitoring service; see "Monitoring Choices" on page 239 for an overview. The services are efficient and include search and filter capabilities for easier analysis. "Ingesting Logs into CloudWatch" on page 264 demonstrates how to set up AWS CloudWatch to ingest an HDFS namenode log as an example.

Another option available in the cloud is to copy log data into an object storage service. You do not gain the benefits of search and monitoring, but you may save on cost. Since logs rarely need to be analyzed, they can be sent to "cold" storage tiers, where costs are even lower.

Suppose all of the Hadoop logs that should be saved are in */var/log/hadoop*. If you are running in AWS or Google Cloud Platform, you can use their respective CLIs to efficiently send new and updated files to a storage bucket:

```
# AWS
$ aws s3 sync /var/log/hadoop s3://myhadooplogs
# Google Cloud Platform
$ gsutil rsync -r /var/log/hadoop gs://myhadooplogs
```

At the time of this writing, there is no equivalent command in the Azure CLI.[2] You can use the CLI to copy individual files via the `azure storage file upload` command, but this does not skip files that are unchanged. A more efficient alternative is to use Azure File storage to mount a file share on the relevant cluster instances, and then employ the standard `rsync` command to perform backups. Consult the Azure

---

1 Both of these components include an audit logger in their Log4J properties.

2 There is an AzCopy utility that can perform copies to Azure Storage, but it works only on Windows.

File storage for Linux (*https://docs.microsoft.com/en-us/azure/storage/storage-how-to-use-files-linux*) documentation to learn how to create a file share and mount it on a Linux virtual machine.

A General Cloud Hadoop Backup Strategy

Your task as the maintainer of critical Hadoop clusters is to combine the usual options for backup with those available in the cloud into a strategy that meets the needs of your organization and the requirements associated with the data the clusters operate on. Every organization is different, but here are some general pointers that can form the seed of your own strategy:

- Identify cluster data that must be backed up, distinct from transient data that can easily be regenerated. Have jobs work with the first set in areas separate from the second set, so that it's easier to target backups.

- Adjust workflows for cloud clusters so that critical data needn't reside in the clusters for long, preferring to save long-term results in object storage services or elsewhere. This reduces the risk of clusters failing and the need to restore backups.

- Designate destination storage for backups, either in DR clusters or object storage services. Make sure that security rules restrict access to protect the data within them, but also allow for backup processes to reach them and write data.

- Establish regular backups, and monitor them so they cannot silently stop working. Use cloud services to set alarms if backups stop occurring.

- Improve the speed and reliability of the process for standing up Hadoop clusters, using images and automation as much as possible, so that restoring from backup takes a reasonable amount of time.

- Practice performing restoration. The time to discover that a backup is incomplete or a restoration process is faulty is not when you need to restore a critical cluster. Regular practice of restoration increases confidence in the backup strategy and leads to faster recovery times.

- Delegate backup responsibilities to cloud services where possible. Your cloud provider has powerful backup, availability, and failover capabilities managed by experts ready for you to use.

Not So Different, But Better

You may notice that some of the advice in this chapter, like identifying the essential data for backup and practicing cluster restoration, is not specific to clusters running on a cloud provider. You should employ the techniques no matter where your clusters are.

The key idea is that, in the cloud, there are services at your disposal that can augment your typical practices. It's one of the most important reasons to move your clusters to the cloud, for it opens up a vast array of resources and versatile services that may be difficult or impossible to create in your organization's own data centers. You don't need to create a robust, resilient, geographically dispersed storage system. You don't need to rig up a network that is flexible to configure yet straightforward to secure. You don't even need to directly manage database servers. All of these responsibilities, and more, are handled by your cloud provider. You just need to figure out how best to take advantage of them.

This doesn't apply just to performing backups, but to every aspect of cluster management. When you begin moving Hadoop clusters to the cloud, it's natural to start with the processes you are already familiar with, and that works. As you grow more comfortable and you explore cloud provider capabilities, those processes can morph and expand, perhaps beginning with a focused change or two, but eventually moving on to embracing provider services to fundamentally change how you manage clusters. This indeed can make cluster management easier and more satisfying, but it also opens up new ways of working for your organization, so you can use clusters to answer questions you couldn't before, and move faster and with more confidence.

The reason to adopt a new technology then, like the cloud, is not merely to check a box. It's to advance to a higher state of functioning, which could be speed, or quantity, or complexity, or quality. The public cloud providers have provided the means to get there; it's a matter of learning about them and building on them.

To the Cloud

When you look up at a cloud, it seems simple enough, and not so mysterious. But when you are in an airplane flying through one, you can barely see anything outside of your window, and the ride gets bumpy. So it is with "the cloud": It doesn't appear that complicated at first, but once you're inside it, it's easy to lose sight of where you are and hard to figure out which way to go.

For moving your Hadoop clusters to the cloud, this book's goal is to be like radar, helping you discern the shape of your cloud provider and all its services, and the path through it to get your clusters up and running. Providers are ever-changing, but with enough experience, your piloting skills will be enough to see you through, as both Hadoop and the cloud continue into the future.

Hadoop Component Start and Stop Scripts

Some Hadoop components, like HDFS and YARN, ship with management scripts that let you start and stop all of their component daemons or servers in one command. Others do not. The scripts here fill those gaps.

Code is available at this book's code repository (*https://github.com/ bhavanki/moving-hadoop-to-the-cloud*).

Apache ZooKeeper

The script in Example A-1 starts and stops Apache ZooKeeper servers, assuming each one is running on a worker instance in the cluster. It should be installed on the manager instance and run under the "zk" account, or any account that has password-less SSH access to an account on each worker that may control ZooKeeper.

Example A-1. Control script for Apache ZooKeeper

```
#!/usr/bin/env bash

if [[ -z $1 ]]; then
  echo "Syntax: $0 (start|stop|status)"
  exit
fi

# Assumption is that each "slave" hosts a ZooKeeper server
SLAVES=( $(cat /etc/hadoop/slaves) )

case "$1" in
```

```
  start)
    echo Starting ZooKeeper
    for s in "${SLAVES[@]}"; do
      ssh "$s" /opt/zookeeper/bin/zkServer.sh start
    done
    ;;
  stop)
    echo Stopping ZooKeeper
    for s in "${SLAVES[@]}"; do
      ssh "$s" /opt/zookeeper/bin/zkServer.sh stop
    done
    ;;
  status)
    echo Checking ZooKeeper status
    for s in "${SLAVES[@]}"; do
      ssh "$s" /opt/zookeeper/bin/zkServer.sh status
    done
    ;;
esac
```

Apache Hive

The scripts in Examples A-2 and A-3 start and stop the Hive server (HiveServer2) and the Hive metastore server, respectively. They should be installed on an instance where Hive is installed, usually a manager, under an account such as "hive" that has permission to run Hive components. The scripts do not require any remote connectivity.

Ensure that the value of SPARK_HOME in the scripts points to a version of Spark that is compatible with Hive.

Example A-2. Control script for Apache Hive server

```
#!/usr/bin/env bash

if [[ -z $1 ]]; then
  echo "Syntax: $0 (start|stop|status)"
  exit
fi

# Define enviroment variables Hive expects
export HADOOP_HOME=/opt/hadoop
export HIVE_HOME=/opt/hive
export SPARK_HOME=/opt/spark
export PATH=${HIVE_HOME}/bin:${HADOOP_HOME}/bin:$PATH
export HADOOP_CONF_DIR=/etc/hadoop

HS2_PID_DIR=/var/run/hadoop
HS2_PID_FILE="${HS2_PID_DIR}"/hs2.pid
```

```
 case "$1" in
   start)
     echo Starting HiveServer2
     "${HIVE_HOME}"/bin/hiveserver2 &
     PID=$!
     echo "${PID}" > "${HS2_PID_FILE}"
     echo "HiveServer2 started [${PID}]"
     ;;
   stop)
     if [[ ! -f "${HS2_PID_FILE}" ]]; then
       echo HiveServer2 not running
       exit
     fi
     echo Stopping HiveServer2
     kill "$(cat "${HS2_PID_FILE}")"
     ;;
   status)
     if [[ ! -f "${HS2_PID_FILE}" ]]; then
       echo Pid file for HiveServer2 not found
       exit 1
     fi
     PID=$(cat "${HS2_PID_FILE}")
     if kill -0 "${PID}" 2>/dev/null; then
       echo "HiveServer2 is running [${PID}]"
     else
       echo "HiveServer2 is not running"
     fi
     ;;
esac
```

Example A-3. Control script for Apache Hive metastore server

```
#!/usr/bin/env bash

if [[ -z $1 ]]; then
  echo "Syntax: $0 (start|stop|status)"
  exit
fi

# Define enviroment variables Hive expects
export HADOOP_HOME=/opt/hadoop
export HIVE_HOME=/opt/hive
export SPARK_HOME=/opt/spark
export PATH=${HIVE_HOME}/bin:${HADOOP_HOME}/bin:$PATH
export HADOOP_CONF_DIR=/etc/hadoop

HIVEMETA_LOG_DIR=/var/log/hive
HIVEMETA_PID_DIR=/var/run/hadoop
HIVEMETA_PID_FILE="${HIVEMETA_PID_DIR}"/hivemeta.pid
PORT=9083

case "$1" in
```

```
start)
  echo Starting Hive Metastore Server
  hive --service metastore -p ${PORT} > ${HIVEMETA_LOG_DIR}/metastore.log &
  PID=$!
  echo "${PID}" > "${HIVEMETA_PID_FILE}"
  echo "Hive Metastore Server started [${PID}]"
  ;;
stop)
  if [[ ! -f "${HIVEMETA_PID_FILE}" ]]; then
    echo Hive Metastore Server not running
    exit
  fi
  echo Stopping Hive Metastore Server
  kill "$(cat "${HIVEMETA_PID_FILE}")"
  ;;
status)
  if [[ ! -f "${HIVEMETA_PID_FILE}" ]]; then
    echo Pid file for Hive Metastore Server not found
    exit 1
  fi
  PID=$(cat "${HIVEMETA_PID_FILE}")
  if kill -0 "${PID}" 2>/dev/null; then
    echo "Hive Metastore Server is running [${PID}]"
  else
    echo "Hive Metastore Server is not running"
  fi
  ;;
esac
```

Hadoop Cluster Configuration Scripts

To speed up the creation of Hadoop clusters in the cloud, you can create an image for one or more representative cluster instances with software already installed and, for the most part, configured. Chapter 16 describes the process. Still, there are configuration steps that can only be done once the cluster instances are running, and the scripts here can automate the work.

A quick glance at the scripts should reveal that even this small slice of automation is not trivial. You might consider borrowing the techniques used here and implementing them using a different scripting language or framework. Central to them is the ability to establish SSH connections into and within the cluster, so look for frameworks that help in that regard, such as Fabric (*http://www.fabfile.org/*).

 Code is available at this book's code repository (*https://github.com/bhavanki/moving-hadoop-to-the-cloud*).

SSH Key Creation and Distribution

The Hadoop installation process in Chapter 9 and elsewhere includes the creation of user accounts specific to services like HDFS, YARN, and ZooKeeper. Those accounts can already be in place in an image, but for greater security they should be configured with unique SSH keys, so that instances in one cluster cannot access instances in other clusters that were built from the same image.

The Bash script in Example B-1 can be run from your local computer to orchestrate the creation of SSH key pairs on the manager instance of a Hadoop cluster for each

Hadoop account, and the distribution of public keys to the manager instance and worker instances.

Example B-1. SSH key pair creation and distribution script

```
#!/usr/bin/env bash

# Generates SSH key pairs for accounts on one instance (manager), and distributes
# public keys to that instance and other instances (workers).

DEFAULT_ACCOUNTS=( ubuntu hdfs yarn zk )

usage() {
  cat << EOF
usage: $0 options manager-ips worker1-ips ...

OPTIONS:
  -a accts   Accounts to configure (default ${DEFAULT_ACCOUNTS[*]})
             Specify as space-separated list, e.g., "acct1 acct2 acct3"
  -G         Do not generate new SSH key pairs; use what is already available
  -i file    Identity file for SSH connections to manager
  -u user    User for SSH connections to manager
  -h         Shows this help message

Run this script on a machine that can connect to the manager instance via SSH.
The user account on the manager instance must have passwordless sudo access.

Pass the public and private IP addresses for each instance in the cluster as
a colon-separated pair, e.g., 203.0.113.101:192.168.1.101.

EXAMPLE:
  $0 -a "hdfs yarn" -i /path/to/key.pem -u ubuntu \\
    203.0.113.101:192.168.1.101 \\
    203.0.113.102:192.168.1.102 \\
    203.0.113.103:192.168.1.103 \\
    203.0.113.104:192.168.1.104
EOF
}

ACCOUNTS=( "${DEFAULT_ACCOUNTS[@]}" )
DO_NOT_GENERATE=
SSH_IDENTITY=
SSH_USER=
while getopts "a:Gi:u:h" opt
do
  case $opt in
    h)
      usage
      exit 0
      ;;
    a)
```

```
      ACCOUNTS=( $OPTARG )
        ;;
    G)
      DO_NOT_GENERATE=1
        ;;
    i)
      SSH_IDENTITY="$OPTARG"
        ;;
    u)
      SSH_USER="$OPTARG"
        ;;
    ?)
      usage
      exit
        ;;
  esac
done
shift $((OPTIND - 1))

if (( $# < 2 )); then
  echo "Supply the manager private IP address and at least one worker IP address"
  usage
  exit 1
fi

if [[ ${#ACCOUNTS[@]} == 0 ]]; then
  echo "No accounts specified"
  usage
  exit 1
fi

# Find manager IP addresses: "public IP:private IP"
MANAGER_PUBLIC_IP="${1%%:*}"
MANAGER_PRIVATE_IP="${1##*:}"
shift
# Collect remaining IP address pairs for workers
WORKER_IPS=( "$@" )

NUM_WORKERS=${#WORKER_IPS[@]}
MANAGER_HOSTNAME="$(hostname --fqdn)"

echo "Manager public IP: $MANAGER_PUBLIC_IP"
echo "Manager private IP: $MANAGER_PRIVATE_IP"
echo "Manager hostname: $MANAGER_HOSTNAME"
echo "${NUM_WORKERS} worker IPs: ${WORKER_IPS[*]}"
echo "Accounts: ${ACCOUNTS[*]}"

# Construct the SSH command with the provided identity file and username
SSH_CMD=( ssh )
if [[ -n $SSH_IDENTITY ]]; then
  SSH_CMD+=( -i "$SSH_IDENTITY" )
fi
```

```
if [[ -n $SSH_USER ]]; then
  SSH_CMD+=( -o "User=$SSH_USER" )
fi

# For each account ...
for acct in "${ACCOUNTS[@]}"; do

  # Note whether this account is the one used for SSH connections by this script
  if [[ -n $SSH_USER && "$acct" == "$SSH_USER" ]]; then
    issshuser=1
  else
    issshuser=
  fi

  echo
  if [[ -z $DO_NOT_GENERATE ]]; then
    # Generate a key pair on the manager instance using ssh-keygen
    echo "[$acct] Generating manager SSH key pair"
    "${SSH_CMD[@]}" -t "${MANAGER_PUBLIC_IP}" "sudo -u \"$acct\" ssh-keygen" \
      "-t rsa -b 2048 -f /home/$acct/.ssh/id_rsa -N ''"

    # Copy the new public key to the authorized_keys file on the manager
    # - If this account is the one being used by this script, then just
    #   append it to authorized_keys, don't outright replace the file
    echo "[$acct] Copying public SSH key to authorized_keys on manager"
    if [[ -n $issshuser ]]; then
      "${SSH_CMD[@]}" -t "${MANAGER_PUBLIC_IP}" \
        "sudo cat /home/$acct/.ssh/id_rsa.pub | sudo -u \"$acct\"" \
        "tee -a /home/$acct/.ssh/authorized_keys > /dev/null"
    else
      "${SSH_CMD[@]}" -t "${MANAGER_PUBLIC_IP}" \
        "sudo cat /home/$acct/.ssh/id_rsa.pub | sudo -u \"$acct\"" \
        "tee /home/$acct/.ssh/authorized_keys > /dev/null"
    fi
    # Set the permissions for authorized_keys appropriately
    "${SSH_CMD[@]}" -t "${MANAGER_PUBLIC_IP}" \
      "sudo chmod 600 /home/$acct/.ssh/authorized_keys"
  else
    echo "[$acct] Skipping manager SSH key pair generation"
  fi

  # Get the new public key
  echo "[$acct] Retrieving public SSH key"
  pubkey="$( "${SSH_CMD[@]}" -t "${MANAGER_PUBLIC_IP}" \
    "sudo cat /home/$acct/.ssh/id_rsa.pub" )"
  echo "[$acct] Public key contents:"
  echo "----"
  echo "$pubkey"
  echo "----"

  # For each worker ...
  for worker_ips in "${WORKER_IPS[@]}"; do
```

```
# Write the public key to the authorized_keys file on the worker, creating
# it and its directory if necessary
# - Again, just append to the file if the account is being used here
worker=${worker_ips%%:*}
echo
echo "[$acct] Installing public SSH key on $worker"
"${SSH_CMD[@]}" -t "${worker}" \
  "sudo -u \"$acct\" mkdir -p -m 0700 /home/$acct/.ssh"
"${SSH_CMD[@]}" "${worker}" "cat >> /tmp/pubkey" <<< "$pubkey"
if [[ -n $issshuser ]]; then
  "${SSH_CMD[@]}" -t "${worker}" "sudo cat /tmp/pubkey | sudo -u \"$acct\"" \
    "tee -a /home/$acct/.ssh/authorized_keys > /dev/null"
else
  "${SSH_CMD[@]}" -t "${worker}" "sudo cat /tmp/pubkey | sudo -u \"$acct\"" \
    "tee /home/$acct/.ssh/authorized_keys > /dev/null"
fi
"${SSH_CMD[@]}" -t "${worker}" "sudo chmod 600 /home/$acct/.ssh/authorized_keys"
"${SSH_CMD[@]}" "${worker}" "rm /tmp/pubkey"

done

# Connect from the manager instance to itself and each worker so that the
# new host keys are accepted now; this avoids being asked interactively later
echo
echo "[$acct] Connecting to each cluster instance from manager to" \
  "accept host keys"
if [[ -n $MANAGER_HOSTNAME ]]; then
  "${SSH_CMD[@]}" -t "${MANAGER_PUBLIC_IP}" "sudo -u \"$acct\"" \
    "ssh -o StrictHostKeyChecking=no \"$MANAGER_HOSTNAME\" date > /dev/null"
fi
"${SSH_CMD[@]}" -t "${MANAGER_PUBLIC_IP}" "sudo -u \"$acct\"" \
  "ssh -o StrictHostKeyChecking=no \"$MANAGER_PRIVATE_IP\" date > /dev/null"
"${SSH_CMD[@]}" -t "${MANAGER_PUBLIC_IP}" "sudo -u \"$acct\"" \
  "ssh -o StrictHostKeyChecking=no 0.0.0.0 date > /dev/null"
for worker_ips in "${WORKER_IPS[@]}"; do
  worker=${worker_ips##*:} # connect from manager to private IP of worker
  "${SSH_CMD[@]}" -t "${MANAGER_PUBLIC_IP}" "sudo -u \"$acct\"" \
    "ssh -o StrictHostKeyChecking=no \"$worker\" date > /dev/null"
done

done
```

Configuration Update Script

The bash script in Example B-2 handles substituting cluster instance private IP addresses for tokens placed into various Hadoop configuration files, as suggested in "Image Preparation" on page 225. The script is run on the manager instance (and, for HA clusters, on the second manager instance as well) and handles configuration on that instance as well as worker instances.

Example B-2. Hadoop configuration update script

```bash
#!/usr/bin/env bash

# Configures Hadoop components on a manager instance and one or more worker
# instances.

usage() {
  cat << EOF
usage: $0 options manager-ip worker-ip ...

OPTIONS:
  -d <name>  Hostname of database server hosting Hive metastore
  -a <keys>  AWS access key and secret access key, separated by a colon
  -H         Initialize for second manager (for HA cluster)
  -m <ip>    IP address of second manager (for HA cluster)
  -h         Shows this help message

For an HA cluster, run this script on the first manager with -m, and then
on the second manager with -m and -H. Use the same manager IP addresses on
each manager; do not reverse them when running on the second manager.

The user account on each manager must have passwordless sudo access.
EOF
}

HIVE_DB_SERVER=
AWS_ACCESS_KEY=
AWS_SECRET_KEY=
ON_SECOND_MANAGER=
MANAGER2_IP=
while getopts "a:d:hHm:" opt
do
  case $opt in
    h)
      usage
      exit 0
      ;;
    a)
      AWS_ACCESS_KEY="${OPTARG%%:*}"
      AWS_SECRET_KEY="${OPTARG##*:}"
      ;;
    d)
      HIVE_DB_SERVER="$OPTARG"
      ;;
    H)
      ON_SECOND_MANAGER=1
      ;;
    m)
      MANAGER2_IP="$OPTARG"
      ;;
    ?)
```

```
        usage
        exit
        ;;
    esac
done
shift $((OPTIND - 1))

if (( $# < 2 )); then
    echo "Supply the manager private IP address and at least one worker IP address"
    usage
    exit 1
fi

if [[ -n $ON_SECOND_MANAGER && -z $MANAGER2_IP ]]; then
    echo "When running on second manager, -m is required"
    usage
    exit 1
fi

# Collect required IP addresses: manager and workers
MANAGER_IP="$1"
shift
WORKER_IPS=( "$@" )

NUM_WORKERS=${#WORKER_IPS[@]}

echo "Manager IP: $MANAGER_IP"
if [[ -n $MANAGER2_IP ]]; then
    echo "HA Manager IP: $MANAGER2_IP"
fi
echo "${NUM_WORKERS} worker IPs: ${WORKER_IPS[*]}"
echo

# Replaces a ${token_string} in a file with a value
swap_in() {
    local f="$1"
    local token_name="$2"
    local repl="$3"

    local token='\${'"${token_name}"'}'

    sudo sed -i "s/${token}/${repl}/g" "$f"
}

echo
echo "Substituting IP addresses and hostnames into Hadoop configurations"
echo

# Replace in core-site.xml files: manager.ip, worker<i>.ip
echo "- /etc/hadoop/core-site.xml"
swap_in /etc/hadoop/core-site.xml manager.ip "${MANAGER_IP}"
for i in $(seq 1 "$NUM_WORKERS"); do
```

```
    w="${WORKER_IPS[$(( i - 1 ))]}"
    swap_in /etc/hadoop/core-site.xml "worker${i}.ip" "$w"
done

# Replace in yarn-site.xml files: manager.ip, manager2.ip, worker<i>.ip
echo "- /etc/hadoop/yarn-site.xml"
swap_in /etc/hadoop/yarn-site.xml manager.ip "${MANAGER_IP}"
swap_in /etc/hadoop/yarn-site.xml manager2.ip "${MANAGER2_IP}"
for i in $(seq 1 "$NUM_WORKERS"); do
    w="${WORKER_IPS[$(( i - 1 ))]}"
    swap_in /etc/hadoop/yarn-site.xml "worker${i}.ip" "$w"
done
if [[ -n $ON_SECOND_MANAGER ]]; then
    # Change YARN RM HA ID to rm2 on the second manager
    sudo sed -i 's/<value>rm1</<value>rm2</' /etc/hadoop/yarn-site.xml
    echo
fi

# Write slaves file based on known worker IP addresses
echo "- /etc/hadoop/slaves"
printf '%s\n' "${WORKER_IPS[@]}" | sudo tee /etc/hadoop/slaves > /dev/null

# Replace in zoo.cfg files: worker<i>.ip
echo "- /opt/zookeeper/conf/zoo.cfg"
for i in $(seq 1 "$NUM_WORKERS"); do
    w="${WORKER_IPS[$(( i - 1 ))]}"
    swap_in /opt/zookeeper/conf/zoo.cfg "worker${i}.ip" "$w"
done

# Replace in hive-site.xml: manager.ip, dbserver.name
echo "- /opt/hive/conf/hive-site.xml"
if [[ -z $ON_SECOND_MANAGER ]]; then
    swap_in /opt/hive/conf/hive-site.xml manager.ip "${MANAGER_IP}"
else
    swap_in /opt/hive/conf/hive-site.xml manager.ip "${MANAGER2_IP}"
fi
if [[ -n $HIVE_DB_SERVER ]]; then
    swap_in /opt/hive/conf/hive-site.xml dbserver.name "${HIVE_DB_SERVER}"
fi

echo
echo "IP address and hostname substitutions complete"

if [[ -n $AWS_ACCESS_KEY ]]; then
    echo
    echo "Substituting AWS keys into Hadoop configurations"
    echo

    # Replace in core-site.xml: AWS keys
    echo "- /etc/hadoop/core-site.xml"
    swap_in /etc/hadoop/core-site.xml aws.access.key "${AWS_ACCESS_KEY}"
    swap_in /etc/hadoop/core-site.xml aws.secret.key "${AWS_SECRET_KEY}"
```

```
    echo
    echo "AWS key substitutions complete"
fi

if [[ -z $ON_SECOND_MANAGER ]]; then
    echo
    echo "Copying configurations out to workers"
    WORKER_FILES=(/etc/hadoop/core-site.xml
                  /etc/hadoop/yarn-site.xml
                  /opt/zookeeper/conf/zoo.cfg)

    # Copy out configuration files to each worker
    for w in "${WORKER_IPS[@]}"; do
      echo "- $w"
      scp "${WORKER_FILES[@]}" "$w":.
      for f in "${WORKER_FILES[@]}"; do
        ssh "$w" sudo cp "$(basename "$f")" "$f"
      done
    done

    # If configuring for HA (and running on first manager), remove
    # yarn.resourcemanager.ha.id from worker copies of yarn-site.xml
    if [[ -n $MANAGER2_IP ]]; then
      echo
      echo "Removing YARN RM HA ID from workers"
      for w in "${WORKER_IPS[@]}"; do
        echo "- $w"
        ssh "$w" sudo sed -i \
          '/\<name\>yarn.resourcemanager.ha.id\</,/\<property\>/d' \
          /etc/hadoop/yarn-site.xml
      done
    fi

    # Create ZooKeeper myid files, assigning a unique number per worker
    echo
    echo "Creating ZooKeeper myid files on workers"
    for i in $(seq 1 "$NUM_WORKERS"); do
      w="${WORKER_IPS[$(( i - 1 ))]}"
      echo "- $w"
      echo "$i" | ssh "$w" "sudo tee /var/lib/zookeeper/myid > /dev/null"
    done
fi
```

New Worker Configuration Update Script

When adding a new worker to an existing cluster, only a small amount of configuration is needed compared to what's done for an entire new cluster. The script in Example B-3 is a cut-down form of the previous script that works for most kinds of new worker instances, such as those hosting an HDFS datanode or a YARN node manager. See "Elastic Compute Using a Custom Metric" on page 260 for how a script like this can help implement the automatic addition of workers to a busy cluster.

Example B-3. Hadoop configuration update script for a new worker

```bash
#!/usr/bin/env bash

# Configures Hadoop components on a new worker instance.

usage() {
  cat << EOF
usage: $0 new-worker-ip worker-ip ...

Run this script on a manager.
EOF
}

if (( $# < 2 )); then
  echo "Supply the new worker private IP address and at least one" \
    "(old) worker IP address"
  usage
  exit 1
fi

# Collect required IP addresses: this worker, and other workers
NEW_WORKER_IP="$1"
shift
WORKER_IPS=( "$@" )
WORKER_IPS+=( "$NEW_WORKER_IP" )

NUM_WORKERS=${#WORKER_IPS[@]}

echo "New worker IP: $NEW_WORKER_IP"
echo "${NUM_WORKERS} worker IPs: ${WORKER_IPS[*]}"
echo

echo
echo "Substituting IP addresses and hostnames into Hadoop configurations"
echo

# Rewrite slaves file based on known worker IP addresses
echo "- /etc/hadoop/slaves"
printf '%s\n' "${WORKER_IPS[@]}" | sudo tee /etc/hadoop/slaves > /dev/null

echo
echo "IP address and hostname substitutions complete"

# Copy out configuration files to the new worker
echo
echo "Copying configurations out to new worker"
WORKER_FILES=(/etc/hadoop/core-site.xml
```

```
            /etc/hadoop/yarn-site.xml
            /opt/zookeeper/conf/zoo.cfg)

echo "- copy to $NEW_WORKER_IP"
scp "${WORKER_FILES[@]}" "$NEW_WORKER_IP":.
for f in "${WORKER_FILES[@]}"; do
  echo "- put $f in place"
  ssh "$NEW_WORKER_IP" sudo cp "$(basename "$f")" "$f"
done
```

Monitoring Cloud Clusters with Nagios

Nagios (*https://www.nagios.org/*) is a popular system for monitoring infrastructure. It can monitor networks, hardware, and applications using its built-in capabilities along with a plug-in architecture.

Nagios is more than capable of monitoring cloud clusters for you, and a great choice if you are already familiar with the tool. It can be configured with custom checks that work with cloud provider infrastructures, Hadoop components, or anything else you can think of.

 Code is available at this book's code repository (*https://github.com/bhavanki/moving-hadoop-to-the-cloud*).

Where Nagios Should Run

As discussed in "Hadoop Daemon Status" on page 248, there are benefits and drawbacks for running a monitoring system within a cloud provider or outside it. These considerations apply to where Nagios runs as well. If you opt to run Nagios outside the cloud provider and outside a VPN with privileged access to the network where the Hadoop cluster runs, you must then loosen security rules to permit Nagios to reach all of the ports necessary for effective cluster monitoring. Also, unless you assign static public IP addresses to your instances, you will need to edit the Nagios configuration as those addresses change over time.

Instance Existence Through Ping

Nagios normally checks if instances exist by attempting to ping them. The security rules set up in your cloud provider may block ping traffic, especially if it is running outside the cloud provider. You have the option of redefining the standard existence check, but you could instead simply permit ping traffic from where Nagios runs.

For EC2 instances running in AWS, add a new inbound rule to the security group containing the cluster to permit pings to enter:

- Type: Custom ICMP Rule (IPv4)
- Protocol: Echo Request
- Port Range: N/A
- Source: An appropriate IP range to cover your Nagios installation

The default firewall rules set up in Google Cloud Platform include one that permits ICMP traffic. Edit the rule if necessary to cover your Nagios installation.

Azure as a whole disallows all ICMP traffic, so pinging a virtual machine in Azure from an outside location such as the internet is not possible. The alternative is to set up a service listening on a TCP or UDP port and check for a response from that port instead. In the host definition for each Azure virtual machine, specify a command for the check_command value that itself uses either check_tcp or check_udp to attempt to connect to your chosen port.

For example, if you choose TCP port 55555 as the port to check, first add a new inbound security rule to the network security group containing the cluster to permit TCP traffic over that port:

- Source: A CIDR block with an appropriate IP range covering your Nagios installation
- Service: Custom
- Protocol: TCP
- Port range: 55555
- Action: Allow

Set up a service listening on port 55555 on each Azure instance. You have many options here, and perhaps the simplest is to use netcat, which can listen on a TCP port for arbitrary traffic. The -k option allows netcat to continue running after each connection from Nagios, instead of terminating after the first one:

```
nc -k -l 55555 > /dev/null &
```

With this command running on a virtual machine, the following check_command in its host definition will configure Nagios to check port 55555 to verify that the instance is up, instead of pinging it:

```
check_command check_tcp!55555
```

A functioning TCP port check is shown in Figure C-1.

| Host Status: | UP (for 0d 0h 0m 27s) |
| Status Information: | TCP OK - 0.035 second response time on 13.90.90.142 port 55555 |

Figure C-1. Checking TCP port connectivity in Nagios for an Azure VM

Hosts and Host Groups

Create a host definition in Nagios for each instance in the Hadoop cluster. As usual, prefer using the private IP address for each instance for security and performance reasons. For ease of tracking, use the cloud provider's name for each instance for the host_name and/or alias of its corresponding host definition.

Every instance in the cluster can be corralled into a single host group representing the cluster. It is also helpful to create host groups for each instance role (see "General Cluster Instance Roles" on page 188) since each role has common characteristics and performance expectations; this makes it easier to target service checks appropriately. For example, if a host group covers all of the worker instances in a cluster, then service checks concerning HDFS datanode disk usage or YARN node manager utilization can be targeted only at those instances.

Nagios allows you to define custom variables for objects. To support service checks involving the cloud provider, define custom variables for each host to convey provider-specific identification.

Here is an example of host and host group definitions for a small Hadoop cluster on AWS. The custom variable _INSTANCEID holds the EC2 instance ID for each instance:

```
define host {
  use            linux-server
  host_name      manager
  alias          manager
  address        203.0.113.101
  _INSTANCEID    i-12345678901234567
}

define host {
  use            linux-server
  host_name      worker1
  alias          worker1
  address        203.0.113.102
  _INSTANCEID    i-23456789012345678
```

```
}

define host {
    use             linux-server
    host_name       worker2
    alias           worker2
    address         203.0.113.103
    _INSTANCEID     i-34567890123456789
}

define host {
    use             linux-server
    host_name       worker3
    alias           worker3
    address         203.0.113.104
    _INSTANCEID     i-45678901234567890
}

define hostgroup {
    hostgroup_name  mycluster
    alias           My Cluster
    members         manager,worker1,worker2,worker3
}

define hostgroup {
    hostgroup_name  mycluster_workers
    alias           My Cluster Workers
    members         worker1,worker2,worker3
}
```

Figure C-2 shows how the defined host groups appear in the Nagios web interface.

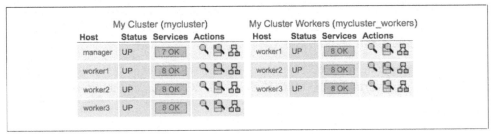

Figure C-2. Host groups for a Hadoop cluster in Nagios

Services and Service Groups

The usual Nagios checks for system health apply to cloud cluster instances. To check on the health of Hadoop daemons, the check_tcp service check works in a similar fashion to netcat for determining if a daemon is listening on a port. For example, to verify that a namenode is running, check on port 8020:

```
define service {
    use                  generic-service
    host_name            manager
    service_description  HDFS Namenode
    servicegroups        HDFS
    check_command        check_tcp!8020
}
```

A service group can collect together all of the service checks relevant to a Hadoop component, so that it is possible to assess the overall health of that component in one spot. Example service groups for a few Hadoop components are shown in Figure C-3.

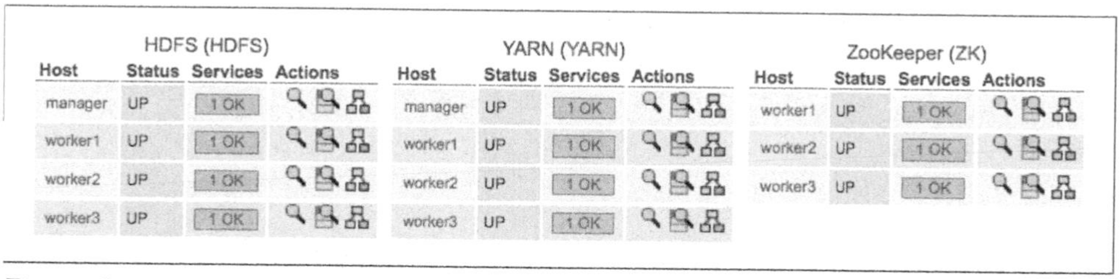

Figure C-3. Service groups for a Hadoop cluster in Nagios

Provider CLI Integration

It is not difficult to define your own scripts for use as Nagios plug-ins. Such a script can perform a specific call to the provider based on host information, interpret the results, and then return one of the expected exit codes that Nagios interprets as the outcome of the service check.

Nagios requires a functioning CLI installation to use such scripts, which implies that Nagios has access to credentials for an account on the cloud provider. It's therefore important to restrict the permissions on the account, in the event that the credentials are compromised, and also to prevent badly behaving Nagios plug-ins from interfering with cluster operations.

Suppose that a Hadoop cluster is running in AWS, and you want a Nagios service check that looks at the instance status of each host. Start by creating a script that uses the `describe-instance-status` command to retrieve the status information. The command requires an instance ID, and so Nagios can pass that information from the custom variable associated with the host being checked. In Example C-1, the host is passed as an ordinary script argument.

Example C-1. A Nagios script for checking the status of an EC2 instance

```bash
#!/usr/bin/env bash

usage() {
  cat << EOF
usage: $0 options instance-id

OPTIONS:
  -p <profile>  AWS profile (no default)
  -h            Shows this help message
EOF
}

PROFILE=

while getopts "p:h" opt
do
  case $opt in
    h)
      usage
      exit 3 # UNKNOWN
      ;;
    p)
      PROFILE="$OPTARG"
      ;;
    ?)
      usage
      exit 3 # UNKNOWN
      ;;
  esac
done
shift $((OPTIND - 1))

INSTANCE_ID="$1"

CMD=(aws)
if [[ -n $PROFILE ]]; then
  CMD+=(--profile "$PROFILE")
fi
CMD+=(ec2 describe-instance-status "--instance-id=${INSTANCE_ID}"\
      --include-all-instances --query 'InstanceStatuses[0].InstanceStatus.Status')

status=$("${CMD[@]}")
echo "Instance $INSTANCE_ID status: $status"

if [[ $status == "\"ok\"" ]]; then
  exit 0 # OK
else
  exit 1 # WARNING
fi
```

This script uses the `--query` option of the AWS CLI to isolate the instance status from the JSON returned by the command.

Place this script somewhere where Nagios can call it. Then, define a command for running the script, passing in the instance ID from the custom variable associated with the host using a custom variable macro (*https://assets.nagios.com/downloads/ nagioscore/docs/nagioscore/3/en/macros.html*):

```
define command {
    command_name    check_aws_instance_status
    command_line    /path/to/check_aws_instance_status -p $ARG1$ $_HOSTINSTANCEID$
}
```

Finally, add a service definition using the new check for the cluster instances. You can use the host group covering the entire cluster:

```
define service {
    use                 generic-service
    hostgroup_name      mycluster
    service_description AWS Instance Status
    check_command       check_aws_instance_status!myprofile
}
```

Be sure to set the interval for provider CLI checks to a reasonable value. If Nagios performs too many calls, the provider may begin to enforce rate limiting and deny some calls, leading to spurious warnings from Nagios.

A functioning instance status check is shown in Figure C-4.

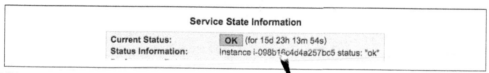

Figure C-4. AWS instance status check in Nagios

Index

cloud provider CLI interfaces for, 241-245
cloud provider services for, 240
creating your own service for, 241
custom metrics in CloudWatch, 253-260
elastic compute using a custom metric, 260-264
Google Cloud Platform CLI for, 242
Hadoop daemon status, 248-250
ingesting logs into CloudWatch, 264-272
instance existence, 245, 298
instance reachability, 246
scripting and, 253
Stackdriver, 251-252
system choices for, 239
system load, 250
system monitoring by Azure, 252
what to monitor, 245-253
MRBench, 140
multitenant clusters, 218

N

Nagios
    cloud cluster monitoring, 297-303
    host and host groups, 299
    instance existence checking, 298
    provider CLI integration, 301-303
    services and service groups, 300
    where to run, 297
network ACL rules, 40-42
network address translation (NAT) gateway, 210
network address translation (NAT) instance, 210
network security groups, 44
network topologies, 197-213
    availability zones, 211-213
    cluster access to Internet/cloud provider services, 209-211
    cluster topologies, 204-211
    gateway instances, 207
    geographic considerations, 211-213
    private cluster, 208
    public cluster, 204
    public/private subnets, 197-204
    regions, 211
    secured public cluster, 205-207
    SOCKS proxy server, 201-203
    SSH tunneling, 199-201
    starting topologies, 213

VPN access, 203
networking, 29-46
    CIDR notation, 29
    combining with security, 45
    routing, 34-38
    security rules, 38-45
    virtual networks, 30-33
new worker configuration update script, 293
next hop, 37
NoSQL databases (see cloud NoSQL databases)

O

object access, 51
object storage, 49-55
    accessing objects in, 51
    basics, 49
    buckets, 50
    containers (Azure), 50
    data objects, 51
    in AWS, 52
    in Azure, 53
    in Google Cloud Platform, 53
on-premise clusters, 4
Oracle JDK, 105
outbound rules, 38

P

Packer, 234-236
page blobs, 49
peered networks, 32
per-team clusters, 218
performance (see pricing and performance)
persistent disks, 48
persistent storage, 47, 190
port scanners, 206
preemptible instances, 26
pricing and performance, 187-196
    as reason not to run Hadoop in the cloud, 7
    availability zones, 195
    cloud provider selection, 17
    cluster usage patterns, 221
    geographic considerations, 195
    instance types and, 187-190
    persistent vs. ephemeral block storage, 190
    regions, 195
    stopping/starting entire clusters, 192-193
    temporary instances, 193
private cloud, 4
private cluster, 208

About the Author

Bill Havanki is a software engineer working for Cloudera, where he has contributed to Hadoop components as well as systems for deploying Hadoop clusters into public Cloud services. Prior to joining Cloudera he worked for 15 years developing software for government contracts, focusing mostly on analytic frameworks and authentication and authorization systems. He earned his B.S. in Electrical Engineering from Rutgers University and his M.S. in Computer Engineering from North Carolina State University. A New Jersey native, he currently lives near Annapolis, Maryland with his family.

Colophon

The animal on the cover of *Moving Hadoop to the Cloud* is a southern reedbuck (*Redunca arundinum*).

Southern reedbucks are typically found in southern Africa. They inhabit areas of tall grass near a source of water. The grass offers camouflage from predators such as lions, leopards, cheetahs, spotted hyenas, pythons, and crocodiles. Being herbivores, the tall grass also provides sustenance. Southern reedbucks need to drink water at least every few days, which is not typical for species in this arid region of Africa.

An elegant antelope, southern reedbucks have distinctive dark lines running down the front of their forelegs and lower hind legs. The color of their coat ranges between light- and greyish-brown and their underparts are white. Only the males bear forward-curving horns, about 35–45 cm (14–18 in) long.

The southern reedbuck is monogamous, a pair inhabits a territory that is defended by the male from other males. A single calf is born after a gestation period of around eight months and remains hidden in the dense grass for the next two months. During this period, the female does not stay with her young but instead visits it for 10 to 30 minutes each day. This antelope has an average lifespan of ten years.

The southern reedbuck makes a number of characteristic noises, including a shrill whistle through the nostrils, a clicking noise to alert others about danger, and a distinctive "popping" sound, caused by the inguinal glands, heard when the southern reedbuck jumps.

Many of the animals on O'Reilly covers are endangered; all of them are important to the world. To learn more about how you can help, go to *animals.oreilly.com*.

The cover image is from *Wood's Animate Creation*. The cover fonts are URW Typewriter and Guardian Sans. The text font is Adobe Minion Pro; the heading font is Adobe Myriad Condensed; and the code font is Dalton Maag's Ubuntu Mono.

Learn from experts.
Find the answers you need.

Sign up for a **10-day free trial** to get **unlimited access** to all of the content on Safari, including Learning Paths, interactive tutorials, and curated playlists that draw from thousands of ebooks and training videos on a wide range of topics, including data, design, DevOps, management, business—and much more.

Start your free trial at:
oreilly.com/safari

(No credit card required.)

CPSIA information can be obtained
at www.ICGtesting.com
Printed in the USA
BVOW09s0738090717
488838BV00003B/3/P